IS
SCIENTIFIC MANAGEMENT
POSSIBLE?

SOCIETY TODAY AND TOMORROW

General Editor: A. H. Halsey

*Fellow of Nuffield College and Head of the Department
of Social and Administrative Studies, Oxford*

*

Is Scientific Management Possible?

A Critical Examination
of Glacier's Theory of Organization

by
JOE KELLY

FABER AND FABER LTD
24 Russell Square
London

First published in 1968
by Faber and Faber Limited
24 Russell Square London WC1
Printed in Great Britain by
Western Printing Services Limited Bristol

SBN 571 08729 9

CONTENTS

5

CONTENTS

3. THE PERSPECTIVES OF THE GLACIER PROJECT: HISTORICAL, ECONOMIC, TECHNOLOGICAL AND THEORETICAL

PART TWO. GLACIER INDUSTRIAL RELATIONS

4. GLACIER REVISITED, A STUDY OF INDUSTRIAL RELATIONS AS A REACTION TO TASK MANAGEMENT

CONTENTS

CONTENTS

PART FOUR. THE GLACIER SUPERVISOR AND GLACIER MEETINGS

8. AN EMPIRICAL EXAMINATION OF THE BEHAVIOUR OF THE GLACIER SUPERVISOR

9. GLACIER MEETINGS

PART FIVE. CONCLUSIONS

10. AN ASSESSMENT OF THE GLACIER SYSTEM OF MANAGEMENT

CONTENTS

APPENDICES

ACKNOWLEDGEMENTS

A book is inevitably the product of many people besides the author. This book is no exception; and special appreciation is due to Professor T. T. Paterson, Head of the Department of Industrial Administration who supervised the actual research exercise and came up with many helpful criticisms and suggestions. I am also indebted to Professor A. J. M. Sykes, also of the University of Strathclyde, whose research suggested the possibility of using activity sampling procedures as a means of studying executive behaviour.

I would like to acknowledge the help and assistance of the various personnel managers and line managers at the Kilmarnock factory of the Glacier Metal Company. A great deal of the actual observational work was done by students from the postgraduate personnel management course at Strathclyde University; in all some thirty students participated in this project. I gratefully acknowledge their labours.

In preparing the manuscript for publication, I must acknowledge the generous advice and encouragement of Dr. A. H. Halsey, especially his comments on the penultimate draft which stimulated a major revision of the whole book. I am grateful to Mr. E. F. L. Brech, for a substantive review of the entire manuscript and whose help significantly improved the text. None of these tough-minded scholars will be quite satisfied with the end-product; all tried to rescue me from lapses of intelligence in terms of analyses and faults in presentation. Sins of factual error, taste or prejudice, either of commission or omission, are therefore mine.

An encompassing debt is owed to my wife who listened, endured, and kept some domestic balance while this thing happened.

FOREWORD

FOREWORD

No teacher of management may neglect the 'Glacier Studies' sponsored by Wilfred Brown and beginning with Jaques' *Changing Culture of a Factory*, rightly received with acclaim shortly after the Second World War. That book might well be regarded as the British equivalent of *Management and the Worker* in its search for 'good human relations'. But, as with *Management and the Worker*, there comes a time when the value of the Glacier experiments needs another assessment, of the nature of Henry Landsberger's *Hawthorne Revisited*.

This re-assessment was, curiously enough, triggered off by Wilfred Brown himself in his book *Exploration in Management*, a statement of the application to Glacier Metal Ltd. of his own views on management. This is a good and stimulating book which, as I have remarked elsewhere, is one of wisdom if not of knowledge. What is exciting in that book is not its unconscious recognition of some fundamentals of management theory–on this score it makes excellent material for student criticism–but its re-orientation away from the 'human relations' fashion of the post-war period. It moved towards the more down-to-earth approach of the concept of 'task management' that appeared in America in the fifties, culminating in Sayle's organization based on work flow and backed by the revival of the older 'functional' approach in the hands of Dale.

Dr. Kelly has commenced this re-assessment; only commenced, for he would be the first to recognize that he has not yet tackled the major analysis of the unity of theoretical background to the apparent duality of views of Glacier, the early and late. Some would argue that the change to task management was a reaction to economic environment stimulated by management consultants. Others would suggest that the change was a reaction to the fashionable movement away from a surfeit of 'good human relations'; although the most cynical believe that

FOREWORD

the Glacier people were learning to become better managers just as that change in fashion, generally, was an appreciation of the harder facts of modern industrial administration.

Dr. Kelly has adopted a careful approach, not too broad in scope to become unmanageable and to lose coherence, not too narrow to miss some of the more outstanding variations in Brown's 'philosophy'. He backs his opinions with facts and makes no leaps into unwarranted speculation. To my theoretically-orientated mind this is both an admirable characteristic and yet a drawback. But he is probably wise to do so in this book and leave us hoping that its successor will provide us with that insight to be expected from him.

T. T. PATERSON,
*Professor of Industrial Administration,
University of Strathclyde
February 1968*

INTRODUCTION

CHAPTER I

IS SCIENTIFIC MANAGEMENT POSSIBLE?

Asking the right question is a necessary first step to finding the right answer. To many people the question 'Is human life possible on the moon?' must seem irrelevant when as yet we cannot give a definitive answer to the question 'Can contemporary man survive in an organizational environment?' Thus the title of this book is misleading, in the sense that while it is the Glacier system of management which is under assessment, the real subject under consideration is best projected in the question, 'Can man in his ingenuity and wisdom devise organizational solutions which give technological and economic effectiveness which in turn will give the affluence he so urgently wants, without offending the human condition?' From organizations, contemporary man expects affluence, generated by technological and organizational innovation, but without anomie and alienation. An impossible dream? But a dream worth exploring. Thus the real subject in the dock is scientific management.

Why was the Glacier system of management selected for this examination? Two obvious reasons suggest themselves. In the late 'forties and early 'fifties Glacier, who incidentally manufacture plain bearings including 'big end' bearings for car engines, were widely recognized as having an international reputation in the fields of human and industrial relations. The other reason was that, in spite of employing only something like 5,000 people, Glacier had developed its own distinctive management philosophy which included a series of concepts about organizational life which are quite different and in many ways unique and which was the result of a penetrating and radical analysis of the problems of organizational life made chiefly by two men, Wilfred Brown* and Elliott Jaques.† Brown joined Glacier in the 'thirties and became Managing Director in 1939. It might be argued that if anyone can bridge the gap between management and labour it would be the managing director who is both a member of his union and the Labour Party. Brown satisfies both of these requirements. In terms of organization theory, Brown represents a kind of industrial philosopher-king.

If industrial relations have been satisfied, what then about human relations? In Elliott Jaques, Brown had the perfect partner. Dr. Jaques, a Canadian psychiatrist, came from the Tavistock Institute of Human Relations which has an outstanding reputation for fusing Freudian psycho-analysis and Lewin's Field Theory to provide fruitful insights into business behaviour. But this is not to imply that Jaques was trapped in the theories of the past as a psycho-analyst; in the early 'fifties he began to describe his work as that of a social analyst and to concern himself in conjunction with Brown with the development and exposition of a theory of management.

Before saying any more about Glacier and working on the premise that a social scientist should declare his prejudices, per-

* Some biographical details in regard to Wilfred Banks Duncan Brown who was created M.B.E. in 1944 may be of interest to the reader. Born in 1908, educated at Rossall School, he was created a life Baron on 22 December 1964 and assumed the title of 'Baron Brown, of Machrihanish'. He joined the Glacier Metal Co. Ltd. in 1931, became Sales Manager in 1935, Joint Managing Director 1937 and Managing Director and Chairman 1939, Chairman only in the period 1959–65, and a member of the Board of Associated Engineering Ltd. 1964–65. He is also Chairman of the Board of Governors of Brunel College, Fellow of the British Institute of Management, member of the International Academy of Management. A member of the Labour Party, he is presently Minister of State, Board of Trade. He is a member of the Reform Club. (Sources: Burke's Peerage 1967 ed., and Dod's Parliamentary Companion, 1965.)

† Elliott Jaques, M.A. (Toronto), M.D. (John Hopkins), Ph.D. (Harvard), was a founder member of the Tavistock Institute of Human Relations. He qualified as a psycho-analyst at the British Psycho-analytical Society, has been its Scientific Secretary, and is presently a member of its Council. Since 1952 he has been in private practice, half-time as a psycho-analyst and the other half as consulting social-analyst on the Glacier Project. He is now Professor and Head of the School of Social Sciences at Brunel University. (Source: Biographical Note in *Human Relations*, Volume 19, Number 2, May 1966, p. 137, following Jaques' article 'The Science of Society'.)

haps it is only fair at this juncture to point out that if there is a theme running through this book, it is the belief that management theory has passed through three phases in its development, and more important that these three developments in management theory have certain cyclical characteristics.

THE CYCLICAL NATURE OF MANAGEMENT THEORY

A large number of business enterprises have been very successful economically despite the lack of rigorous theories of organization from which the principles of executive behaviour may be deduced. In spite of this fact, considerable effort is being expended to develop a theory of organization. The possibility of a scientific approach to organizational problems is an exceedingly attractive proposition for research resources and funds. The practical value of a theory is not always immediately recognized; a 'good' theory, which must have empirical reference, logical interconnections with other 'good' theories, and have the power of prediction, is important in management in the sense that it structures the perceptions of the executive, enabling him to codify his experience and thus frees him for the exploration and charting of unexplored empirical data. Secondly, even a minor advance in the analysis of organization has a major pay-off in all sections of administration including military, industrial, hospital, public, ecclesiastic etc. But, first, it would be of considerable value to delimit the discourse by defining organization.

Perhaps, it would be more appropriate to sink a number of critical shafts into the mass of definitions that concern themselves with organization. But first a comment about the building blocks of such a definition. In the physical sciences, the sequence is electron, proton, atom, molecule; in the biological sciences the sequence is gene, chromosome, nucleus, cell, tissue, organ, organism; in the social science the sequence is reflex, instinct, learning, personality, role, group, organization, institution and society. In considering the various behaviour options available to the researcher, it is necessary to restrict the inquiry to the sequence that includes role, group and organization.

Roles represent the basic building blocks in any definition of organization. The concept of role implies that the pattern of behaviour and attitudes which is expected of everybody in a particular position, varies only to a slight extent, irrespective of who the actual role holder is. Therefore, the behaviour and to a lesser extent the attitudes of the role holder are socially ordained and thus the role serves to delimit the types of personality expressions possible in any given situation. Formal organizations which may be thought of as giant molecules with roles for atoms have the effect of circumscribing and defining the individual's activities. Role theory minimizes differences in personality.

If roles represent the basic blocks in building organizations, then groups represent the frames within which these blocks are placed. Groups refer to two or more people who have come together to achieve some purpose and who bear an explicit psychological relationship to one another (i.e. people are in roles). The effect of a group working on tasks creates a logic and dynamic which, after a time, requires the spontaneous invention of values, norms and the specification of sanctions which are peculiar to that group. It is possible to think of a group as a relatively small molecule of roles which when linked together form giant molecules called organizations.

In this context, the term organization must not be regarded as a mechanical edifice. The term 'social institution' is sometimes used instead of organization, e.g the anthropologist Bronislaw Malinowski has used the term social institution to describe a 'group of people united in a given task or tasks, bound to a determined portion of the environment, wielding together some technical apparatus, and obeying a body of rules'. According to such a definition, a social institution could be a factory, a batallion, a hospital or a school. In this way, the anthropologist has provided a framework for studying management organization, which emphasizes that an organization is more than a collection of individuals in a group of groups.

The modern analysis of organization is predicated on the distinction between formal and informal organization. A formal organization refers to the social entity which has been specifically designed by its designers to achieve a particular purpose which requires the exploitation of the principles of specialization which, in turn, calls forth a need for co-ordination. To achieve their mission, formal organizations are usually hierarchically structured which has the effect of defining communication routes, thus spelling out who can speak to whom, who can initiate contacts and further to guard against chaos and preserve predictability, a well developed authority system is required. Informal organization is, on the other hand, the spontaneous backlash of the organized against the organizers and refers to the unplanned set of group and relations which inevitably emerge as a reaction to the restrictive structure of formal organization.

The norms of an organization not only prescribe action patterns for its members, but also prescribe the role–behaviour of its members. As organizations become larger the rules and regulations specifying the behaviour become more and more standardized. Communicating and relations become depersonalized. Such organizations are referred to as bureaucracies. The term bureaucracy, which is sometimes equated with red tape, in this context has no derogatory connotations and is used as a technical term to refer to an 'ideal type' of organization. The monumental work of the German sociologist Max Weber, because of its ponderously legalistic language, has often been ignored, while, in fact, it provides the basic description of this type of ideal organization.

THE LITERATURE OF ORGANIZATION THEORY*

Any attempt to produce a systematic summary of the literature of organization theory must take cognisance of three difficulties: firstly the diversity of the sources of material of such theories; secondly the considerable repetition encountered in the literature on account of the absence of a common technical language; and thirdly the great disparity between the effort directed to theory building and the collection of evidence.

Many executives have recorded their managerial experience in the form of a theory of organization. To some extent Brown's theory of organization falls into this category. Such theories fail

* An excellent summary of the literature of management is contained in E. F. L. Brech's *Organisation: The Framework of Management* (Longman's, 1965).

ultimately because of their lack of rigorous scientific scrutiny in terms of method and their excessive reliance on anecdotal material.

Most books on organization theory take as their point of departure a statement of the principles of scientific management in the tradition of Frederick Winslow Taylor. Taylor's approach is sometimes described as a 'physiological organization theory' because it is concerned with a narrow range of relatively simple 'physiological' tasks and emphasizes a limited number of variables. An example of the research generated by this theoretical stand is the study of the relationship between temperature and productivity of the worker. In this theory the tasks are relatively routine and simple and can be described in terms of overt behaviour without significant reference to the mental processes of the operators.

If Taylorism represents one strand of the 'classical' organization, then the other strand is the 'Administrative Management' Theory which refers to the work of Urwick, an early disciple of Taylor. The theory of departmentalization assumes that an organization, given a general purpose, will be able to identify the required tasks, to organize the jobs in sections, to place the sections within units, to unite the units within departments and to co-ordinate departments under a board all in the most economic manner.

March and Simon in *Organization* have argued that

'Propositions about organizational behaviour can be grouped in three broad classes, on the basis of their assumptions:

1. Propositions assuming that organization members, and particularly employees, are primarily *passive instruments*, capable of performing work and accepting directions but not initiating action or exerting influence in any significant way.
2. Propositions assuming that members bring to their organization *attitudes*, *values* and *goals*; that they have to be motivated or induced to participate in the system of organization behaviour; that there is incomplete parallelism between their personal goals and organization goals; and that actual or potential goal conflicts make power phenomena, attitudes, and morale centrally important in the explanation of organizational behaviour.
3. Propositions assuming that organization members are *decision makers and problem solvers*, and that perception and thought pro-

cesses are central to the explanation of behaviour in organizations.'

Putting names to these classes of propositions:

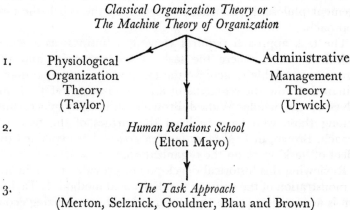

Classical Organization Theory or
The Machine Theory of Organization

I. Physiological
    Organization
    Theory
    (Taylor)

Administrative
Management
Theory
(Urwick)

2. *Human Relations School*
    (Elton Mayo)

3. *The Task Approach*
    (Merton, Selznick, Gouldner, Blau and Brown)

The classical theory of organization tends to ignore or at least to minimize the importance of the human factor, treats the worker primarily as an economic animal, is obsessed with the scientific measurement of a fair day's work and pays little or no heed to the human aspect of work. The human agent is regarded exclusively as an instrument.

The classicists' theory of motivation sometimes described as the 'carrot and stick' philosophy was predicated on the principle that the 'best man for the job' employing 'the one best way' working under piecework would give of his best. But he did not. The classicists' oversimplified motivational assumption gave no weight to the worker's need 'to belong' to his primary working group which is the central tenet of the human relations school. The human relations approach, initiated by Elton Mayo with the Hawthorne Experiment, may be regarded as a counterbalance to the excesses of Taylorism. Roethlisberger and Dickson in *Management and the Worker* argue that an industrial organization should be seen as a social system, which has two main functions – 'That of producing a product and that of creating and distributing satisfaction among the individual members of the organization'. The first which is essentially economic was, in their opinion, adequately developed while the second, which is associated with developing good human relationships, they regarded as inadequately developed. They base their whole theory of management on the development of the social organization of the plant. In turn 'good human relations' as a management philosophy is being succeeded by the third, the task approach.

The task approach requires viewing a business as a sociotechnical system where the task of the enterprise and the resources available to achieve the task are the principal determinants of how the segments of an organization relate themselves to the whole. Wilfred Brown's philosophy places him among those who have realized the virtues of the task approach. Brown, in *Exploration in Management*, has explained the effect of 'task' work on the organization.

Reviewing this historical development provides a convincing demonstration of the value of the dialectical method. If Taylorism is accepted as primarily concerned with maximizing economic effectiveness and Mayo's human relations approach is concerned with human happiness through making him feel that he belongs at the expense of the economic and technical, then it is possible to view the task approach as the fusion of the two previous systems.

The modern discipline, group dynamics, is based on the notion that there are two basic types of group function. The assumption is that most group objectives can be placed under one of two headings:

(*a*) the achievement of some specific group goal (The Task) or
(*b*) the maintenance or strengthening of the group itself; (Human Relations).

In an over-simplified picture it might be argued that management theory seems to oscillate between an over-emphasis on goal achievement, i.e. the economic well-being of the firm, to a preoccupation with the group maintenance function, i.e. the development of 'good human relations' within the firm. While this may be true of the work of Taylor and Mayo the task approach represents a synthesis of the two functions which Mayo calls the logic of efficiency and the logic of sentiment.

IS SCIENTIFIC MANAGEMENT POSSIBLE?

THE GLACIER PHILOSOPHY

By any standards the Glacier Studies must be regarded as a tremendous contribution to management knowledge on account of their scope, significance and design. These studies, which began in 1948, arose from the collaboration of Tavistock with Glacier. Although the Glacier Studies are not to be considered the acme of perfection, they nevertheless represent a considerable improvement over most of the work that has been done in this field.

The objective of this book is to make a critical assessment of the Glacier system of management. To achieve this aim, it is necessary first of all to state the postulates of Glacier philosophy; secondly the application of these postulates within the Company, require to be ascertained and the inevitable divergence between theory and practice recorded.

The Glacier Metal Company occupies a special position in the esteem of those who study organizational theory; for its pioneering experiments in management science it has rarely been bettered. The opinion might be ventured that in scope, length, theoretical significance and general impact, the Glacier studies merit comparison with the famous Hawthorne investigations which were carried out in the 'twenties by a team of social scientists from the Harvard Business School led by Elton Mayo. But it is not as experiments competing for prestige that they warrant our attention. What is specially significant in both the Glacier and Hawthorne investigations is the transformation of theory in the face of fresh empirical data. The Hawthorne Experiment began as a study of the relationship between illumination and productivity. An implicit assumption of the first experiments was the belief that the human agent may be regarded as a tool and a variation in the physical environment such as illumination would affect the efficiency of the tool, viz. the productivity of the operator. The actual experimental evidence showed that there was no relationship between these two variables: illumination and productivity. The first scientific blow had been struck against the machine theory of organization. In its place, the Hawthorne researchers placed the human relations approach. Implicit in this approach is the idea that a business should be treated as a social organization. It was precisely this view, that the firm must be regarded as a social organization, which provided the starting point for the Glacier Experiment reported by Elliott Jaques in *Changing Culture of a Factory*, published in 1951.

In Glacier, this essentially human relations view of management is in turn giving way to Brown's conception of 'task management'. The flavour and economy of task management may be gathered from two of Brown's fundamental propositions; one positive and the other negative. In 'task management' effective organization is a function of the work to be done (task) and the resources available to do it, personnel, technical and economic. In considering the question of optimal organization personality, according to Brown, plays no part. But nowhere in *Exploration in Management* is the term 'optimal' defined. In the Foreword E. L. Trist argues that 'a fundamental distinction has to be made between the adequate and the optimum: adequate solutions enable one to get by: optimum solutions enable one to attain the highest results'. The overall impression created by Brown is that optimal would be defined in terms of task effectiveness: this, in itself, would be a considerable help to management theorists and no small achievement. But what about optimal human satisfaction? The difficulties of defining this latter term are formidable. This proposition is asserted but never proved. It must remain an act of faith until it is proven.

The object of my research is to study the effect of this type of management on the attitudes and informal organization of Glacier employees. But before we proceed further it might be as well to say something about the culture prevailing at Glacier which in fact it might be better to describe as two cultures; 1950 provides an arbitrary but convenient date separating these cultures.

The Two Cultures: the Pre-1950 Culture

Before the Second World War, Glacier was no different from any other industrial organization. Brown tells us that when he became Managing Director in 1939, he was upset by the quality of relations between management and labour. Repelled and disturbed by the impact which capitalism had had on the thinking and behaviour of the workers, Brown fastened on to the idea 'that democracy should permeate into industry'. Spurred by this wave of idealism, Brown in 1942 seized upon the opportunity presented by the war of introducing a Works Council at Glacier.

From 1942 onwards at least until 1950, much of what Brown wrote, said and did was coloured by his beliefs that it was only possible 'to achieve efficiency through happiness' and the impossibility of doing efficient work 'while suffering a sense of injustice, grievance or frustration' (*Managers, Men and Morale,* 1948). With such a philosophy it can come as no surprise that before 1948 Glacier had established a liaison with Tavistock, some of whose members, as I have already mentioned, exploited an intellectual approach, which combined concepts drawn from the emergent disciples of group dynamics with some of the methods of the psycho-analysts, and whose outlook, according to their critics, was essentially therapeutic; these same critics summed up the Tavistock philosophy in the optimistic if somewhat oversimplified aphorism—when all is known, all will be well.

With this essentially optimistic view of industrial life, it was assumed that all that was needed was to set free the infinite goodwill which had been bottled up inside working men by capitalism for nearly a century. 'Working through', the technique favoured by Jaques, would help to discover the nature of the forces, both conscious and unconscious, holding in the stopper. Inside was a heady mixture, composed mainly of a desperate need for human relations which in some curious and unknown way, if got right, could also improve industrial efficiency.

In holding these views, Brown was only reflecting the culture of the times. For Britain and the United States, the 'forties had seen the vindication of democracy with its triumph over autocracy. Social scientists such as Lippitt and White had 'proved' the supremacy of democratic over both authoritarian and *laisser-faire* forms of leadership 'in the laboratory'. The Hawthorne researchers had proved that 'people matter'. These happy tidings were finding their way across the Atlantic in the attaché cases of the managers and trade unionists of the Anglo-American Productivity Teams who had gone to the Mecca of Efficiency (alias the Arsenal of Democracy) to discover the secret of this new industrial alchemy. The problem was productivity (it was a sellers' market) and the answer was human relations.

Glacier epitomized this culture. Under Brown's direction the Company began the process of transforming itself into a demo-cratic organization. Just as in Marx's ideal communist state the classes will wither away, so in Glacier, the general atmos-phere at this time seemed to imply that the conflict between management and labour was on the wane and that both sides of industry recognized that 'really we are all one big happy family'.

The best account of Glacier culture before 1950 is contained in Elliott Jaques' *Changing Culture of a Factory*. Referring to the outstanding reputation for industrial and human relations which Glacier enjoyed, Jaques, writing in 1950, makes the point that 'The quality of group relations has steadily improved over the past ten years and the firm is now accepted generally by its members at all levels as a very satisfactory place in which to work.' (Page 3.) To my mind, this was undoubtedly true of Glacier in the 'forties; indeed it was for this very reason that the Company was selected by Tavistock as the setting for their study of the social life of one industrial community.

A major Glacier achievement was the decision to give the Works Council legislative authority. While this transforming of the Works Council into a policy-making body is typical of the radical approach adopted by Wilfred Brown to organizational problems, it is worth remembering that Elliott Jaques concluded *The Changing Culture of a Factory* on a note of interrogation:

> The big remaining question is whether history is to repeat itself in a phase of technological development, proceeding independently and leaving organisation stresses to be caught up with later; or whether the experience of the past years has struck home sufficiently deeply to allow the social-technical split to be eliminated, and for organisational flexibility and skill to accompany and facilitate technological health and development. (p. 320.)

The Two Cultures: the Post-1950 Culture

Measurement of Responsibility, the title that Jaques gave to the book reporting his next piece of research at Glacier, reflects the changing Glacier attitudes of the early 'fifties, and presents a new and radical approach to the problems of payment, involv-ing a new method of analysing the work content of roles. In this novel approach all work is regarded as capable of analysis into two parts, a prescribed and a discretionary element. Jaques then makes the intriguing and exciting point that this latter part could be measured by the time span of discretion, which is the 'maximum period of time that a subordinate may continuously use sub-standard discretion in carrying out his work before this fact became apparent to his manager'. Jaques has also argued that the time span of discretion is a measure of level of work and of responsibility and that it is directly related to salary. While in this explicit sense, this revolutionary approach to the problem of payment has not been accepted in Glacier's factories, it did provide an excellent device for developing role specifications and thereby classifying organizational problems. The use of the concept 'Review Mechanism', which refers to the systematic means by which a superior becomes aware of his subordinate's use of his discretion, reveals an underlying preoccupation with efficiency, particularly the assessment of task efficiency. Indeed much of Jaques' thinking, as shown in *Measurement of Responsibility*, is in fact a necessary intellectual preliminary for the 'task themes' revealed by Brown in *Exploration in Management*.

In *Exploration in Management* (published in 1960) Brown states his faith in the task approach to organization problems. An excellent illustration of Brown's use of task management is provided by his thoughts on meetings as revealed in *Exploration in Management*. Two types of meetings are considered: the command meeting and the Works Council. It is an interesting commentary on the Glacier project which began as an experiment largely concerned with making committees more effective, should now be so heavily involved in making the order-giving session, the command meeting, effective. In essence, this preoccupation with making command meetings effective must be compared with Jaques' interest in committees and provides a neat example of the switch from human relations to task management. *Changing Culture of a Factory* is largely concerned with giving an account of how the Glacier Works Council was transformed from a two-sided to a multi-sided meeting whose principal function was now policy-making and matters of democracy were of paramount importance: *Exploration in Management* develops the ideas of task management as applied to the meeting of the manager and his subordinates in the form of the command meeting; the term 'industrial democracy' has been dropped. A new Glacier era has been ushered in where the committee, if not in disrepute, has given way to the command meeting where the manager carries full responsibility and the importance of group participation in the decision-making process has been minimized.

The use of the term 'command meeting' with all its military overtones for the Glacier order-giving session was no accident; much Glacier language has a martial ring about it. Official Glacier dogma recognizes only three levels of management within a factory. These are General Manager, unit manager and section manager. Phrases such as 'Immediate Command' and 'Extended Command' are freely bandied about. The phrase 'contraction of executive lines' has been minted which means that formal recognition has been given to the fact that management could by-pass the stewards and speak directly to the shop floor. At this juncture Glacier's need was for personnel officers who were skilled in the technique of writing role descriptions to fit the 'optimal organization' and the human relations aspect of personnel receives scant attention.

In task management, personal factors are minimized. Personality is regarded as no longer relevant in developing the 'optimal organization'. Definitions, concepts, organizational shapes and standing orders will 'structure' (a favourite Glacier word) the behaviour of organizational members. Tight control appears to be the answer to most industrial problems. In Glacier communications are couched in a new organizational argot. For those who have had military, especially, officer training, it has a somewhat familiar ring. In *Exploration in Management* Brown quotes himself as saying to a staff officer

'Well, make them, give instructions, use your authority. You are trying to get me to do your job for you. You are a Staff Officer responsible for seeing that my policy goes, get cracking, your authority is clear. If they are in real difficulties, find out and let me know, but otherwise see that they get on with it quickly.'

It is possible to summarize the post-1950 Glacier culture by saying—at the risk of oversimplification and in anticipation of the evidence—that in this period Glacier had developed into a pocket bureaucracy, with fixed routes of communication which required the use of a cryptic argot with a military ring about it; efficiency was in; and happiness, if not out, received no mention.

GLACIER ACTUALITIES: STRUCTURAL FACTORS

While the Glacier philosophy of management has its own distinctive characteristics, the behaviour of Glacier executives and workers is much more similar to their counterparts in other firms than Glacier's theory would lead one to expect. Presumably, this is because management attitudes have a minimal effect on behaviour compared with economic, social and cultural factors. These latter considerations are major determinants of organizational behaviour irrespective of the company.

Glacier is the largest manufacturer of plain bearings in Europe, and was formed in 1899 by two Americans to manufacture anti-friction metals. During the First World War, it was drawn into the making of bearings for internal combustion engines. This became a major interest of the Company as the British car industry expanded. During the Second World War,

Framework for the Present Study of the Glacier

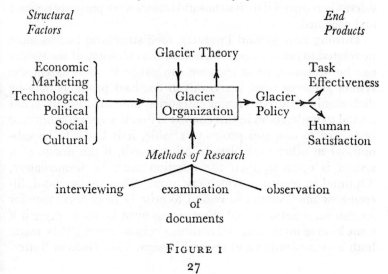

FIGURE I

27

Glacier set up a shadow factory at Ayr. After the War, this factory, known as No. 3 factory, was shifted to Kilmarnock.

Figure 1 provides a diagrammatic explanation of the framework which I propose to use to study the Glacier organization. A word of explanation about this framework may not be inappropriate at this point. The rationale of this model is to be found in the belief that three things matter in talking about organization input factors, output factors and the method employed for studying the complex relations between these two variables.

Input factors refer to the structural determinants of organizational behaviour and focus attention on the need to recognize that economics matters (levels of capital intensity), marketing consideration (a buyers' v. a sellers' market), technological developments (rate of obsolescence, need for innovation), political climate (e.g. W.A.S.P. theme of 'work is salvation' is not the same as Japanese paternalism), social setting (Ford's at Dagenham compared with Vauxhall's at Luton) and cultural considerations (e.g. Muscovite Stakanovite attitude of 'Total Push' compared with a 'presbyterian catholic' demarcation dispute torn atmosphere of a Clyde shipyard on a Monday morning after Celtic had beaten Rangers on the Saturday) are the vital, if frequently unacknowledged, determinants which, all too often, pre-empt the organizational choices of executives. The apparent contradictions in the literature of management would be considerably reduced if such structural factors were properly defined and specified.

Turning now to End Products, such structural factors must be related to output variables so that the efficiency of the system can be measured or at least we can gauge to what extent the system achieves what it sets out to do. End products may be dichotomized into two major categories, task and human. What is vital to understand in this context is that if a system is optimal in regard to one end product variable, it is likely to be suboptimal in other variables. In other words, if the design of a system is optimal, then the question must be immediately, 'Optimal in regard to which criterion?' This fundamental dilemma or multilemma in regard to criteria of performance for measuring organizational effectiveness must be made explicit if some kind of intelligent and realistic decision is going to be made both in organization and research design. This 'Guns or Butter' type model of end products becomes much more interesting when the choice the organization planners have is between high profitability in the short term, extending one's share of the market or diversifying into a new technical field.

The third major consideration in regard to this framework is the matter of research methods. In general terms, inadequate recognition in the past has been given to the proposition that the procedures for collecting data affects which 'facts' are selected, how they are recorded and what accuracy can be attached to the findings. For example, asking (interviewing) subordinates how they regard their 'highly effective' boss frequently produces a picture of leadership emphasizing the importance of democratic styles which involves them in frequent consultation and which is essentially non-threatening. Whereas watching (observing) managers in action may produce a portrait of the effective executive where the emphasis is on structure, channelling of communications, role definition and task specification. This equivalent of the Heisenberg principle of uncertainty in the behavioural science has the effect of structuring the experimenter's readings so that if he measures one variable exactly, it is usually at the expense of the accuracy of others. To facilitate the discussion, the material is presented under the following headings:

Structural Factors

Methods of Research

and End Products

(1) Structural Factors	—Part I of the Book
(2) Glacier Industrial Relations	—Part II of the Book
(3) The Section Manager	—Part III of the Book
(4) Glacier Meetings ⎱	—Part IV of the Book
(5) The Supervisor ⎰	
(6) An Assessment of the Glacier System	—Part V of the Book

The fundamental contention of this research is that the Glacier System is more determined by structural factors than any theoretical prognostications produced by its own management theorists. The major determinants of Glacier policy and behaviour are economic, marketing, technological, political, social and cultural factors.

What is being asserted is that the Glacier System is too finely balanced as constituted to stand the rigours of the British economic climate, particularly finding itself part of the most sensitive sector of the economy, namely the notoriously unstable motor car industry. The present stop-go aspects of the economy make it particularly difficult for Glacier to pursue long-term policies. Contractions produce short-time working, redundancies and sometimes strikes: booms demand the recruitment of new labour and the working of more overtime which can also stress a business and produce industrial conflict, overtime bans, walk-outs and strikes.

The present study reported in this book began in a very simple way when the opportunity became available to collect empirical data which would enable a comparison to be made between Glacier's section managers and the foremen of other companies in matters of salaries, duties, responsibilities and conditions of employment. The problem was tackled in two ways: by a postal questionnaire answered by 21 firms and by interviewing the personnel managers of these firms. The section manager role in Glacier was created in 1953 to transform the foreman's role by injecting some managerial authority into this supervisory role.

One of the most interesting points to emerge from the study was the fact that the Glacier section managers who were relatively highly paid were also very highly unionized as were the most highly paid foremen in the sample who were employed by an American manufacturing firm. These Glacier section managers provided a certain fascination for me. How did they operate? What did they do? Were they just traditional foremen with a more glamorous name? It seemed to me that they should be studied. But what would be the most appropriate method?

About this time, A. J. M. Sykes,* who had been experimenting with the technique of observation as a method of studying organizational behaviour, pointed out to me the virtues of using direct observation as a means of studying executive life. If some of these questions regarding Glacier section managers were to be answered might not an observational study be the ideal way of tackling this problem? In fact, it was decided that the section managers' behaviour should be studied by activity sampling.

The subjects of this observational study were four section managers in the Wrapped Bushes Unit whose behaviour was

* Professor A. J. M. Sykes, Head of the Department of Sociology, University of Strathclyde.

studied for three weeks using the technique of activity sampling. This behaviour sampling technique requires instantaneous observations to be made at randomly determined times. Nearly 3,000 separate observations were made. At the outset, this investigation was mainly concerned with assessing the practical possibilities of activity sampling as a method of collecting data about executive behaviour. In fact, reliability and validity checks confirmed its usefulness. A full account of this behavioural study is presented in Part III of this book.

One of the difficulties encountered in setting up this exercise was that the section managers who were the subjects of the study kept referring to a strike which had taken place the previous year in the Kilmarnock plant where the vital issue had been whether managers ought to work machines when the operatives are on strike. It seemed to me impossible to form a proper assessment of the section manager's role without considering this strike.

It is perhaps just as well to remember that the chroniclers of the Glacier Experiment have a curious attitude towards industrial conflict. In *Changing Culture of a Factory* there is reference to a strike which took place in the 'thirties at the London factory. The whole matter is treated as a sort of anachronism which is unlikely to trouble Glacier again. In fact, two strikes which took place at Glacier's Kilmarnock factory in 1957 and 1962 are described here.

It was becoming obvious as the study proceeded that there was no question of achieving finality by looking at one particular role or event. The whole system required to be considered. If the research was going to have any meaning, then the area under investigation would have to be widened.

With the limited research resources at my disposal, it was decided to focus attention on four different Glacier themes, Glacier Meetings, the Glacier Supervisor, Glacier Shop Stewards and a Glacier Wage Negotiation.

To this end, observational studies were made of two different kinds of Glacier meeting. The role, function and effectiveness of one particular command meeting was studied. The other part of this research on meetings was concerned with the study of a particular Works Council meeting at Kilmarnock.

On the Glacier Supervisor, the aim of this part of the investigation was to produce an objective record of the behaviour of eight supervisors. Again the method was the technique of activity sampling. During the three weeks of the study 6,000 observations were made.

A self-recording and observational study of a group of Glacier Shop Stewards was conducted. On account of the limited resources available for this project, it was only possible to produce a 'behavioural snapshot' of the Glacier Steward.

While these various behavioural studies were proceeding the opportunity presented itself for one complete Glacier wage negotiation to be recorded in detail.

In this study of Glacier it was necessary to supplement the empirical studies of the behaviour of the section managers and supervisors, by surveys, interviewing, and by examining Company documents. An extensive interviewing programme was initiated. Among those interviewed were the General Manager, many unit managers, a large number of section managers, and a considerable number of machine operators. Intensive interviews were conducted with the personnel staff, the Convener and his deputy of the Joint Shop Stewards Committee.

The documents examined included the minutes of the Works Committee, many official job descriptions, various Company memoranda on a wide variety of topics and the Annual Abstracts of Accounts. The many publications, concerned with the Glacier experiment, were also examined.

METHODS OF RESEARCH

It is necessary to say something about research methods for the reason that an informed, realistic and objective assessment of research findings is only possible if the techniques used in the study for gathering the evidence, their reliability and validity are specified.

To describe an activity as scientific is to confer great prestige on it; and there are many candidates for this form of canonization. To establish professional probity is the aim of every emerging occupation, and probity is measured ultimately by the degree of penetration of science into the activity. Management likewise has fastened on to science. Lacking the paraphernalia of science, viz. a definitive language, fundamental concepts and a theoretical structure, the study of management has developed slowly.

Today, it is becoming increasingly obvious that what is required is theoretically significant empirical research into organizational behaviour. But we must start with the facts. Unfortunately many managers mistakenly take their intuitive prejudices to be facts. As Carlson, a Swedish social scientist who pioneered observational studies of managerial activities, points out in *Executive Behaviour*,

> In the literature on administration most of the writing is not even concerned with results in the form of observed and classified facts, but merely with generalizations from limited experience and with principles which in some instances are clearly stated as 'axioms' or 'propositions', but which in most cases are nothing else but personal opinions. . . ./Further/ concepts like planning, co-ordination and control are of very limited use when we want to describe in an observational study the daily work and actual patterns of behaviour of a managing director. Most of these concepts do not fulfil the qualification of operational concepts that they should be synonymous with a clearly defined set of operations. . . . A fact can be established only through the careful use of objective methods of observation, measurement and experimentation. These methods must be used to provide a dependable body of knowledge about organizations.

Carlson's brilliant observation study of Swedish managing directors is the most seminal piece of research reported in the literature of executive behaviour but unfortunately, presumably because of the laborious and undramatic nature of the technique and no doubt partly on account of the difficulty of gaining access, only a handful of researchers have used observation as their method.

In the present study, early on, I decided, perhaps rather naively, that observation would be the principal technique of my research. I use the term 'rather naïvely' advisedly and in retrospect because at the beginning of the investigation, I had not fully realized the limitations of the technique; that it would most likely confirm the cliché, tell us what everybody already knew. I was also unaware of the sheer bewilderment of being confronted with a mountain of data without the help of a realistic theory into which I could pigeon-hole my facts.

Nevertheless, in spite of these difficulties, empirical studies of executive behaviour are slowly appearing in management literature, both in the United States and in Great Britain. Instead of being content with speculation about executive behaviour, social scientists are beginning to seek out the facts and to attempt to distinguish between objective data and subjective impression. A great deal of effort has been expended in the development and proving of the techniques for recording data on executive behaviour.

An entirely different approach is adopted by Glacier researchers in their approach to organizational problems.

Glacier Research Methods

The principal research method used by Glacier social scientists is the technique of 'working through'. This effort to apply psycho-analytical methods to social research requires the consultant to enter an organization only after being requested to do so. The analogy of a sick person calling in his doctor is sometimes invoked. As Jaques observes in *Changing Culture of a Factory* (p. 307):

> This process of helping a group to unearth and identify some of the less obvious influences affecting its behaviour is one which is borrowed from medical psychotherapy, from which is borrowed also the technical term *working through*. It presupposes access by a consultant trained in group methods to a group accepting the task of examining its own behaviour as and while it occurs, and a group able to learn, with the aid of interpretive comment, to recognize an increasing number of the forces, both internal and external, that are influencing its behaviour. The expectation, then, is that the group will acquire a better capacity to tolerate initially painful insights into phenomena such as scapegoating, rivalry, dependency, jealousy, futility, and despair, and thence a greater ability to deal effectively with difficult reality problems.

Advantages of 'working through' include the fact that it emphasizes the importance of negotiating 'entry' into an organization. It also has considerable diagnostic value, in the sense that it enables a researcher to identify *some* of the forces operating in a social situation. And it is as well to keep in mind that those who have taken part in these 'working through' exercises, as in psycho-analysis, report that they have enjoyed the experience. The practitioners of this technique give the impression that 'When all is known, all will be well'. This must be regarded as an over-optimistic oversimplification. Knowledge, by itself, is not the only or even the most important factor in changing attitudes. From a social science point of view 'working through' must be thought of as an essentially semantic technique and is lacking in any real efforts at reliability and validity testing. Worst of all, it is ascriptive of motive. The point is that there is a real danger that the consultant, through the process of suggestion, may project his anxieties, tensions and hostilities on to the 'solution' to the problem. Again 'working through' may be criticized on the basis that the technique approximates to a psycho-analytical interview in that the material collected is not used for predictive purposes and the facts cannot be checked because the interviews are confidential. Again, 'working through' has also been criticized on the grounds that the material produced is described as a case study. *Changing Culture of a Factory* on page 3 is described by Jaques as 'A case study; the book is not intended to be a statement of precise and definite conclusions'.

The method most frequently employed by Brown in the dialogue. These dialogues are, in fact, anecdotes, i.e.

> an account of an observation from which no conclusion can be drawn either because the observation is badly controlled, with perhaps an unreliable observer or because it is a single observation made under conditions in which numerous similar observations would be necessary for the drawing of a valid conclusion. (R. W. Thouless, *General and Social Psychology*.)

Most case studies are, in fact, anecdotes, yet they are extensively used by Brown as a basis for extracting the principles of administrative behaviour which are held to be valid not only for his particular firm in the engineering industry, with its own particular historical and geographical idiosyncrasies, but are held to be valid for all administrative behaviour.

For management teachers the case study is a favourite source of data about organizational life. The case study is usually rich in detail and depth of information and hence is particularly relevant for questions involving aetiology and development. Unfortunately most case studies seem, from a methodological point of view, naïve. Usually, the selection of the organization to be studied, the data to be collected, and the methods of its collection are treated in a casual manner. The chief limitation of the case study is that the results are based on a sample of one, so that the degree of generality of the conclusions is not known. Nevertheless, while case studies rarely prove anything, they are frequently rich in clues and insights for further investigation.

Studying Executive Behaviour by Activity Sampling

It is possible to classify research methods according to the techniques employed in the collection of data. Basically, the methods of gathering information about people are three: by observing them, by questioning them and by examining their written records. These are the basic categories of research in the social sciences, viz.: observation, interviewing and the analysis of documents. The major technique in this study is observation.

Management studies seem to be slowly moving beyond the phases of armchair theorizing and casual empiricism. This change has been expedited by the use of research techniques which require the systematic collection of behavioural data. In terms of methodology, the key question is 'who collects what?' 'Who' in this context can either be a member of the organization being studied or an outside researcher who has spent enough time in the company to ensure his acceptability. 'What' refers to the behavioural data, but says nothing about the method of collection, which can vary from observations which are strictly controlled, requiring careful definition of terms, training of observers and careful cross-checking of events with other executives by the observer, to the crudest of methods where the observations are entirely impressionistic.

In the study of executive behaviour three different methods have been used. The first, the self-recording technique, has been extensively used. The second method is the objective study of executive behaviour by a qualified outside observer. This approach has not been used so frequently as the first for the following reasons. Even if the executive to be studied has no objections to the presence of an observer, it is extremely likely that others concerned might raise objections. Again, it may be that the executive is involved in important negotiations or delicate interviews. Further, the fact that someone is under observation, may cause him to alter his behaviour. In this respect, executives are indistinguishable from machine operators. Some of these objections may be overcome if an activity sampling procedure is used where a series of intermittent observations are made.

This method requires that the behaviour to be studied should be broken into categories, and then a large number of momentary observations are made. To be effective the following conditions should be fulfilled: the observations must be momentary; they must be made at randomly selected times; the manager should not be affected by the observer's presence; and the types of event and behaviour to be observed should be carefully defined.

To test the accuracy of the activity sampling technique, it was decided to compare the results from three different phases of an observational study. A high degree of reliability was found.

It may be appropriate to ask what special virtue flows from using an elaborate technique like activity sampling as a means of studying executive behaviour. This technique has to be thought of primarily as a diagnostic technique. Behaviouristic studies of this type provide the necessary data to enable the work of the executive to be more efficiently planned, facilitate his selection and training and spotlight any weaknesses in his behaviour. As Carlson notes with approval in *Executive Behaviour*:

> In many cases this laborious recording showed only what 'everyone already knew'. Observational studies do frequently show only what was generally suspected, but call attention to the degree to which the suspicion was correct and under what conditions the facts are as 'everyone known'. The distinction is an important one, because social scientists frequently fail to distinguish between what they know (as science defines knowledge, i.e. demonstrable fact) and what they 'know' as a matter of private conviction, belief and feeling.

In this study of Glacier, the main problem was to analyse the behaviour of the executive by functions. This was achieved by using the functions programming, technical and personnel.

While these categories were carefully defined, checks of reliability showed that the greatest agreement was found between observers on the events that were labelled technical. Nevertheless, certain limitations, inherent in the technique of controlled observation, require comment. These include:

(a) the selection of the episode that defines the period of study;

(b) the assumption that the episode selected is typical;

(c) the assumption that the categories selected are exclusive, e.g. a personnel item such as manning the line may just as easily be noted under programming.

Activity Sampling or Ratio Delay Technique was developed by L. H. C. Tippett of the Shirely Institute of the British Cotton Research Association in approximately 1927. It was used by him in the textile industry to obtain information on a large number of machines and workers spread over a large area. Activity sampling has these advantages: several managers can be studied simultaneously; observations can be made over a period of days or weeks, which reduces the chance of day-to-day or week-to-week variations affecting the result; managers are not under close observation for long periods of time; measurements may be made with a pre-assigned degree of accuracy; and the results are easier to analyse. The disadvantages are that the manager being studied may change his behaviour in the presence of the observer; activity sampling does not provide as much detailed information as a continuous study. There are, in addition, the dangers of using an incorrect sample size or of failing to ensure the randomness of the observations; and the study may also be invalidated through lack of careful definition of the behaviour to be studied.

END-PRODUCTS

In management literature, in economic theory and in operations research, a significant effort is being made to state numerically as many as possible of the variables with which management must deal. This is particularly true of measures of end-products. In general, to achieve these end-products, organizational behaviour has to be supervised to ensure some correspondence between performance and plan.

In the most general sense, end-products are of two types, task and human. Task end-products refer to measures of productivity, cost, quality, scrap, safety and so forth. An ultimate measure of the human aspect of the organization is impossible to make without damaging the sacred concept of individual personality. Interim measures of the human variable might be provided by assessments of morale which in turn could be supported by measures of labour turnover, absenteeism, sickness, accidents and neurosis. The technique of cost benefit analysis could be applied here to form composite criteria which would combine measures of these separate quantities which would be weighted in some fashion and then added or averaged. Research on management control is very far from this point of composite criteria of performance which includes both task and human factors. A simpler starting point would be to consider measures of productivity and to examine the dysfunctional consequences of their over-rigid application.

Indeed the whole question of productivity warrants closer examination; particularly so as industry is being continuously exhorted by the government to increase productivity. The key question here is how can productivity be measured. Paul Chambers, chairman of I.C.I., is sceptical of the value of any traditional measure of productivity. In his 1965 presidential address to the Royal Statistical Society, he said: 'Today there is a great emphasis on productivity and there are laudable efforts not only to increase productivity but to measure it. I have yet to see a productivity index (as distinct from an efficiency input/output index for a specific industrial operation) which is both reliable and useful.' He further argued that these indices are 'sometimes useless and sometimes deliberately misleading because the designers of such measures fail to define exactly what they are measuring and why. More sophisticated measures of productivity are required which take into consideration such factors *inter alia* as the availability and cost of raw materials, power, labour and capital.' Even with such refinements the index is unlikely to be reliable. Chambers quoted the example of an experimental index in one of his divisions which had 'the awkward habit of showing an increase in productivity when the division was doing badly and slowing to a fall when the division was doing better and making larger profits'. Indeed, Chambers noted, 'No method of measuring the productivity of I.C.I. as a whole, or of a division, has been devised which is meaningful, of practical use, and reasonably simple to compile.'

Turning now to the consequences of applying these controls, the literature is replete with examples of short term compliance with standards that had bad long term consequences. Argyris gives many illustrations of people fulfilling quotas by choosing easy, quickly completed jobs towards the end of a quota period (*The Impact of Budgets on People*). Blau in his famous study of law enforcement officers in *Dynamics of a Bureaucracy* illustrates the same phenomenon by the behaviour of these officers in selecting fast, easy cases towards the end of a quota period. Berliner's reports of Soviet industry and commerce show that this phenomenon variously referred to as 'making out with a pencil', 'bleeding the line' and 'storming production' is not culture bound.

In Glacier the 'end product mix' has varied from time to time. In *Changing Culture of a Factory*, the emphasis was undoubtedly on the human measure. Starting with *Measurement of Responsibility* but more so with *Exploration in Management* the emphasis in the 'end product mix' shifted to the task. This was facilitated by the introduction first of the methods of the management consultants, particularly programming, budgetary control and work study, and by the appointment of consultants to the jobs of Managing Director and General Manager of the Kilmarnock factory. Glacier's emphasis on role descriptions, time span of discretion and review mechanism can be regarded as control devices.

An example of the 'rachet principle', where demands are increased without any corresponding increase in resources, can be seen in the demand of the General Manager to be told a unit manager's scrap figure. When the answer 'x per cent' was given the latter was told to reduce it to 'y per cent'. The dysfunctional consequence in this case is the anxiety experienced by the unit manager.

In another unit which had a very large number of batches on the shop floor at any time, both the unit manager and the section manager were spending too much of their time in programming. When a new unit manager took over, the through-put of production information and sales demand was increased to such a level by the factory programming manager that the new unit manager could not cope; another dysfunctional consequence of the over-application of a control system.

Many illustrations of the slavish application of Glacier principles to situations which the architects of the system would have considered wrong, can be provided. Two examples must suffice. The Glacier assessment system provides a good illustration of how concern for ends can be displaced on to means. Briefly, the semantic background to this problem is to be found in the Company Policy Document where the managerial authority is defined in such a way that the manager 'can determine differential rewards'. All operators are assessed quarterly. During a wage review the section manager spends a considerable proportion of his time on personnel matters, viz. completing the review of his subordinates. If he is realistic, he checks with his boss, the unit manager. These assessments are impossible to make, impossible to justify and cause trouble everywhere. As soon as the workers are told their fate the appeals start. The first level of appeal is to the unit manager whom the section manager consulted. Neither the managers nor the men believe this method to be realistic. Glacier came recently to the brink of a strike on this sacred principle. Theoretically, this policy could be changed by the managers taking the initiative in discussion. But why should ugly facts destroy a beautiful hypothesis?

More briefly, much the same discussion could be repeated concerning whether the managers should operate machines (especially if the workers are out on, say, a one day National Strike). Again, slavish application of the concept that 'his delegation of part of his work in no way effects his total responsibility' (*Exploration in Management*, p. 49) produced the unrealistic instruction for those managers who had not joined A.S.S.E.T.*
to work machines with which they were not familiar; a total strike followed.

In other words, the rigid application of these quantitative performance measurements and the slavish application of inappropriate policy have undesirable consequences for overall

* The Association of Supervisory Staffs, Executives and Technicians.

organizational performance. V. F. Ridgway in an article entitled 'Dysfunctional Consequences of Performance Measurement' in referring to the application of a composite measure of performance in U.S. Air Force wings concludes, 'When the organization was put under pressure to raise their composite score without proportionate increases in the organization's means of achieving them, there were observable unanticipated consequences in the squadrons. Under a system of multiple criteria, pressure to increase performance on one criterion might be relieved by a slackening of effort toward other criteria. But with a composite criteria, this does not seem as likely to occur ... individuals were subjected to tension, role and value conflicts, and reduced morale; air crews suffered from inter-crew antagonism, apathy, and reduced morale; organization and power structures underwent changes; communications distortions and blockages occurred; integration decreased; culture patterns changed; and norms were violated. Some of these consequences may be desirable, some undesirable. The net result, however, might easily be less effective overall performance.'

In Glacier, the same dysfunctional consequences may be observed with morale affected and anxiety generated. This is particularly true of Glacier executives whose position demands commitment to the Company philosophy–there exists a compulsion to meet formal criteria of performance, even if in so doing, high but hidden costs are produced.

A major objective of this book is to document this process by which Glacier emerged in the 'sixties as a task oriented organization, which had the exclusive right to manufacture its own organization theory and then to insist on the application by its employees.

Any assessment of the Glacier system must take cognisance of two facts: (1) that the system of philosophy, labelled Glacier, is in a continuous state of flux and still in the process of development; (2) there exists a symbiotic relationship between the Company's credos and Tavistock's research findings.

The thesis, argued here, is that the two-culture concept is the most appropriate model to explain historical developments within the Company since 1945. *Changing Culture of a Factory* illustrates the human relations approach, while *Exploration in Management* presents the task approach. The historical background to these theoretical changes requires exploration. The importance of the Company's record of poor profitability in the mid-'fifties is related to the need for the introduction of consultants into the Company. In essence, this amounted to an injection of Taylorism (work study, budgetary control and programming) into the body politic of human relations. This represented a convincing demonstration of the practical possibilities of the task approach, which essentially requires the synthesis of the two previous systems. The thesis being argued here is that in the process of absorbing the task approach, Glacier has emerged as a 'pocket bureaucracy'.

Bureaucracy, as theoretically the ideal type of organization, has no derogatory connotations in this context and is linked with the Glacier form of management. Empirical evidence from Glacier may be used to illustrate Weber's characteristics of a bureaucracy. The marks of a bureaucracy illustrated include specialization of task, specified areas of competence, established norms of conduct, and the appeals system. Glacier, by its emphasis on written policy, role definitions, depersonalized strategies and its glossary of bureaucratic terms has all the hallmarks of a bureaucracy.

The resurrection of Weber's monumental work on bureaucracy is but one symptom of the growing realization that the proper focus of a management science is neither the individual nor the group but the organization.

By presenting a series of empirical studies of organizational behaviour, which were carried out at Glacier's Kilmarnock factory, this research hopes to prepare the reader to make his own assessment of the validity of the Glacier system of management. In terms of methodology, this research sets out to ascertain the value of the technique of activity sampling as a means of examining executive behaviour. The justification of this inquiry into the efficacy of Glacier is to be found in the fact that the role of social science research is not only to produce new theories but also to examine critically the correctness and usefulness of existing organization theories.

PART I

THE GLACIER PROJECT

CHAPTER 2

THE GLACIER PROJECT

THE GLACIER SWITCH FROM HUMAN RELATIONS APPROACH TO THE TASK APPROACH

The famous Glacier Project began in 1948 and is still going on. This celebrated research project, widely admired by both academics and experienced managers alike, raises a number of intriguing questions; such as what is the correlation between theory and practice in Glacier itself; does Glacier theory produce significant economic advantages; and can the Glacier theory be applied in other industrial organizations? Before these questions can be answered, it is necessary to spell out the postulates of Glacier theory.

The two principal architects of the Glacier theory are Wilfred Brown and Elliott Jaques. In 1948, Jaques brought a team of social scientists from the Tavistock Institute of Human Relations to Glacier's London factory to make a study of the psychological and social forces affecting the social structure of one factory. This research generated a number of concepts and hypotheses about organizational behaviour which are distinctly different from those found in contemporary management literature.

But it is difficult to understand Glacier thinking unless cognisance is taken of the fact that the theory is continually evolving. Basically, the Glacier approach is dynamic and somewhat instrumental, in the sense that ideas and concepts are used as tools to achieve practical goals as well as to define theoretical concepts and as such, they are influenced both by internal organizational changes and external cultural considerations. A good example of this latter influence is provided by the idea of 'industrial democracy' which was once regarded as vital if not sacred by Wilfred Brown and is now virtually anathema to him. This change of values is but one indication of the fact that the Glacier Project which began in the human relations phase has moved into the phase of task management. Another good illustration of this point is provided by Brown's attitude to happiness and efficiency.

In 1948, when the human relation movement was at its zenith in the Company, there was published *Managers, Men and Morale*[46] which states on pages 4 and 5:

> If we attempt to achieve efficiency in the hope that happiness will follow, we are usually putting the cart before the horse. Nobody can work efficiently while suffering a sense of injustice, grievance or frustration. Good work cannot be turned out under such conditions. It is clear, therefore, that the task of the manager is to achieve efficiency through happiness. It is useless to look at the group we command and say to ourselves: 'I have done everything that a man can reasonably be expected to do to make these people happy, and consequently they should be happy. Now I can forget that issue and concentrate on efficiency.' A manager must continually observe his subordinates and courageously face the facts. If they are not happy, it is useless to escape from the responsibility which that fact imposes upon him by assuring himself that they ought to be happy. His job is to find out why they are dissatisfied; then to do everything possible to eliminate the causes of their dissatisfaction.

This plea for happiness contrasts strangely with the following extract from the Glacier Bible of task management, *Exploration in Management*, published in 1960. On page 29, Brown notes:

> In concluding this chapter, and by way of summing-up, I will now try to state in a slightly different manner the assumptions on which we base our organizational and social approach:
>
> (a)   That the Company's organization and social institutions exist primarily to facilitate the optimal discharge of the Company's work with the resources and techniques at its disposal;
>
> (b)   That changes in the work itself–the methods of doing it or of the resources available–set up pressures for change in the pattern of roles in the Executive System and of the distribution of work between roles;
>
> (c)   That a company which is unable to adapt itself, consciously

or unconsciously, to those pressures will cease to be a viable economic proposition;

(d) That our continued existence as a competitive unit is evidence of the fact that we have introduced at least some of the changes implied by changes of work, resources and methods available;

(e) That the degree of our adaptation to these pressures is one determinant of our state of competence to discharge our work as compared to the optimum attainable;

(f) That with our present lack of insight into these matters, much of our adaptation is done not as a piece of conscious planning, but is forced upon us by feelings of pressure whose source is not always recognized;

(g) That our approach to the problem of establishing better organization and more appropriate social organization is by analysing the way in which work, resources and methods have changed and are likely to change; the adjustments implied by these changes; and the extent to which these adjustments have already taken place.

The Company in the 'forties was preoccupied with the happiness of the employees, with efficiency only of secondary importance. By the 'sixties, 'the optimal discharge of the Company's work' is the prime responsibility and happiness, social justice and industrial democracy are no longer part of the official Glacier terminology.

The same point regarding the switch from 'maximizing happiness to optimizing effectiveness' has been made by Austen Albu,[2] in the introduction to his essay *Glacier's Experiment in Management*, observes 'Over the door of the building which until recently housed the main offices of the Glacier Metal Company, there is carved in large letters: "Life without industry is guilt; industry without art is brutality". Although these words were the expression of faith by the previous owner, they might well serve to explain the psychological drive which has made Glacier one of the most famous and controversial names in the study and teaching of management methods. For what started as a fumbling attempt to find a reasonable relationship between employer and worker, with vague ideas of industrial democracy as an ultimate target, has by now become a full-scale experiment in the application of a theory of work and its organization in an employment situation.'

THE GLACIER PROJECT

The Glacier Metal Company was selected because the Institute regarded it as fulfilling the conditions necessary for a project of this type. The Institute insisted that management, supervision and workers should each independently agree to co-operate in any projected experiment.

The Independent Role of the Research Team

Great care was taken by the Tavistock researchers to protect the independent role of the research team. They argued, on scientific as well as theoretical grounds, that if an independent relationship was to be achieved then it was necessary not to become involved with members, including management and workers of the factory, in leisure time activities. To facilitate this an agreed set of principles was drawn up to define the relationship between the research team and the firm. A number of investigations were carried out by the team.

While all of these researches are of importance and interest, the flavour of Jaques' penetrating powers of analysis can be gained from his study of the Works Council. But first a word about methods. The methods used by the Tavistock team are described on page 306 of *Changing Culture in a Factory* under the heading 'Group Tensions and Working-through'. In this approach, groups who had asked the assistance '. . . of the team in exploring underlying and concealed forces–whether psychological, cultural, structural, or technological–that were impeding their progress or otherwise reducing their efficiency. So far as this meant uncovering forces that had gone unrecognized either through being consciously or unconsciously ignored or denied, resistances were encountered. For to put up with the continuation of the problem was often felt to be less painful than to undergo the changes required for its resolution. The method used was to draw attention to the nature of the resistance on a basis of facts known to those concerned. Opportunities were taken to illuminate in the specific situation the meaning of the feelings (whether of fear, guilt or suspicion) that constituted the unpalatable background to anxieties that were present about undergoing changes that were necessary. When successful, interpretations of this kind allowed group members to express feelings which they had been suppressing sometimes for years, and then to develop an altered attitude to the problem under consideration. Even awkward or over-blunt comments often came as a relief.'

This therapeutic approach to social organizations is an extremely daring and unorthodox method whereby supposedly unconscious anxieties and hostilities are mobilized and then released. It can provoke considerable resistance. How should this resistance be dealt with? Jaques' answer on page 308 of *Changing Culture of a Factory* is reminiscent of Freud's rejoinder to those who cannot accept the principles of psycho-analysis, 'that there are no logical difficulties in psycho-analysis, only psychological difficulties'. For Jaques, 'The function of the consultant was to make such observations as would help those concerned to recognize some of the less apparent factors affecting the immediate situation, particularly the stresses in the face-to-face group. There was resistance to his interpretations, varying from polite denial or ignoring of his remarks to expressed annoyance or irritation. Where he felt justified, he used these reactions to himself to show the group how uncomfortable they felt about their own relationships, and that they were transferring on to him, as the person bringing these problems into the open, their own attitudes towards each other.'

THE HISTORY OF JOINT CONSULTATION IN THE GLACIER METAL COMPANY

Formal Consultation Committees date from 1941. In introducing formal consultation at this time, the Glacier Metal Company like many other companies was reacting to war-time needs.

In December 1941, the Managing Director circulated a memorandum proposing that the 'non-staff and staff employees should democratically elect from among their members a Works Committee composed of 24, of whom not less than five shall be women . . . and that a works council shall be formed as follows. The Works Committee shall select from their members four men and two women to form part of the Works Council and five members of management as follows: one director, a works manager, an assistant manager, a production manager, one departmental manager representing the foremen of the company.'[65]

At this stage there was no insistence that members of the works committee should be members of recognized trade unions but, in fact, the trade unionists began to insist on this point. As in the case of I.C.I., membership of a recognized trade union was in fact made a necessary condition for election to the works committee. In 1947, the managing director who had until then held the position of chairman of the Council, relinquished this post in favour of the medical officer. This was done to allow the managing director to speak freely. It is interesting to note that the medical officer was selected partly on account of his skill as a chairman and partly on account of the neutral position which he occupied in the factory.

Before proceeding further in discussing the development of the consultative procedures in this Company, it might be as well to say something about the progressive reputation for which this Company is noted. All observers seem to have been impressed by the good morale prevailing at Glacier's London factory. As Jaques notes on page 36 of *Changing Culture in a Factory*, 'The first impression of Institute staff members, like that of the psychologist two years before, was that a remarkably sound morale existed in the concern. There appeared to be an overall sense of security, and a marked feeling of freedom to bring up those things which caused trouble or bother. Accordingly, in spite of the many difficulties that were expressed by the employees, the factory was described as a fine place in which to work, in which everyone was "treated as a human being", in a manner unfamiliar to many who had worked elsewhere.'

The high morale, whether it was a consequence of the Company's attitude towards profits or their unusual joint consultative procedures, was certainly a characteristic of the organization until the early 'fifties. Even in the mid-'fifties, the Company's advertisements emphasized the firm's international reputation for good human and industrial relations. Many of the firm's best managers and technologists joined Glacier for this reason. The Company's advertisements have since dropped this approach. A good illustration of the relationships at Glacier in the immediate post-war era is provided by the Courtenay Plan.

Following a period of prosperity, the Board of Directors in 1947 decided that an additional £30,000 per annum could be added to the firm's wages and salaries. The question arose as to how this increase was to be distributed. The problem was referred to the Works Council. They promptly appointed a committee to deal with the matter. This body became known as the 'Gold Brick Committee'. It invited members of the firm to make suggestions on this question of distribution, and the 'Courtenay Plan' was the result. The Plan made the following proposals:

1. There was to be an increase in wages and salaries ranging from 2s. 6d. to 10s. per week, which was awarded in proportion to the person's total income.
2. An extensive sickness benefit scheme was introduced under which 88 hours' sickness absence per annum with full pay was provided.
3. On the suggestion of management, formal time keeping in the form of clocking on and clocking off was abolished.

According to Jaques, it can be taken as indicative of the high morale prevailing in this factory that there was only a slight increase in the sickness absence when this scheme was introduced. Again, the abolition of clocking on produced no obvious increase in lateness. This plan was implemented in June 1948.

In January 1949 the Council was made up of eighteen members, a chairman and a minutes secretary. The nine works committee members were elected directly to that body and the nine management members, with the exception of the representative from the superintendents' committee, were appointed by the managing director. The council usually met once a month, immediately after working hours. According to Jaques there was a certain measure of dissatisfaction among the Works Council members regarding the problems of consultation. They therefore invited the research team to help in solving 'the outstanding problems generally relating to joint consultative machinery throughout the company'. Social scientists from Tavistock were soon made aware of the very complex undertaking which had been presented to them.

The research team began their investigation by surveying the Council Minutes. They found that when the Council had started in 1942 it had dealt mainly with matters of principle which it had been able to resolve, but it had then turned to the rather simpler problems concerned with the canteen, overtime work, holidays, lateness and absenteeism. However, over the years the Council's interest began to move back towards more important matters of policy. Elliott Jaques interpreted these findings as supportive of the view that with the complex, difficult problems of policy, it was impossible for the Council to obtain 'satisfying and clear cut solutions'.

There seemed to be a fair degree of confusion about the functions and responsibilities of the Works Council. This confusion was reflected particularly in the powers of the standing committees. To overcome this difficulty it was suggested that a comprehensive organization of standing committees be set up; it was also recommended that every member of the Council be on one of these committees.

These changes produced a considerable measure of disquiet and anxiety among the members of the Council. Two main fears were voiced:

1. That the proposed changes would increase the status and authority of the Council.
2. It was felt on the other hand that the standing committees might usurp the work of the Council.

Again when each member realized on seeing his own name listed that he himself would become either chairman or member of one of these committees, it produced a certain measure of anxiety. But according to Jaques, more fundamental than all of this was the fear that to accept the responsibilities involved in the new arrangements was beyond the abilities and qualifications of the members. This attitude of Jaques that the workers' representatives were basically frightened of accepting responsibility is one that should be viewed with some reservation.

A more plausible view would be that the representatives intuitively realized that they could never fully control the policy of the Company. For example, surely the Company's policy of trebling the rate of ordinary dividend over a period of fourteen years is one which affects the firm's employees in a significant way; yet this is an area over which the workers have virtually no control. Again, have the workers' representatives the necessary training and experience to make policy for the firm? The essence of the matter is that the representatives lack the necessary structural and sapiential authority to make policy. In this comment the word 'plausible' is used advisedly because, in questions of motive, certainty can never be achieved.

This reservation about the accuracy of Jaques' interpretation of shopfloor behaviour exemplifies a frequently cited criticism of the Tavistock method of 'working through'. By the same token, when a consultant encounters resistance from a client, he may ascribe whatever motive he wishes, including scapegoating, aggression, withdrawal, displacement, anxiety or hostility.

THE WORKS COUNCIL AND
POLICY MAKING

In May 1949, the Managing Director introduced a revolutionary change in the Works Council. He proposed that the Council should become a policy-making body for the Company so that 'every major policy decision would become a matter for consultation with the entire Works Council'. The Managing Director rightly argued that there were two stages in management: policy making and executive action. He further argued that the Works Council should be responsible for policy and management for executive action. These revolutionary proposals produced such a shock in the Council that the meeting, in order to avoid considering the awkward implications of this radical innovation, turned to the problem of electing members to the standing committees. But the Managing Director insisted that they should first consider this question as to whether the Council was a policy-making body before dealing with the problem of nominations. This created an impasse. It was obvious that some time was required to allow the Council to adapt itself to such a proposal. To facilitate this adaptation the research team presented a special report to the Council in July 1949. They noted that reconstruction of the Council's function was required. In their report they drew attention to a number of symptoms, indicative of the inadequacy of the Council, 'Concern about the demands on people's time; feelings that being an elected representative lowered rather than raised prestige; fear of victimization or of upsetting other people if you said what you felt; the recurrence of the same problems year after year at Works Conferences, and nothing done about them; reporting the good features of Glacier to others as an escape from dealing with internal problems.'[65] It was felt that these were only symptoms of underlying problems such as evasion of its executive responsibility and 'the failure to work out effective face-to-face relations between persons and groups in the executive and consultative channels'.[65] This report was not discussed on the evening when it was presented. It was decided that the Council should go away *en bloc* for a weekend to discuss the significance of this report. A weekend conference was held in a centre near London to discuss this problem of policy-making and joint consultation. Some notion of the atmosphere of uncertainty and insecurity may be gained from the fact that before the main discussion, there was an ordinary meeting to settle the date for a two-week holiday shut-down which the Council was unable to resolve.

The main discussion started on the Saturday morning with Brown making a statement on the functions of the Council, in relation to the roles of the executive and the managing director. Somewhat idealistically he defined the purpose of the Company as 'the continuity and expansion of a working community which aimed at the establishment of such internal conditions as would enable its members to serve society, to serve their own dependents, and to serve each other, and to do these things with a sense of creative satisfaction'.[65] Some idea of the 'democratic' flavour of the 'forties can be caught in his view that this aim could be achieved by 'concentrating on the subsidiary aims of seeking the maximum technological efficiency and the greatest organizational efficiency; by seeking to establish an increasingly democratic government of the factory which would award fair responsibilities, rights, and opportunities to the producers, executives, consumers, and shareholders, and by seeking through work to earn such revenue as would enable the Company to achieve those objects mentioned under the Financial Policy of the Principles of Organisation'.[65]

He then defined the functions of the Council as 'to carry the responsibility of deciding in the light of opinions of producers and managers, and in the light of the interests of consumers and the nation at large, the principles and policies which should govern the executive management of the company . . .'[65] The management of the firm would operate within the framework of the policy as agreed by the Works Council.

In spite of the exhortations of management, most of the workers' representatives despaired of having to accept further responsibilities. They were frightened of the criticisms of their constituents and of being overwhelmed by management. A very heated discussion developed. The question also arose as to whether the Council members were delegates or representatives. It appeared that members oscillated between these two roles. When the going was hard they sought refuge in the more easily defined role of representative (i.e. they required to return to their constituents to be briefed on their views), but when things improved they assumed the more difficult role of delegate (i.e. they felt free to speak for their constituents without immediate further consultation). In general terms, it appeared that the members of the Council were going to elaborate lengths to avoid facing the realities involved in the new role.

On Sunday morning the standing committee reported a series of recommendations for the conference. According to Jaques these recommendations were both numerous and constructive and as each report was given, the morale of the members improved steadily. It was apparently only at this stage that the Council slowly began to accept its responsibility as a policy-making organization.

THE STRUCTURE OF THE WORKS COUNCIL

A consideration of the structure of the Works Council indicated that it was not an appropriate organization for policy making. In the factory there were three levels of staff known as Grade I (general managers and unit managers*), Grade II (section manager*), and Grade III (supervisors*). Grade III staff was only indirectly represented through the works committee at the divisional manager's meeting. To overcome these difficulties, a

* These are the current terms for these roles and not necessarily those in use in 1949.

new structure was proposed. It was proposed that a fourteen-member Works Council be set up as follows:

Grade I	Staff	1
Grade II	Staff	2
Grade III	Staff	3
Hourly paid operatives		7
General Manager		1
TOTAL		14

In August the new Council constitution, with a few minor amendments, was adopted; the role of the Council as a policy-making body has been clearly defined. All decisions had to be unanimous before they were accepted as policy. The role of unanimity in this context is to ensure, after the discussions in the Council, factory-wide commitment to the decision finally agreed. As Jacques notes on page 266 of *Changing Culture of a Factory*, 'It is precisely because power relations may shift, while the authority structure remains unchanged, that the firm's unanimity principle is of such value, for it allows the continuous testing-out and exploration of the power situation by means of constructive discussion, instead of the intermittent testing of power which accompanies executive policies and actions which have not been agreed and which when unacceptable lead to a piling up of stress and to explosive outcomes. Not that the unanimity principle automatically solves questions of power relationships; rather is it to be seen as a mechanism for facilitating more constructive relationships and ensuring more realistic compromises when the necessary motivations and skills exist in those concerned.' As an example of the efficacy of this new approach the Council at its August meeting tackled two major questions: (1) the problem of redundancy, (2) the wage policy of the factory as a whole.

In conclusion, the study of the Works Council presents an excellent illustration of the approach favoured by Elliott Jaques; it involved an extensive work-through lasting nearly a year and was predicated on the principle that first reactions in many cases can only be superficial symptoms which show a certain reluctance to face the reality of the problem. But, by virtue of this difficult process of working through to an all-factory representational body, it had become possible to create a sound basis for the democratic sanctioning of executive authority.

THEORETICAL BASIS OF CHANGING CULTURE OF A FACTORY

In Jaques' view, the unique character of a factory arises as a consequence of the connection between the factors of structure, culture and personality. Social structure is defined as the more or less identifiable and stable pattern of organization of the firm including the executive system, consultative system and grading system. Structure in this sense is made up of a network of roles. For every defined position in the organization there is an expectation, which is held by members of the organization, of what should be the *behaviour* of the person carrying the position. A major criticism of Jaques' theoretical work is his failure to distinguish between role and role behaviour. This distinction is more fully discussed at a later stage in this Chapter. A role encompasses among other things duties and obligations. Roles are necessarily interdependent. To define the role associated with any given position in an organization necessitates defining related roles. Closely associated with the term role is the concept of status. Jaques defines status as the value attached to a role or stratum of roles.

He defines 'the culture of the factory' as its customary and traditional way of thinking and of doing things, which is shared to a greater or lesser degree by all its members, and which new members must learn, and at least partially accept, in order to be accepted into service in the firm.[65] Personality is defined as the total psychological make-up of the individual. It is the interaction of these three factors, structure, culture and personality, that gives each industrial community its own peculiar flavour.

The executive system is regarded as the hierarchy of executive roles. In this context, a manager is defined as the occupant of an executive role that carries the responsibility for subordinates and authority over them. In dealing with the problem of role relationships, two types are specified; line relationships and functional relationships. Line relationships refer to the vertical relationships between superior and inferior roles within the same line of command. Functional relations refer to horizontal or diagonal relationships in an executive system. According to Jaques' narrow definitions line relationship arises when a person in a superior role instructs or issues an order to a subordinate. The functional relationship develops when a manager is authorized by his superior to seek a prescription or advice from a specialist outside his line of command.

Jaques provides many illustrations of how role theory may be used to explain how executives evade responsibility. Jaques observes on page 300 of *Changing Culture of a Factory* that 'A person who occupies a number of roles acquires relationships with a number of different sets of people, not to mention different relations with the same people'. At this point Jaques introduces the somewhat startling and disturbing idea of dividing a role and argues 'A role divided between two or more persons imposes on those concerned the necessity of co-operating as a role-carrying group. Changes in social structure entail changes in formally established relations and, hence, also require the working out of new personal networks. These potentially confusing and difficult inter-personal connections demonstrate the necessity of adhering rigorously to the role required by each particular situation. Accomplishment of such behaviour becomes possible only when the roles themselves have been precisely defined.' It is difficult to accept the need to introduce the idea of 'dividing roles'. The confusion is between role and function. If a number of people share a function, then a group or meeting has been created. Jaques is on much safer ground when he turns to practical illustrations. An excellent example of Jaques' technique of analysis is his penetrating observation of the confusion generated by the Managing Director's behaviour when he held two roles, as Managing Director, as well as being General Manager of No. 1 factory. Apparently it was not uncommon for him when facing his departmental managers, *qua* General Manager, for him to withdraw into his role of Managing Director. Having two roles in this way provided him with an excellent defence mechanism.

A casual reader of *Exploration in Management* might be forgiven for wondering if Wilfred Brown paid much heed to this rather penetrating insight into his capacity for exploiting a number of roles. The point that is being made that many of the examples given in *Exploration in Management* represent dialogues with the author playing the heavy uncle, remonstrating with some Company executive. It is impossible to tell from these anecdotes in which role the author is. Is he Chairman, Managing Director, or General Manager? From the contents of the conversations, it is possible to guess that the other person acts as if he is at a considerable disadvantage in terms of status.

The descriptions given of the command meeting and techniques such as 'the contraction of executive lines' seem more realistic if it is accepted that a person, who is the Chairman of the Company and possibly the Managing Director, decides to convene a meeting of managers. Surely the status gradient is too steep to permit much participation. Since a great deal of *Exploration in Management* appears to be drawn from autobiographical case studies, it is possible to argue that the principles developed from such case material are only valid in the limited context from which they are derived. Their validity, if established, relates only to the upper echelons of a medium sized light engineering company when the Chairman or Managing Director contacts an unspecified manager of his company. This would impose a severe restriction on what, after all, in any case is regarded by most management scientists as a rather inferior research method, viz. the autobiographical case study.

Further, it may be noted that Jaques' study which was concerned with examining the social organization of one factory, ended by stressing the importance of role definition and clarification. Much of Jaques' work was concerned with specifying and defining roles and making explicit the relations between roles. In this context, not unexpectedly a great deal of resistance was encountered clarifying roles. This problem, of course, is not one of intellectual clarification alone, but inevitably involves emotional problems as well. In some cases, role confusion may be used as a defence mechanism.

Another penetrating example of defensive behaviour which Jaques spotlighted is adaptive segregation, which he neatly defines as 'the process of keeping communications between groups at an optimal level by the creative use of selective barriers'. An example of this type of behaviour is the apparent lack of interest of workers in the Works Councils. There seems to be in this behaviour a certain measure of survival value, in the sense that the workers are content to get on with their own jobs provided the processes of consultation are working reasonably well. Adaptive segregation in this case is functionally significant. Jaques' notion of adaptive segregation has considerable explanatory value in the field of executive behaviour. A good illustration of the relevance of this proposition is provided by the fact that many managers ignore certain parts of the work in the absence of negative feed-back. But should the situation change and they become aware of negative evidence from an area within their command which they have been unconsciously ignoring then they will take the necessary action to meet this situation. Because ultimately the manager cannot attend to everything all of the time, he is compelled to pursue a policy of adaptive segregation.

Jaques brings *The Changing Culture of a Factory* to a close by referring on pages 418–19 to 'The constructive attitudes of those who brought about changes in the factory were sufficiently tough and resilient to survive the difficulties encountered. The developments in the executive structure and joint consultation had combined to lay the basis for solid morale in the firm.'

THE GLACIER CONCEPT OF MANAGEMENT

The most comprehensive and detailed exposition of the Glacier system of management has been provided by Wilfred Brown in *Exploration in Management*. It is greatly to the credit of the present Glacier system of management that it puts such great emphasis on written policy. In the Policy Document for the Company, which represents something of a *tour de force* and which occupies twenty-seven printed pages, there are outlined four systems of organization:

> The Legislative System
> The Executive System
> The Representative System
> The Appeals System.

Referring to these four systems, Brown observes, 'We know now that there are a number of different systems of interconnected roles in operation in the Company: the Executive System, the Representative System and the Legislative System. People move, in the course of their daily work, from a role in one system to a different role in another system; and it is essential that this be recognised and that behaviour appropriate to the role be adopted if trouble is to be avoided'. Within this extremely elegant framework provided by these four systems, Brown's distinctive approach to the theory of organization is revealed in what Trist calls Brown's 'credo', the task approach'. It is vital to keep in mind at all times that in the task approach, optimal organization is a function of the work to be done (the task) and the resources available to do the work, personnel, technical and economic resources, and apparently factors such as personality are irrelevant. On the other hand, the background against which the task management operates is provided by the workings of the four systems.

In a way these four systems are analogous to those operating at a national level, e.g. the Legislative System to Parliament, the Executive System to the Civil Service, the Representative System to the Trade Unions, and the Appeals System to that part of the Legal System which specifies the right that everyone has to appeal from a lower court to a higher court. Or, putting it another way, the development of these four systems by Glacier represents an attempt to introduce the principal institutions of the nation, albeit, writ small, at a factory level. This brilliant industrial model of the city state represents a radical, novel and fundamental approach to the problem of making policy explicit, of ensuring democratic acceptance of this policy and operating it within a framework that is both honest and just.

The Legislative System

The function of the Legislative System is to make policy for the whole organization. Theoretically the policy-making institutions in Glacier are the Works Councils. The Legislative System is made up of the Councils where the executive and representative systems meet and 'by means of which every member can participate in formulating policy and in assessing the result and implementation of that policy'. In the Councils a proposal must be passed unanimously before it is accepted. Examples of the policies which have been produced by the Legislative System are the Redundancy Policy and the Policy on Appointments. For example, the Policy on Appointments specifies that all appointments will be made from within, that the most scientific methods of selection will be used and that the personnel department will be involved in the process of appointments and so on.

The Executive System

In *Exploration in Management* Brown points out that ' "The Executive System" is defined in our Company Policy Document as: "The network of positions to which the Company's work is assigned. It is made up of positions which shall be called Executive Roles. The Executive System includes all members of the Operating Organisations, a member being in his Executive Role while he is carrying out his job responsibility".'

The Executive System represents a network of roles for carrying out the day-to-day work of the Company within the framework of the Company policy. Brown himself is not unaware of the theoretical imperfections of this model. For example, in *Exploration in Management* (p. 197) Brown criticizes the definition of policy given in the Company Policy Document. As he points out in a footnote on page 197, 'I think that this definition can be validly criticized on two counts–on the one hand, it can be seen that the attempt has been made to define policy largely by reference to its source, rather than to its inherent nature; and, on the other hand, the definition is, in any case, incorrect, since policy emanates also from the Board of Directors.' Brown goes on to say, 'Policy, as the term is used in this book, means the prescribed part of a role, or group of roles'. Brown further argues that, 'A policy instruction is quite simply a communication from a manager to any or all of his subordinates, stating the policies which they must observe'. Thus Brown appears to identify policy with instructions. This is a virtual *volte-face* from the position adopted by Jaques in *Changing Culture of a Factory*, where it is assumed that policy is always a consequence of consultation.

This matter of how policy is in fact made requires further analysis. In general terms, policy refers to the established, accepted and codified framework of rules which are intended to structure the behavioural choices of a member of an organizaion and thus enable him to discharge his function. The assumpion on which Glacier's earlier concept of policy-making was ased was that the authority to make policy could be abrogated o the Works Council. Implicit in this approach was the notion hat a Board of Directors (in Glacier, the Works Council) could nake policy, from which the General Manager could fashion lirectives, which unit managers could translate into prorammes, which in sections would be seen as loads and which

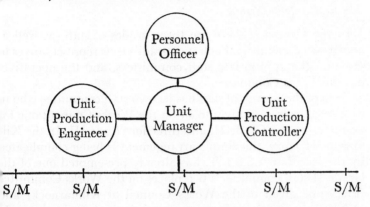

ltimately would take the form of instructions for the shopfloor perative. Brown's present position on policy making challenges his essentially theological picture of policy making and is redicated on the realistic assumption that policy making happens at all levels in a business and sometimes the policies flow p the organization.

Brown defines the terms 'Operational Manager' and 'Specialst'. 'An Operational Manager is one who carries out the whole, r some part, of the operational work of the Company. Specialist ole: a role in which the occupant is accountable for assisting a nanager through the discharge of one or more of the following: Advisory; Service-providing; Staff; Technical Co-ordination.'

In this system, great pains are taken to ensure harmonious elationships between the executive managers and specialists nd, above all, to resolve the problems that arise when there is failure to apply the principle of 'one man, one boss'. To solve his problem, Brown introduces the concept of the nuclear command structure in which the line manager has three staff officers, rogramming, technical and personnel. This means, in fact, that

the line manager carries executive responsibility for his sub
ordinates (who are responsible to him and no one else), but i
this task he has three colleagues to advise him. Their advice i
related to when to do it (programming), how to do it (technical
and who is to do it (personnel). The structure is represented a
every level in the organization. An example of this type o
organization is provided at unit manager level (see page 65)

The Representative System

In the Company there are three grades of staff, as well a
hourly rated members. Each staff grade elects representatives t
serve on the appropriate staff committees, and the operative
have a Works Committee.

Each of these levels of staff has its own staff committee who i
turn select representatives to sit on the Works Council; one fo
Grade I, two for Grade II, and three for Grade III. In the Kil
marnock factory, this simple arrangement is being complicate
by the fact that A.S.S.E.T. has already pre-empted one of th
Grade II staff committee's two places on the Works Committe
(the name given to the Works Council at Kilmarnock) an
D.A.T.A. are applying pressure to gain a similar advantage. I
the factory there are four representative committees.

At Kilmarnock, the workers are represented by shop steward
Committees are formed by Units. There are 42 stewards in th
Kilmarnock factory. At factory level there is a Joint Sho
Stewards Committee (J.S.S.C.). The J.S.S.C. has an executiv
of seven who are known as the Executive Seven. The J.S.S.C
elects seven representatives who sit on the Works Committee.

The Covener of the J.S.S.C. is provided with an office, tele
phone and clerical assistance. He is completely free from h
operative duties and has substantial control over his move
ments. Generally, the stewards appear to have real freedom an
are very heavily involved in stewards' duties. Victimization
stewards is virtually unknown.

The Appeal System

The Appeal System was introduced in writing in 1949, i.
during the human relations period. Its main provisions are a
follows:

1. Every member has the right to appeal against the decision of his manager through the successive levels of the company.
2. Subject to special provisions he can appeal to an Appeal Tribunal consisting of an independent outside chairman (appointed by the Works Council), a management member and a representative.
3. At each hearing the member may be represented and the relevant manager present.
4. Either party may refer the dispute for counselling to the Personnel Officer but if this fails the appeal can proceed.
5. The procedure may be shortened by taking the appeal straight to the chief executive.

It is interesting to note that the Appeal Tribunal has never been used – that the vast majority of appeals reaching the Managing Director are disallowed.

In general, the attitude of general managers and unit managers to the Appeals System is to back up the decision of their subordinate managers. This view is reflected in the minds of the workers who are somewhat sceptical of the virtues of this system. The shop stewards lack confidence in the Appeals System for appeals against wage assessments. The explanation for this attitude is to be found in the somewhat arbitrary way appeals against wage assessments are handled by senior managers – fifty per cent are settled in favour of the appellant, fifty per cent against. (This matter of the Workers' attitudes to the Appeals System is discussed more fully in Chapter 5.) For appeals against dismissals, on the other hand, there is considerable respect.

At first the Appeals procedure was regarded as a separate system. The implication of this proposition was that the manager had a 'judicial' role. Wilfred Brown now accepts that the Appeals procedure is part of the Executive System. In *Exploration in Management*, page 253, Wilfred Brown concludes by saying, 'I have, therefore, come to the conclusion that an appeal process is part of the Executive System; and that it can be described quite simply as a mechanism which allows a person to make contacts at every higher level without by-passing his immediate manager. This changed conception does not, however, seem to call for any amendment of the detailed provisions for handling appeals set out in our Policy Document.'

It is this type of unilateral action that minimizes the importance of moral consideration that is the most worrying feature of Glacier in the task phase. Moral considerations are of prime importance in the social life of industry, T. T. Paterson in 'Towards a theory of retribution in industry'. (*The Manager*,[110] March 1961) observes, 'Retribution can be imposed only in situations where the relations are responsibility and accountability. That is to say retribution is an activity restricted to the system of structural authority, which involves the imperatives of obligation and expectation in terms of rightness. This rightness is inherent in the social contract expressed in written, verbal or traditional agreements. It is this contract with which the trade unions are very concerned. It is indeed the first concern of a trade union to scrutinize the rightfulness of managerial activity, wherefore trade unions are constantly on the alert for reputedly wrongful retribution.'

On the method of hearing an appeal Wilfred Brown on page 253 notes that, 'A manager hearing an appeal does so in his managerial role. It is executive terms of reference which insist that he must: behave impartially, listen carefully to all the evidence, base his decisions on policy rather than his own feelings, and so on.'

Robert McCusker,[96] an official of A.S.S.E.T. in 'Ice Cold at Glacier Metal' (*Trade Union Affairs No. 4*) referring to the Appeals System, notes, 'Here again, we would seem to have the ideal of industrial democracy, but again there are some snags to it. For example, although the appellant can be represented at various stages of appeal by one of his colleagues, he is not allowed to be represented by a full-time trade union officer.'

Analysing Organizational Behaviour

Within the framework of these systems Wilfred Brown has developed a method for analysing organizational behaviour. As usual in *Exploration in Management* some definitions are required. First he defines a decision as a commitment to action. A role 'is a position into which decision making work is allocated'.

This is a somewhat inadequate definition of role. When con-

rasted with Jaques' definition of this term, it is distinctly con-
using. Brown's definition of a role is a major weakness in his
heorizing and represents a fundamental difficulty which illum-
nates the faulty logic underlying much of his thinking about
organization. To clarify this difficulty, it is necessary to intro-
luce and define two terms: role and role-behaviour.

Roles only arise in groups and organizations, and only have
neaning in relation to other roles. A role refers to the function
of the role holder (and can only be defined in relation to the
unction of other roles with which the role-holder is required to
nteract) which is *expected* of the person in the role, irrespective
of who he is. Thus a role is socially ordained by the other roles
vith which the role is formally linked. Role-behaviour refers to
1ow the role-holder interprets the role or part he has been
assigned. This involves consideration of two aspects which
3rown chooses to ignore; personality, and the attitudes a person
orings to work. The former can be illustrated by his definition
of optimal organization which explicitly excludes personality,
and the latter by his insistence on the concept of 'contraction of
executive lines' which is an euphemism for bypassing the shop
stewards, anathema to most active trade unionists.

An Executive System is made up of a hierarchy of inter-
related roles. To facilitate analysis Brown introduces on page 24
of *Exploration in Management* four useful terms. These are:

Manifest – the situation as formally described and displayed.
Assumed – the situation as it is assumed to be by the individual
             concerned. There may or may not be consistency
             between the 'assumed' and the 'manifest' situation.
Extant   – the situation as revealed by systematic exploration
             and analysis. (It can never be completely known.)
Requisite – the situation as it would have to be to accord with
             the real properties of the field in which it exists.

Using these four possible analyses of an organization, the
manifest (what it is supposed to be), the assumed (what it
appears to be), the extant (what it is) and the requisite (what
it should be), Brown proceeds to solve a number of practical
problems that have arisen in his Company. Incidentally trans-
lating these four terms into the formal/informal language
would produce the following legend:

$$\left.\begin{array}{l}\text{manifest} \\ \text{assumed}\end{array}\right\} = \text{formal}$$

$$\text{extant} \quad = \text{informal}$$

$$\text{requisite} \quad = \text{ideal}$$

Nevertheless, once this analysis has been made, Brown proceeds to apply these principles in his search for an executive system. As Brown[26] says, 'The chapters that follow are in themselves examples of how the ideas which have been discussed so far can be used' (p. 44).

APPLYING THESE IDEAS TO GLACIER

The chapters where Brown uses this technique of analysis to clarify the role of specialists are among the best in his book. In these chapters on specialists' work, he redefines the traditional concepts of line and staff management in terms of the task approach. Staff work or specialist work, as Brown terms it, is analysable into three functions, programming, technical and personnel. Having defined these functions he then re-organized the organization structure of the firm so that both the general manager and the unit manager have a nuclear command group of these specialists. To illustrate this relationship, the example could be taken of the unit personnel officer who, in Glacier language, is executively responsible to the unit manager and functionally responsible to the personnel manager.

Brown's discussion of the manager and his subordinates is stated in the following terms (p. 49) – 'Historically, a manager was a person who was put in charge of a venture by a company of people who, in order to finance it, had joined together and subscribed the necessary money. If he could "manage" the venture single-handed, then he was not a manager in the full sense in which we in the Company now use the word. But if he required the assistance of others in his task and chose subordinates to whom he could delegate some part of his work, then his function corresponded to the managerial position we have in mind. His delegation of part of the work in no way affected his total responsibility. He alone remained responsible to the Company of shareholders. He was, in fact, completely answerable for any failure on the part of his subordinates.'

Having defined the manager's role, Brown proceeds to deal with the problem of selecting subordinates. He describes the procedure used in the company which requires the drawing up of a job specification and the advertising of the vacancy within the organization. Then follows a discussion on the possible disagreements between executives. A discussion is given of 'collateral relationships', i.e. relationships between two peers who have the same superior but who have to interact in carrying out their responsibilities.

On the subject of communications he introduces the concept of 'contraction of executive lines' which he defines on page 109. 'A manager shall, when he feels such action[26] to be necessary, contract the executive lines in his command; i.e., make executive contact with any member or members of his extended command, either directly or indirectly, through the intermediate subordinates.' This procedure has caused considerable confusion in Glacier as representatives (the shop stewards) resent this form of semantic alchemy which transforms them into non-representatives when the manager uses the magic phrase, 'I am going to contract executive lines'.

Part three of *Exploration in Management* which deals with communication is completed by a discussion of 'The Manager and Meetings'. This is discussed in detail in Chapter 9.

CRITIQUE OF
EXPLORATION IN MANAGEMENT

The principal virtue of *Exploration in Management* lies in the fact that it represents the conclusions of an experienced and inquiring manager. On matters such as defining the manager's job, writing job descriptions, defining policy and clarifying relations between line and functional management, as far as it goes, it is very good. But Brown's approach is essentially linguistic or semantic. What is vital to remember is that the process of definition is only the first step in theory building. The subsequent steps of developing the hypothesis, its evaluation by experiment or controlled observation, the formation of a new hypothesis, further experimentation and the subsequent development of a comprehensive theoretical structure with a firm empirical base requires further development.

It is this failure in methodology that lies at the root of the trouble. It is this faith in making the implicit explicit that most academics fear. Glacier researchers leave themselves open to the charge of being too introverted. Aside from references to the work of Dr. Jaques there is practically no mention in *Exploration in Management* of any other work in the field.

The difficulty is not only theoretical, it is also practical. Glacier does not have the personnel researchers to carry through this exercise to its logical and expensive conclusion. Wilfred Brown[26] acknowledges these criticisms when he observes that:

> The period during which this book has been written has, in a sense, been one of considerable frustration for me, and maybe for many others in the Company, because I have known what we have to do in the field of personnel and organizational work, and yet economic factors have prevented us from doing it. We need a Personnel Division, containing the same order of resources of people, brains and facilities as we have deployed in our Technical Division or in our Product Research and Development Organization, in order to implement fully the findings already achieved, and to take the exploration further. Unfortunately, the Company has, during the last few years, been engaged in a more than usually virulent competitive fight for its markets.

Exploration in Management may be criticized for applying a normative approach (describing behaviour as it ought to be) rather than a positive approach (describing behaviour as it is).

THE JAQUES THEORY OF PAYMENT

Dr. Elliott Jaques, in his approach to the problems of payment, has developed three instruments: the time span of discretion; the equitable work-payment scale; and the standard earning progression curves. It is necessary to accept his view that all work can be broken into two elements, the prescribed and the discretionary. The prescribed content of work arises from the rules and regulations which set the external limits within which discretion has to be exercised. The discretionary content refers to the exercise of discretion which the individual doing the work is expected to carry out. In *Measurement of Responsibility*,[67] work is defined as 'the exercise of discretion within prescribed limits in order to reach a goal or objective'.

An employee is paid nothing at all for the prescribed element, that is for carrying out that part of the work about which he is given definite instructions. It is the discretionary element that determines the salary differential. The more important the post the more latitude for discretion, and Elliott Jaques measures this latitude in the temporal sense which he calls the time span of discretion.

The time span of discretion is the 'maximum time lapse over which a person is required to exercise discretion in his job without that discretion being reviewed'.[67] The concept of 'review mechanism', which Jaques introduced, refers to the systematic means whereby a superior becomes aware of his subordinate's use of discretion. These are of two types; the direct review, where the completed work of a subordinate is inspected and the indirect review, where intelligence is deliberately and positively collected from outside sources regarding a subordinate's use of discretion. If the superior makes no effort to get information in this manner, but assumes that he will hear of his subordinate's ineptitude, then this type of review has been categorized as 'Indirect Negative' while the former is referred to as the 'Indirect Positive'.

The Equitable Work-Payment Scale

Jaques claims to be able to specify 'the differential distribution of payment which corresponds to the individual sense of fairness of pay in connection with the level of work carried in a job'.[29] This distribution is referred to as the Equitable Work-Payment Scale.

The Standard Earning Progression Curves is the array of curves which follow the growth in capacity for the individual to bear responsibility; broadly speaking these curves conform to the pattern of biological growth. Jaques claims that he has analysed some 3,000 jobs of all kinds, from 5s. 6d. per hour to £18,000 per annum. From this analysis, Jaques concludes that there exists, albeit intuitively, known norms of fair payment and further that employees share the knowledge of these norms. According to Jaques when an individual is paid in accord with the scale for their level of work, then he feels fairly paid; if above, he feels 'very favourably paid'; and if below, he feels under-paid.

Example of Time-span equitable payment levels, June 1963

Period	Earnings
1 day	£12 12s. p.w.
1 week	£15 p.w.
1 month	£17 p.w.
6 months	£1,150 p.a.
1 year	£1,550 p.a.
2 years	£3,200 p.a.
5 years	£6,500 p.a.

Jaques claims that the equitable work payment, used in conjunction with his time-span instrument, can be used to construct a national incomes policy. In this scheme it would be possible:

1. To maintain full employment and a buoyant economy.
2. To relate the structure of payment to level of work.
3. To recognize individual effort and achievement with a wage bracket.
4. To allow changes in differentials only in response to changes of level of work.
5. To encourage mobility of labour.

In his scheme, no salary increase would be allowed for scarcity value. If for any reason, special awards were granted to employees, then they would be made as explicit *ex gratia* payments.

AN ASSESSMENT OF THIS THEORY OF PAYMENT

This approach to payment represents a rejection of the formulas of the past; for example it rejects the market forces of supply and demand, piecework and bonus systems of payments and management-union negotiations over wage rates. Instead, Jaques argues that the most striking finding of his research into pay is that 'employed persons whose work is shown by measurement to be at the same level of responsibility, privately state the same wage or salary to be fair for the work they are doing; this finding holds regardless of a person's actual earnings, or occupation, of current market values, or of income tax levels'. The crucial issue at stake then is, 'can this level of responsibility be measured?' Jaques' answer to this question lies in the time span of discretion. This warrants closer examination.

One very perplexing aspect of the Glacier project has been the reactions of employee representatives to the introduction to this system of achieving equality. In *Equitable Payment*, page 141, Jaques[71] notes:

> The Works Council has not so far accepted, even on an exploratory basis, the notion of the time-span yardstick and the associated equitable work-payment scale whose development it initiated. The Managing Director and the Grade III Staff representatives have argued in favour of slow advance to try out and test the instruments, in order to examine the problems of executive implementation and to discover whether the measuring instrument and payment method are likely to work out in practice. The Grade I and II Staff representatives have, however, adopted the view that more work needs to be done to establish the time-span instrument in generally understandable form before it is tested further; and the Works Committee representatives, while not wanting to stand in the way of staff members, have opted out of any participation in the use of these notions in connexion with hourly-rated roles. In the absence of all-round agreement in the Company, it has not been possible to make open comparison of level of work measured in time-span as between all types of role within the Company.

Not only has it been impossible to achieve the necessary sanction to introduce this system into the Company, there have been other difficulties. A major difficulty has been the training of personnel officers in the use of these techniques. Even after training in these procedures, the Kilmarnock personnel staff made little use of this system. In discussions with personnel officers, the view most frequently expressed is the hope that the handbook which has been published will simplify the complexities of the system.

A limited number of 'show-jobs' have been analysed using the time-span technique. The jobs of progress officer and design engineer are the ones usually selected for analysis. On the other hand, doing 'a time-span' of an operator's job is a monumental task and rarely inspiring in results. Likewise, attempts to do the same for staff roles produce many complex issues. It is difficult to devise a time-span analysis for a personnel officer role which makes any sense, particularly, if it is related to his earnings.

One of the major criticisms of this system concerns Jaques' failure to offer an adequate explanation of the techniques used in his investigation. The key question relates to the curves shown on page 125 of *Equitable Payment*.[71] The curves in the diagram were constructed by plotting the time-span felt fair pay from 1,000 analyses. How do you measure 'felt-fair' pay? Ultimately, this involves the prompting of the interviewee by questions, such as 'What were you earning then?' '£1,550 p.a., you say. Did you feel that was a fair salary for your work?' 'No? What would you regard as a fair salary?' And so on, until figures are produced, that fit graphs. In this way, the interviewee lands on a figure which approximates to the salary determined by time-span analysis. A considerable number of subjective judgments are involved in this type of assessment.

Is Jaques' System Impractical?

In an article entitled 'Jaques System: Impractical?' (*New Society*, 19 December 1963) T. T. Paterson [115] criticizes the Jaques approach by noting that '. . . Dr. Jaques makes this comprehensive claim on the basis of the analysis of 3,000 jobs in different industries in both the private and nationalized sectors; a similar statement appeared in 1961 in his book *Equitable Payment*.[71] So far the figures have not yet been published, nor the figures for comparison with structures in Holland, America and Canada.' But the main criticism levelled by Paterson[115] against the scheme concerns its practicality, where he observes:

There are other great difficulties in introducing such a system, quite apart from the lack of theoretical premise and applicability. . . . For one thing the method is difficult to understand. One of Dr. Jaques' ablest disciples, at a meeting of experts on job evaluation, declared that it requires three years of study with Dr. Jaques to understand it properly. This must be an exaggeration. In order to give a comprehensive picture of the distribution of job time spans in different regions and different industries a tremendous amount of research would be required and, over and above that, retitling of jobs would be necessary. . . . To apply the scheme throughout the country every job would have to be laboriously time-span measured—there is no possibility of rank categorization for a short cut—nearly impossible in a country so industrialized as ours. . . . It is certainly impossible to apply the Jaques principle.

To be able to understand the Jaques' system it is necessary to understand the basic concepts (*Measurement of Responsibility*[67]) and the theoretical background (*Equitable Payment*[71]). Jaques has now produced a manual for practitioners, entitled *Time-Span Handbook* (Heinemann, 1964)[72], which includes a number of practical examples. Most Glacier executives are confused by this complicated theory of payments. One major company, which sent a senior manager on a Glacier course on time-span and had been assisted by the Glacier social science consultant were unable to make practical use of the Jaques' system.

Lisl Klein[76(b)], a research social scientist of Esso Petroleum Company Limited, reviewing this handbook in the *Journal of Management Studies*, has argued:

It is perhaps unfair to criticise a practitioner's manual if one does not wholly accept the basic premise of the method, but I cannot help feeling that no-one who wishes to learn the time-span technique will be equipped to set up a wage structure by a short training course and by reading this very short manual. There are too few examples, and most of them leave the impression that one could argue just as cogently for different parts of the job as being the crucial indicators of the time-span involved as for those which are included. Some consensus about the cash value of jobs already exists before the measurement of any task is undertaken, and it is hard to believe that the practitioner has cleared his mind of any such preconceived ideas before embarking on measurement.

Is Time-Span Valid?

Paul S. Goodman in *An Empirical Examination of Elliott Jaques' Concept of Time Span* (Human Relations, Vol. 20, No. 2, 1967), reports a very carefully conducted investigation where he measured Individual Time Span Capacity in two ways, level of abstraction, organizational level and job satisfaction and the correlation between these variables involving 168 managerial personnel in an American company with rather a similar struc ture to the Glacier Metal Company. Goodman, before he pres ents his empirical findings, argues that Jaques' theory 'is based on at least four assumptions: (1) individuals are aware of their time span capacities; (2) individuals are aware of the time span requirements of the jobs they seek; (3) individuals attempt to achieve congruency between their own propensities and job requirements and (4) individuals prefer to maximize congruency on the time dimension as opposed to other criteria (e.g. status money). *A priori*, it seems unlikely that all four assumption would hold for all individuals.' While his data agreed with Jaques' in that 'individuals whose job time span is congruent with their time span propensities are more satisfied with their jobs than individuals whose job time span is less than their individual propensities,' Goodman concludes that 'the result in this study do not generally support Jaques' hypotheses on the relationship between individual time span and characteristic of the organization structure.'

Many independent social scientists regard the Jaques' System of Payment as complicated, involved, impractical and unproven they are disturbed by the fact that it is not used in the Glacier Metal Company. Yet, Jaques' concept of time-span and more especially the idea of the review mechanism, are extremely useful analytical tools for defining work roles which are the natural building blocks of any organizational structure. In this important matter of role definition, Jaques has made a useful contribution to management theory. Lisl Klein[76(b)] concludes her review by observing:

> If only one could accept the analysis of the time-span of discretion as a fruitful way of thinking about work, and of helping manager to think about the work they allocate, without having to accept i as a way of deciding payment. The concepts which Dr. Jaques ha developed can help one to investigate and assess and describe task and roles in much greater depth and with much more realism than has happened under any other system.

Some Questions relating to Glacier Actualities

In the light of the fact that Wilfred Brown regards the Glacier System as generally applicable to British industry, there are certain questions managers and social scientists would like to ask about Glacier actualities. At this stage, it may be useful to list these questions. They include:

1. What is the Company's level of profitability?
2. What caused the switch from human relations to task Management?
3. Are there strikes at Glacier?
4. How are wages settled?
5. Has piecework really been abandoned?
6. How do appeals work out in practice?
7. How do shop stewards react to the 'contraction of executive lines'?
8. What happens in the Works Council?
9. What happens in the command meeting?
10. How does the role of the section manager work out in practice?
11. What are supervisors and what do they do?
12. Does personality count with Glacier?
13. Is there a Glacier type of executive?
14. What is the human reaction to task management?
15. How different is Glacier?
16. How much of the Glacier philosophy as expounded by Brown and Jaques in their books is in actual use in the Company?

The present research sets out to provide answers to some of these questions.

CHAPTER 3

THE PERSPECTIVES OF THE GLACIER PROJECT: HISTORICAL, ECONOMIC, TECHNOLOGICAL AND THEORETICAL

To a business executive a theory of organization is a tool, an intellectual device, whose use enables him to operate his business more effectively. To the thoughtful and hard-pressed industrial manager, the Glacier Project represents a theory. But how does it work out in practice? The remaining chapters of this book are devoted to delineating Glacier actualities, based mainly on researches conducted at the Kilmarnock factory of Glacier. But before we proceed to examine Glacier actualities, it is necessary to examine the perspectives of the Glacier Project. Three questions should be in the forefront of any unbiased but realistic analysis of the Glacier System. How does Glacier reality compare with Glacier theory? Secondly, what are the economic or human advantages of this theory? And finally, does the Project have any useful lessons for executives in other companies?

But in trying to answer these questions it is perhaps as well to remember that all research involves a degree of distortion. Examining a segment of an organism under the high-power lens of a microscope requires the suppression of the remainder of the field. The selection of the focus of the investigation always involves factors of convenience and practicality and the methods employed depend to a large extent on the resources available; particularly important are financial and personnel considerations. The result is that modern research is frequently described in the truism as 'getting to know more and more about less and less'.

Nevertheless, if the research is going to have meaning in other contexts, there is a need to define the perspectives of the investigation. Nowhere is this truer than in the case of research into the nature of organizations. The dissonance between different research findings in this field would be considerably reduced if the cultural frames of the various studies were known. Capturing a picture of a business enterprise is complicated by the fact that it is not a physical object such as a building which interacts only to a slight extent with its environment. An organization may be regarded as a myriad of processes and interactions, embedded in a cultural environment which places a system of constraints or limits on its development. The traffic of effects between organizations and society is a two-way affair. Thus, it is necessary to accept that organization cannot be studied in isolation from its cultural background. Again, a business organization will inevitably develop its own peculiar culture, which is characterized by its own particular way of doing things and its own patterns of communications. In the ecology of administration, historical, economic, technological and cultural forces are of major importance.

GLACIER'S ECONOMIC ACHIEVEMENTS

The Glacier Metal Company, which is probably the most studied, best documented and most heavily dissected organization, is a successful public company, employing 4,500 people in six locations, is the largest manufacturer of plain bearings in Europe, and in Britain has only one important competitor. A first impression of its economic effectiveness can be gauged from the fact that in the financial year which ended on 28 February 1962, the Company made a profit of just over half a million pounds.

It is worth remembering that these results were achieved at a time when the motor-car industry had been producing below full volume. For a long time the Company has been dependent to a very considerable extent on the automotive markets for placing many of its products; some Company executives have argued that the Company was too dependent on this rather unpredictable sector of the economy. The margin on the supply of bearings to the car industry is extremely small. Today's current prices of supplies to motor-car manufacturers are nearly at the same level as they were in 1939. To meet this situation the Company has been steadily pursuing a policy of product diversification and extension and has developed new materials and techniques of manufacture. So in recent years a decreasing proportion of the Company's total output has been sold to vehicle manufacturers. In fact the Company's almost total dependence on the car industry has been reduced and a significant part of Glacier's turnover is now in thick-wall bearings for the capital goods industry. This type of development which requires batch production as opposed to the fairly long runs which are a characteristic of the manufacturers of the thin-wall bearings for the car industry certainly complicates life for production planners at Glacier. Nevertheless, perhaps some measure of Glacier's success can be got from the fact that while the Company overall is less dependent on the critical automotive industry, Glacier has managed to raise its share of this difficult market from 15 to 50 per cent in a little over a decade.

Perhaps it is as well to point out that to achieve this kind of efficiency the Company is frequently reorganized. Arising from the departure of the Managing Director, the Company has recently been reorganized. The Company's operations are now grouped under three chief executives. The first group consists of those units which are supplying bearings as original equipment. This includes No. 1 London factory, No. 3 factory Kilmarnock, Dualloys Limited, Home Sales, Automotive Sales, and Export Sales. The second group comprises the research and development organization, a new group for the manufacture and sale of machine tools and bearing process plant, the Company's licensing organization and a group of service stations in the United Kingdom. The third group, known as the Stock Products Organization, is responsible for selling replacement bearings, both on home and overseas markets.

The Glacier Metal Company has a number of subsidiary companies. These include Dualloys Limited, Chard, Somerset, which is a wholly owned subsidiary of the main company where 300 people are employed and is concerned with the manufacture of cast copper lead and other bearings. Another wholly owned subsidiary of the Company is Scottish Precision Castings Limited of Glasgow where 140 people are employed manufacturing aluminium and brass die-castings, using both gravity and pressure techniques.

The parent Company has two overseas subsidiaries, one in Natal and the other in New Zealand. Glacier Bearings (Proprietary) Limited, where 51 per cent of the share capital is held by the parent Company, has been established in Durban, South Africa. This factory, of 10,000 square feet, finishes semiprocessed bearing materials which are dispatched to it from the United Kingdom. Glacier Bearings, New Zealand, Limited, where again the parent Company holds 51 per cent of the share capital, has been established in Auckland, New Zealand; this Company was set up to meet competition from an Australian company which was established in New Zealand to manufacture plain bearings.

A more unusual type of subsidiary is the Glacier Institute of Management (G.I.M.) which is concerned with the training of senior executives. The principles of administration, taught in the Institute, are based on the research work carried out at Glacier over the last 15 years. More than 50 per cent of the students are drawn from outside the Company. G.I.M., a self-supporting management school, was set up by Brown to operate quite independently of the Company. But managers attending G.I.M.'s courses may wonder how does the Company make out economically; the answer to this question is in fact highly complex.

For example, Glacier's record in the export field is good. An increasing proportion of the Company's products is now exported directly to most countries in the world. A significant area of interest for the Company has been the marketing of process plant and special machine tools for the manufacture of bearings. The Eastern European countries, especially the Soviet Union, are particularly interested in supplies of this type.

The Company also warehouses a large stock of replacement bearings. To achieve this they hold in stock approximately 12,000 different sets of bearings which the Company claims to dispatch regularly to 130 different markets.

Yet another interesting aspect of economic activity is the sale of Company-built machine tools to licensees in Germany, France, Italy, Spain, the U.S.A., Japan, Brazil and India. The licensee agreements which the Company has with the Common Market countries, Italy, Germany and France, have insulated them from any ill-effects of Britain's failure to enter the Common Market. The Company has also recently concluded agreements with Tractor Export U.S.S.R. which allows them to export, as part of other machinery, filters which fall within the ambit of Glacier patents. These licensing arrangements represent a rapidly developing side of the business.

The Company has expended considerable effort on research and development facilities for scientific work on bearing materials and bearings. One particularly striking contribution of this research activity has been the production of dry bearings which, because of the use of polytetrafluoride ethylene, do not require lubrication. These dry bearings have the additional advantage of being able to function satisfactorily at temperature extremes and are also resistant to water. Glacier research and development has produced a centrifugal oil filter which works on the jet reaction principle and as such has no mechanical drive. The device is now being widely used in a number of applications in heavy engines.

Thus even a casual glance directed at gauging the economic effectiveness of Glacier must be reassuring. A Company which can earn over half a million a year, which is also capable of diversifying to mitigate a dangerous dependence on the car industry, yet gain a substantial increase of the car market, while managing to achieve a good export record can scarcely be regarded as an economic weakling. 'All very well', might be the answer of the sceptical executive, 'But, what about dividends? Doesn't democracy damn dividends?'

DIVIDENDS VERSUS DEMOCRACY

The Glacier Metal Company was formed in 1899 by two Americans to produce anti-friction white metal. The Company took the name Glacier, so the story goes, because its anti-friction metals were white, cool and slippery. One of the founders soon returned to the United States. The Company began the manufacture of plain bearings during the First World War. The Company developed and grew with the expansion of the motor-car industry in the post-war era. In 1923 the factory was moved to its present site at Alperton, North London. In 1929 the Company began the manufacture of steel-backed bearings which necessitated the introduction of power presses. This also involved the recruitment of a number of semi-skilled workers. By 1933, on account of the depression, the factory was forced to

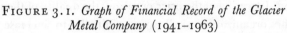

FIGURE 3.1. *Graph of Financial Record of the Glacier Metal Company* (1941–1963)

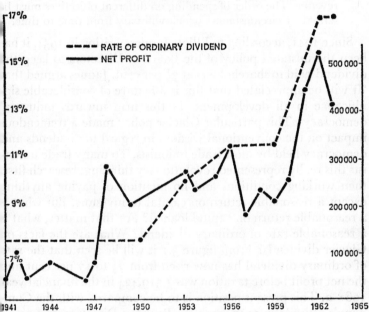

work short-time for a period of six months. To meet the fall-off in business, an effort was made to reduce costs. But at the beginning of World War Two, the productive capacity of the Company was expanded quickly. This expansion continued after the War.

Just after the War, Glacier put out, what was regarded by many business executives and trade unionists, a somewhat unusual policy statement on dividends. On page 57 of *Changing Culture of a Factory* the economic and social policy of the Company is stated. Paragraph one of this policy statement states:

1. So long as shareholders are in receipt of a reasonable return on their investment, the surplus revenue of the organization shall be spent in the following five ways:

   (i) Research and development
  (ii) Betterment of working conditions
 (iii) Betterment of equipment
 (iv) Raising of wages and salaries
  (v) Lowering of the price or raising the quality of the product.

The organization shall strive unitedly to increase surplus revenue. The order of spending on different objectives must be settled by circumstances which will vary from time to time.

Since 1941, according to Elliott Jaques, writing in 1951, it has been the unstated policy of the Board of Directors to keep the dividend paid to shareholders at $7\frac{1}{2}$ per cent. Jaques argued that 'It will be appreciated that this is a feature of considerable significance in all developments in this firm towards industrial democracy'. This particular Glacier policy made a tremendous impact on the conventional wisdom in regard to dividends and democracy held by most trade unionists. To many trade unionists this really represented revolutionary thinking; research first, then working conditions and no mention of paying anything except a reasonable return on capital to investors. But what is a reasonable return on capital loaned? For that matter, what is a reasonable rate of ordinary dividend? What are the facts on Glacier dividends? From figure 3.1 it will be seen that the rate of ordinary dividend has now risen from $7\frac{1}{2}$ to 17 per cent and the net profit before taxation was £519,424 in the financial year 1961–2. This present position is to be compared with the Company's attitude in 1947 when the Board of Directors, as a result of a period of prosperity, decided that an additional £30,000 could be added to the organization's wage expenditure. This enabled them to honour the fourth point of the economic and social policy quoted above. To decide how this increase should be distributed, the problem was referred to the Works Council who, as I have already mentioned, responded by appointing a committee that came to be known as the 'Gold Brick Committee', who came up with the Courtenay Plan. The Glacier Metal Company deservedly received credit for introducing this bold and imaginative plan.

Since then, the Company's financial policies have changed in a dramatic way, moving away from an idealistic approach and taking up a more realistic commercial stance. In the mid-'fifties Glacier made recourse to the money market to increase its supply of capital. Not unnaturally this necessitated increasing the dividend rate to ensure this inflow of capital. Again in 1956 when the Company faced a sharp fall in earnings, Glacier reacted like many other commercial organizations and brought in management consultants who applied their standard techniques, namely work study, programming, and budgetary control as a means of improving profitability. Incidentally, it was through the work of these consultants that the Kilmarnock plant was able to solve a perennial problem, namely that of finding a General Manager. A consultant was appointed General Manager of this factory. Though it was widely held that he was a non-believer of the 'Glacier cult' he was able rapidly to put the plant on a sound financial footing. In fact, he was so successful in this role that he was soon promoted to the position of Managing Director of the whole Company. With this new Managing Director, Glacier was able to achieve an unparalleled increase in profits from 1959 onwards. Unfortunately, this particular Managing Director decided to leave the Company in 1964.

The question has already been posed as to what represents a reasonable and fair return for capital invested in a company. In particular what does the phrase 'Providing such dividends for its shareholders as will represent a reasonable and fair return for the capital invested' mean? There are a variety of ways in which the rate of return earned by companies may be measured. One such measure could be the actual reported profits. This is not satisfactory as these do not necessarily reflect true profitability. Profits need to be assessed in relation to the investment that generated them. The most effective yardstick would be a composite criterion which somehow combined the dividends paid out by the firm with the increase in the value of their shares over a fairly long period.

There seems to be some evidence that it is necessary for firms to maintain their rate of return at a minimal level to ensure support by shareholders. Merrett and Sykes[104] have argued that companies in an effort to gain new equity capital, try to maintain a minimum rate of return required by their shareholders.

They have argued that 'an additional strong reason for doing so is the need to earn a rate of return which will give them adequate after-tax resources (1) to provide sufficient retained earnings for growth and (2) to provide earnings sufficient to ride out temporary periods of adversity. Both these factors would tend to keep up the *real* return on investment. This trend would appear to be only indicative of the classical economic mechanism whereby general pressure from the side of profits tends to hold investment and prices at levels which in the long term will give a viable minimum return.'

TABLE 3.1. FINANCIAL RECORD OF THE COMPANY
SINCE 1946*

Year	Issued Ordinary Capital £	Net Profit before Taxation £	Ordinary Dividends (Gross) £	Rate of Ordinary Dividend %	Earned on Ordinary Capital %
1946	189,500	78,278	14,212	$7\frac{1}{2}$	37·4
1947	189,500	(adjusted) 92,537	14,212	$7\frac{1}{2}$	44·0
1948	189,500	288,499	14,212	$7\frac{1}{2}$	130·0
1949	189,500	223,226	14,212	$7\frac{1}{2}$	98·2
1950	189,500	242,790	14,212	$7\frac{1}{2}$	128·6
1951	300,000	307,922	22,500	$7\frac{1}{2}$	90·8
1952	520,406	492,176	52,040	10	78·6
1953	520,406	270,649	52,040	10	44·7
1954	520,406	231,217	52,040	10	34·1
1955	650,508	247,279	65,051	10	34·1
1956	750,000	321,468	86,250	$11\frac{1}{2}$	37·6
1957	750,000	184,217	86,250	$11\frac{1}{2}$	13·1
1958	750,000	229,018	86,250	$11\frac{1}{2}$	16·3
1959	750,000	212,464	86,250	$11\frac{1}{2}$	21·8
1960	750,000	258,694	97,500	13	30·8
1961	937,500	440,052	131,250	15	43·5
1962	937,500	519,424	159,375	17	51·9
1963	937,500	405,542	159,375	17	39·8
1964	937,500	663,129	187,500	20	66·3

It is as well to remember that in the immediate post-war period, the Labour government's policy had been to reduce the share of profits in the National Income and to increase that of

* All tables shown in this chapter are adapted from Glacier Annual Reports.

wages. In particular, since 1945, the Labour administration had through the tax mechanism steadily squeezed profits and also reduced through income tax what shareholders got in dividends. In 1945 the profits tax was 5 per cent on distributed profits and also 5 per cent on undistributed profits. In the 1947 budget, the tax on distributed profits was raised to 12½ per cent. This was raised in the October 1947 budget to 25 per cent and again in September 1949 to 30 per cent. It was within this political and economic climate that the Glacier policy involved paying 7½ per cent rate of Ordinary Dividend. To claim credit for this is merely to make a virtue of necessity. An additional reason for maintaining such a low rate of Ordinary Dividend is provided when it is realized that the Company was going through a period of patent difficulties. To understand the significance of this statement is is necessary to unravel the legal and technical aspects of the patent struggle in which the Company was involved from 1935 to 1950.

The Problem of Patents

A new method of making plain bearings in which pre-manufactured bimetal strip was shaped into bearings of the specified design instead of producing the shape of the bearing with one metal and then introducing the other was developed by Clevite, an American company, in 1931. Clevite appointed Vandervell, a competitor of Glacier, as its licensee in Great Britain. The Glacier Metal Company became aware in 1936 that they were challenging these patents which their legal advisers informed them were weak. An extended process of litigation ensued involving five hearings before different courts which Glacier alternately won and lost. Glacier's defence was founded on three counts: ambiguity (what does thin mean?–the patent referred to 'thin bearings'), publication of the process before the issue of the patent and the fact that the process was operated in the United Kingdom before the patent was issued. In 1950 the final verdict was given in the House of Lords. Because of the difficulties of interpreting the Lords' verdict, the matter was settled out of court. In 1953 the controller of patents was to consider the renewal of the patents. At this stage, Glacier's competitors pursued their application for an extension of these patents. While the chances of this being granted were considered slight, the Company had to provide itself with considerable finances, in case further royalties were required in the event of a renewal being granted and secondly to provide the financial support for the manufacture of a complete range of equipment. Fortunately, the patent controller disallowed the renewal of these patents. The way ahead was clear for the Company to develop its own manufacturing techniques; these included the development and design of a complete range of bimetal strip mills and machine tools. At this point, it is pertinent to quote from the Annual Report and Accounts of the Glacier Metal Company for 1960 which notes 'It is in the light of these historical events that you have to judge the Board's decision in the years after the war to curtail the distribution of profits'.

Until 1956 the Company succeeded in providing the necessary

TABLE 3.2. PERIOD OF PATENT DIFFICULTIES
(1935–1950)

Year	Event	Dividend
1935	Competitor obtains Licence from U.S.A. Company	15
1936		10
1937	Patent Court rescinds American Company's Patent	15
1938	Patent Appeal Court reinstates Patent with amendment	6
1939–1946	Wartime period. Glacier continues manufacture under Ministry of Supply indemnity	
1947		$7\frac{1}{2}$
1948	Patent expires, but renewal applied for. High Court declares Patent invalid	$7\frac{1}{2}$
1949	Appeal Court reverses High Court decision	$7\frac{1}{2}$
1950	House of Lords upholds Appeal Court decision. Application for renewal goes forward, but is lost in 1953	

Development work concentrated on alternative methods of manufacture capital by issuing additional shares and by retention of a high proportion of profits. Perhaps it is relevant at this point to remember what a difficult financial time the Glacier Metal Company had passed through. This critical situation had arisen from being involved in the fight over patents which turned out to be the second longest patent case in British history (beginning in the 'thirties and only finally settled in 1952) and of such a magnitude that the Company could raise no outside capital; the market was convinced that Glacier would close. The nub of the matter is that in the late 'forties, Glacier was near the brink of financial ruin. It is against such a financial frame of reference that Brown's decision to go 'democratic' and limit dividends must be judged. The only conclusion possible is that the decision and explanation to limit ordinary dividends to a modest figure of $7\frac{1}{2}$ per cent reveal an economic acumen and entrepreneurial *savoir-faire* on the part of Brown that takes him right out of the ranks of the average chief executive of British companies.

TECHNOLOGICAL DEVELOPMENTS

Economically the performance of the Glacier Metal Company is at least adequate. But Glacier executives have never forgotten how close they came to disaster by virtue of not having generated the necessary technological 'know how' in the 'thirties. Since the war Glacier has developed the Research and Development function (R and D) with a vengeance. R and D is currently costing between $4\frac{1}{2}$ and 5 per cent of turnover. Glacier has profited from a bitter experience and recognizes that the only effective way to fight competition is to make a substantial investment in effective R and D.

To cope with the increasing competition the Company initiated the following policies. The management set out:

1. to increase investment in product development to establish a stronger technological base for the Company;
2. to develop the complete range of special machine tools and large process plant;
3. 'to increase our attention to the subject of organization and labour relations in an attempt to ensure, during the period

of stress that lay ahead, a high degree of co-operation and optimum effectiveness from those employed in the Company.

As a result of this policy Glacier is today Europe's largest manufacturer of plain bearings. This involved the expenditure of £1 million in research in the period 1950–60. Up until 1951, the Company had been losing business in the motor industry. Since 1951, this process has been reversed; the Company now supplies about 50 per cent of the requirements of the British motor industry for plain bearings.

TABLE 3.3 TECHNOLOGICAL HISTORY OF THE COMPANY (1950–1960)

Year	Production Processes	Major New Products	Dividend
1950	Foundry mechanization		$7\frac{1}{2}$
1951	Cast iron lining process	Wrapped bush manufacture	$7\frac{1}{2}$
1952			10
1953	Mass production copper-lead bearings	Centrifugal oil filters	10
1954	Plant for bearings up to 4 ft. diameter		10
1955	Mechanized production of automobile bearings		10
1956		Dry bearings	$11\frac{1}{2}$
1957	New white metal strip lining mill	Reticular-tin aluminium	$11\frac{1}{2}$
1958	Reticular-tin aluminium bi-metal mill	Anti-whirl turbine bearings	$11\frac{1}{2}$
1959	Super micro bearings	Ramrod	$11\frac{1}{2}$
1960		Railway bearings Rolling mill bearings	13

A good example of the pay-offs that inevitably flow from properly developed R and D programmes is the fact that the Company has developed a new bearing material which consists of a steel-backed bi-metal with a lining of reticular-tin aluminium alloy. This material is much in demand, especially by licensees in other countries.

Glacier R and D people have also developed the Glacier D.U.

Dry Bearings which run without lubrication at relatively high speeds and loads and are recognized by technologists as a major breakthrough in this area. The Company also manufactures centrifugal oil cleaners for diesel and petrol engines. A great deal of research has been carried out by the Company into the operation of bearings, with a view to providing precise data at a fundamental level of their mode of operation. Through these technological developments, the Company has been able to interest manufacturers in other countries to become licensees of Glacier, paying a royalty to the Company in return for technical 'know how'.

From the above account of the Company's economic and technological history, it will be seen that from 1937 till 1950 because of the patents difficulties the Company had been forced onto the defensive, in an effort to guarantee its continued existence. From 1950 onwards, there has been a period of technological development and expansion which has necessitated financial policies that would bring capital into the Company. In general terms it would seem, based on the above analysis of the Company's operations, that the *Company has always pursued commercial policies*. In particular, paying a 7½ per cent rate of Ordinary Dividend between 1941 and 1950 indicated considerable business acumen and should not be interpreted as an act of generosity, born of idealism or a preoccupation with democratic processes in industry.

A good example of this business acumen is provided by the fact that in 1964, the Glacier Metal Company announced a three point increase in dividend, raising it to 20 per cent. This represented a 63 per cent increase in pre-tax profit over 1963. The results were declared at a time when the Board had declared its intention of raising £650,000 by a 'rights' issue.

While few trade unionists would be prepared to admit it, questions of profitability are related not only to the problems of expansion, with the consequent need to raise funds on the money market, but also to that most traumatic of business experiences – the takeover. In fact, in 1964, Glacier was taken over, with Brown's full approval, by the Leamington piston group, Associated Engineering.

This defensive merger arose from the takeover hunting tactics of two major American bearing manufacturers, Clevite (for whom Vandervell Products were, until March 1964, their British licensees) and the Federal-Mogul group. What happened was that one or other of these American companies had been picking up Glacier's Italian, German and Dutch licensees and all the signs indicated that an attempt was going to be made to pick up the Glacier Metal Company as well; this was particularly neces- sary since Vandervell had decided to carry on on its own. This merger with A.E. will bring capital, diversification and valuable wholesaling distribution outlets to Glacier.

Two points of comment are relevant here. First, inadequate recognition has been paid, especially by management theorists and trade unionists, to the importance of technological and economic factors in their effect on organizational matters. In the case of Glacier, patent problems, the change from a sellers' market to a buyers' market, the need to raise money on the money market, and the threat of takeover bids have all been potent factors in affecting the profitability of the organization, and consequently organizational postures within the Company. Secondly, no sooner had Glacier been taken over than Brown and Jaques showed how instrumental* their philosophy can be when they announced in an article entitled 'The Crippling Fear of Bigness' that

> Every year trade becomes more international, and every year such trade tends to be carried on by larger and larger corporations, both privately owned and nationalised. In Britain, however, there is a strongly held attitude, both among the public and among all the major political parties, which fears industrial concentration as leading to 'monopoly' and the worst kind of unrestrained tycoonery. It is the purpose of this memorandum to question this attitude– to suggest that the fears are largely unfounded, that they are inhibiting necessary efforts to deal with our balance of payments, that there is, in fact, a strong case for supposing that firms should be encouraged, rather than discouraged, in the formation of larger more efficient, more economically viable units. (*Sunday Times*, 7 Feb. 1965.)

What does this brief look at Glacier's economic history prove? To my mind this quick look at Glacier's development over the

---

* Used in the sense that John Dewey uses this term, i.e. as a tool to get somewhere. In Dewey's philosophy, a theory is 'good' as judged by whether it has the appropriate effects.

last thirty years and in particular from the time when Brown took over as chief executive in 1939 at the age of thirty, makes a very strong case for accepting the notion that external economic forces are the dominant considerations in determining how a company develops. In other words I accept a Marxist interpretation of Glacier's history rather than a psychological or political explanation. This is but to say that it makes more sense to regard Glacier behaviour and attitudes as effects arising from the nature of the economic system and its financial institutions rather than to think of them as ideas which human psychology or political ideology required. The alternative is to regard as a coincidence the fact that the greatest period of industrial democracy (subsequently regarded as anathema by Brown) took place at a time when the Company could not pursue appropriate economic and financial policies because the financial gnomes of the 'forties and early 'fifties thought Glacier was unlikely to survive. The gnomes were proved wrong and Brown established Glacier as a viable economic unit, but a unit which could only survive as part of a larger economic unit. At the risk of over-simplification, the moral of the Glacier saga appears to be that economic realities are larger than political realities and pragmatism is the best philosophy for the hard-pressed top executive, for at least he can make a virtue out of necessity.

THE KILMARNOCK FACTORY

The actual empirical data for this research was collected at the Kilmarnock factory of the Glacier Metal Company. The official title for this plant is No. 3 factory. In fact Glacier's productive capacity was concentrated at two sites, London and Kilmarnock. These two plants were approximately the same size and at the time of the research reported here their functions were broadly similar. (This has since changed.) Organizationally the most important difference was the fact that the headquarters of the Company, which included not only Brown, but a considerable number of management specialists, was located at the London factory site.

Basically the Kilmarnock plant looked like many another

'medium sized plus' British light engineering plant. The Cook's tour of the plant usually started in the Foundry, then the Sinter Plant, a look at the presses, a walk round the semi-automatic plant of the Thin Wall Unit and so on. In many ways a typical light engineering plant.

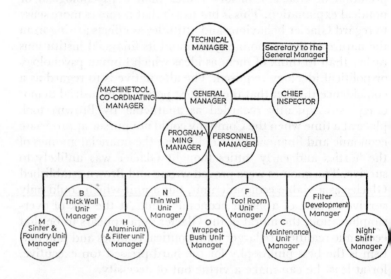

The General Manager of No. 3 factory has five subordinate operational unit managers each in charge of a complete manufacturing unit:

Sinter and Foundry Unit
  Manufactures copper-lead-tin on steel bi-metal strip and plastic-impregnated bronze on steel strip, by continuous process using sintering methods; casts copper-lead on to steel shells and recovers metal from swarf and scrap.
Thin Wall Unit
  Presses and machines thin-walled bearings from the bi-metal strip. Runs in this unit are fairly long. The products, plain bearings, are required in all car engines.
Thick Wall Unit
  Presses and machines thick-walled bearings from forgings and bi-metal strip. Batch production is the order of the day here.

Aluminium and Filter Unit
   Machines solid aluminium bearings; machines and assembles
   oil filters.
Wrapped Bush Unit
   Presses, bends and finishes bushes and thrust washers from
   bi-metal strip lined with lead-bronze and white metal.

   These units are supported by a maintenance unit and by a
tool-room unit which also builds machine tools and process
plant.
   To enable him to operate efficiently the General Manager is
assisted by three specialist staff officers–technical, programming
and personnel–and also by a chief inspector. Accounting and
financial services are provided for him by a chief accountant. A
unit manager's command is organized into a number of sections,
each in the charge of a manager assisted by supervisors. The
unit manager himself is assisted by his own specialist staff officers
in the technical and programming fields.

ECONOMIC AND SOCIAL BACKGROUND
AT KILMARNOCK

Kilmarnock is a busy and thriving community which stands at
the confluence of the Kilmarnock Water and the River Irvine.
The town itself, with a population of 45,000, is situated near the
Ayrshire coalfields; it is also the focal centre of a number of
smaller towns and communities. A tremendous transformation
has been brought about in Kilmarnock since the end of the war.
At the time of writing, February 1964, more than 9,000 new
municipal houses have been built–enough to house more than
half the town's population. The town has a tradition of industrial
development and within the boundaries or very close by are to
be found the workshops of nearly a score of different crafts. Any
investigation, warranting comparisons with the London factory
of the Glacier Metal Company, necessitates some assessment of
the local social and economic factors. The statistics on unemployment provide a measure of economic activity. In this

respect Kilmarnock like many other Scottish communities has more than its share of unemployment. Figures from the local Labour Exchange for Kilmarnock and District, 13 January 1964, show that 1,136 people were unemployed, i.e. 3·6 per cent of the insured population. While in Kilmarnock itself, the unemployment statistics are bad enough, in the surrounding area some of the figures are among the worst to be found in the country. For example, in North Ayrshire, which falls within the catchment area from which Glacier recruits its labour, 7·8 per cent of the insured population were unemployed at that date. This is to be compared with a figure of 4·2 per cent for the whole of Scotland, and 2·1 per cent for Great Britain as a whole and just over 1 per cent (1·1 per cent) for the London area. Inevitably these statistics on unemployment have their effects on the work people and their attitudes towards management. For example, the threat of redundancy has a more terrible meaning for the Kilmarnock employee of the Glacier Metal Company than for his London counterpart. Indeed, even the slightest rumour of a lay-off or short time working has the immediate effect of mobilizing the anxieties of the work force. Two examples of this anxiety may suffice at this stage. One may be seen in the selection by the workers of tougher leaders at the time of crisis (this is a reserve role which many Communist shop stewards hold in less anxious times). Another example of this reaction may be seen in the large number of applications for the relatively safe position of storeman which is received in times of redundancy crises. In general terms it would appear that Kilmarnock workers are more suspicious and anxious than their London colleagues in dealing with management.

It is a truism to say that the Scottish culture is different from the English and it is also true that the Scots take great pains to distinguish themselves from the English. This antipathy towards the English is an attitude widely held by Scots. Irish immigrants to Scotland, of which there are many in the Kilmarnock area, have helped to strengthen this attitude. Many of the Irish moved into the Kilmarnock area after the great famine of the 1840s. A very big proportion of these Irish immigrants were Roman Catholics who have inter-married and tend to have large families. There is always a certain amount of religious conflict between Catholics and Protestants which tends to spill over and become one of the forces of conflict in industrial organizations.

For long the Clyde has been dubbed the 'Red Clyde'. While there is a certain amount of Communist organization of trade unions in the West of Scotland, they represent a diminishing force both in the unions and local government, except in times of industrial crisis in the former. A great deal of this anti-government attitude that originates in Scotland springs from the depressed economic and social circumstances of the people. T. T. Paterson[114] in *Glasgow Limited* has given a perceptive sociological account of the growth of the anti-authoritarian personality in the West of Scotland. He suggests that this anti-authoritarian culture has its core in the ship-building industry, which by the character of the product, the ship, cannot lead to continuous employment so there is frequent dismissal of men who must seek work elsewhere until another ship is at that stage of construction when they can again seek employment.

This irregularity of employment in both ship-building and the industries who are its subcontractors (80 per cent of a ship is 'bought in') produces a loss of confidence in the social and economic system and induces a feeling of insecurity in the Scots; this insecurity reinforced by the Scottish presbyterian sense of independence frequently finds relief in the scapegoating of authority.

Paterson has shown how children in growing up in this culture develop a sort of aggressive independence. He[114] notes 'there are no leaders in the usually accepted sense of that word; there is more of a "pecking-order". The order does not seem to depend on brute strength or size but on aggressive belligerence'. A boy who grows up in Scotland learns that he must be tough, that he must be prepared at a moment's notice to take up the challenge. A lot of this hostility is siphoned off in the scapegoating of strangers, who do not conform to his idea of toughness. There is also an obsession with what is 'right' in the sense of being 'fair', which means that a framework of values is conceived against which behaviour is judged.

At school, this over-developed sense of maleness is further developed. Indeed, one who has worked in Scottish schools is continually reminded of Murchison's[106] experiments on the 'pecking hierarchy' of chickens, where leadership depends on the capacity to elicit unfavourable responses from the members of the same sex and favourable responses from the opposite sex and the ability to defeat others in combat and sexual prowess. In fact, in Scottish schools, such linear hierarchies as Murchison observed can still be noted. These linear hierarchies based on overt dominance seen in Scottish schools are remarkably reminiscent of the experiments carried out by Whyte[151] (into the structure of gangs in Chicago). It is in an atmosphere like this that Scottish boys grow up. T. T. Paterson[114] catches the primitive mores of the Scottish working-class boy as he moves towards some form of maturity – 'Adolescent, he apes his elders, smoking, going to the football match, lounging, frequenting billiard saloons, because he is barred from the holy of holies, the pub. And he clashes with that other great external authority, society, in the form of the police. It is the law of his gang and his neighbourhood which matters to him, not the law of the nation. He is judged by his neighbours, not by the nation. Sent here by "they", the policeman is punitive, not protective. The neighbourhood is protective even though, as his mother did, it may reject him when he seeks security in it. He needs to "go about in droves of his own kind".'

All these factors: social, economic, geographical, contribute to produce the Scottish worker. As an adult, he is inclined to be authoritarian yet hostile to authority, aggressive and sometimes suspicious of the boss with a natural antipathy to all things English. In the words of T. T. Paterson[114] he is 'more concerned with being "a richt" (a "regular guy") than with getting up in the world and so being a non-conformist, for being "a richt" makes life in the pub and factory so much more easy and pleasant'.

The relevance of this discussion of the Kilmarnock culture may not be immediately obvious in its impact on the industrial relations within the factory. But surely the attitudes the employees *bring* to their place of work are at least as important as those arising from within the organization. It can be argued that Kilmarnock is a working-class community with all the virtues and vices already mentioned. If the workers have a multi-class background as I believe the London factory workers have, then they will have a different attitude from the Company's Kilmarnock employees who come from an essentially working-class culture. Class attitudes create insulating barriers between the needs of society as a whole and the workers' own best interests.

This problem of working-class identification and its consequences for the factory has been spotlighted by Peter Willmott[154] in *The Evolution of a Community*. This study of Dagenham shows it to be an essentially working-class community where nearly all parents assume children will leave school at fifteen and care nothing for higher education; where the workers have no desire to advance themselves either at work or elsewhere. For example, at Dagenham hire purchase is less common than elsewhere and relatively few families possess cars. The significance of these attitudes of the Ford workers can be best seen when they are compared with those at Vauxhall's. In Luton where the employees come from a multi-class community all those old working-class attitudes are almost dead. An interesting postscript on this scene is perhaps provided by the fact that many Scottish workers have emigrated to Dagenham.

A similar comparison can be made between Glacier's London factory and their Kilmarnock factory.

THEORETICAL CONSIDERATIONS

Before World War Two, Glacier was no different from any other engineering company. In 1935, Glacier became a public company; at the same time, Wilfred Brown became responsible for the administration of the Company. In 1939, he became Managing Director.

The management-labour relations in the Company disturbed him. In an article entitled 'Can there be industrial democracy?', Brown[25] expressed his concern 'with the apparent dominance of those who owned industry, over those who worked in it. . . . It seemed proper that democracy, the basis of our political institutions, should permeate into industry and form the basis upon which we regulated our working lives also.' (*Fabian Journal*, 1956.) While today it is extremely improbable that Brown would stress the importance of democracy in industry, it is not surprising that Brown joined Sir Richard Acland's war-time Commonwealth Party and afterwards, with Acland, moved into the Labour Party.

Near the end of the war, Wilfred Brown asked the Nationa Institute of Industrial Psychology to carry out a series of attitud surveys. Two facts emerged from these surveys: the factory wa considered a good place in which to work and among middl management there was a feeling that qualities of leadershi were more important than technical qualifications.

In 1947, the Tavistock Institute of Human Relations wa asked to come in and help in dealing with the Company socio logical problems. In 1948, after receiving a grant from th Human Factors Panel of the Cabinet Committee on Industria Productivity set up by Herbert Morrison, then Lord Presiden of the Council, the Tavistock research team investigation wa put on a longer-term basis. In fact, a very close relationshi exists between the Tavistock Institute and Glacier. This sym biotic relationship has contributed greatly towards the develop ment of the task approach.

Tavistock Research and the Task Approach

Research in the behavioural sciences at the Tavistock Institut of Human Relations has provided many of the necessary intel lectual constructs to enable Glacier to establish a theoretica basis for its management operations. Therefore, it is particularl important to examine the contributions of this Institute to th work of social scientists in industry. The Tavistock Institute c Human Relations developed from the Tavistock Clinic whic from its earliest days always has had an interest in the psycho analytical approach to psychotherapy. As well as drawing it concepts from the field of psycho-analysis, many of the conceptua models have been developed from the holistic approach t human problems–Gestalt psychology, Kurt Lewin's[90] fiel theory, the functional anthropology of Malinowski[99] and th open system theory of Von Bertalanffy[15]. Inherent in this ap proach is the acceptance of the complexity of interacting force at work in any situation. This complex of forces may involv personal, social and historical factors. Implicit in this approac is a reluctance to accept that chance can enter significantly int the explanation as to how an organization developed in a par ticular way. This optimistic view demands an approach that is dynamic rather than static.

Again, even a cursory examination of the professions from which the staff of the Tavistock Institute of Human Relations are recruited, shows that they accept that problems do not present themselves to investigators neatly parcelled according to academic function. Thus, in the Institute there are to be found psychiatrists, psychologists, sociologists, statisticians, and economists working in teams exploiting a multi-disciplinary approach when tackling a particular problem.

Lewin's Field Theory

Research workers at Tavistock readily acknowledge their debt of gratitude to Kurt Lewin.[90] Lewin's most important work was done in the 'thirties after he had left Germany for the United States. Influenced by his mathematical training and his association with the early Gestalt psychologists, he tried to develop his ideas about group dynamics in terms of vectors. Lewin coined the term 'group dynamics' as well as introducing the concept of life space. Life space refers to the whole system of the group and its environment; this includes the real aspects of the individuals' personalities, the physical environment, the individuals' concepts of one another and the unreal elements including their hopes, fears, ambitions etc. Central to field theory is the idea that individual group members have goals which they desire to achieve and by moving towards these goals they may gain release from tension. Field theory requires that a group be viewed as a field of forces which is in a state of equilibrium.

Bion's Contribution

Based on his experience in the War Office Selection Board and his experience with group therapy at the Tavistock Clinic, Bion[17,18] developed a psycho-dynamic approach which has proved valuable in areas outside its original clinical setting.

Elliott Jaques has applied Bion's technique of 'working through a problem' to gain insight into the attitudes and beliefs of employees.

According to Bion, when a group is brought together it goes through a period of confusion before it settles down to the actual task. How successful it is in solving the problem, depends on the group's sophistication. If the group is sophisticated and mature, it will deal with the realities of the situation and 'work through' to a solution. On the other hand, less sophisticated groups are likely to respond emotionally to stress. They may respond–by fight or flight, by dependency or by pairing. Bion's techniques were extensively used in the early stage of the Glacier experiment.

Socio-Technical Systems

There is a growing recognition that simple statements of the enterprise's objectives are no longer possible. The proposition that a firm exists simply to make a profit is no longer generally accepted. There is a developing realization that the enterprise has a number of tasks, that include social and personal objectives, even if these only exist as limitations and constraints. The term mission has been suggested as a single name for this complex of tasks. To develop this argument further the Tavistock workers have developed the concept of the socio-technical system. Trist and Bamforth as a result of their study of the introduction of the mechanized long wall system of mining did the early work in the development of the socio-technical theory. A socio-technical system is concerned with the interaction between the technical aspects and social aspects of the problem. Rice,[125] in *Productivity and Social Organisation*, continues more generally: 'The concept of a production system as a socio-technical system designates a general field of study concerned with the inter-relations of the technical and socio-psychological organization of industrial production systems. . . . The concept of a socio-technical system arose from the consideration that any production system requires both a technological organization–equipment and process layout–and a work organization relating to each other those who carry out the necessary tasks. The technological demands place limits on the type of work organization possible; but a work organization has social and psychological properties of its own that are independent of technology. . . . A socio-technical system must also satisfy the financial conditions of the industry of which it is a part. It must have economic dimensions, all of which are interdependent but all of which have independent values of their own.'

It has been further argued that a more comprehensive picture of an enterprise will be gained by viewing it as an open socio-technical system. This assumes than an organization both operates on the environment and is influenced by the environment. Open system theory, which is based on the work of the biologist Von Bertalanffy,[15] has been developed by Trist and others. An 'open system' is characterized by a spontaneous reorganization towards a greater degree of heterogeneity and complexity and a 'closed system' is characterized by a tendency to develop towards maximum homogeneity; the analogy for the former is 'the organism in its environment' and for the latter the physical model is more appropriate. Emery and Trist[44] in 'Socio-Technical Systems' have argued 'Considering enterprises as "open socio-technical systems" helps to provide a more realistic picture of how they are both influenced by and able to act back on their environment. It points in particular to the various ways in which enterprises are enabled by their structural and functional characteristics ("system constants") to cope with the "lacks" and "gluts" in their available environment.' Emery and Trist have also suggested that 'In general the leadership of an enterprise must be willing to break down an old integrity or create profound discontinuity if such steps are required to take advantage of changes in technology and markets. The very survival of an enterprise may be threatened by its inability to face up to such demands, as for instance, switching the main effort from production of processed goods to marketing or from production of heavy industrial goods to consumer goods.' This latter suggestion has a rather ominous ring about it when applied to the Glacier form of leadership.

Thus, from the Tavistock Institute Glacier adopted the following ideas:

1. That the individual's behaviour can be explained through the analysis of the complex of forces acting on him. These

forces can involve personal, social, and historical factors. Some of these forces may be unconscious.

2. Making these forces explicit is the technique of 'working through'. Inherent in this approach is the optimistic view that chance factors are of minimal significance.

3. When all is known (by working through), then all will be well.

4. The socio-technical systems approach provides the basis of task management.

PART II

GLACIER INDUSTRIAL RELATIONS

CHAPTER 4

GLACIER REVISITED:
A STUDY OF INDUSTRIAL
RELATIONS AS A REACTION
TO TASK MANAGEMENT

Two conclusions, both inescapable consequences of any objective examination of Glacier actualities, require to be
tated at this juncture. The first assertion is that the Glacier
ystem of management is too finely balanced with its four
ystems, the legislative system, the executive system, the repre-
entative systems, and the appeals system, to stand the buffeting
f a relatively unstable economy such as that prevailing in
iritain; the second assertion is that the Glacier philosophy has
lways been a reflection of the economic circumstance prevailing
t the time.

To understand the Glacier industrial relations, it is necessary
o understand the Company's theory of work. This theory rightly
ssumes that all managerial authority is subject to limits imposed
y extrinsic considerations. Thus Company policies must receive
anction from three sources, the shareholders who provide the
apital, the customers who determine the scale and quality of
roduction, and the employees who, by withholding their labour,
an bring production to a halt. All contractual arrangements
a the Company make explicit use of the sanctioning principle.
n the Works Council, major changes in policy must be unanim-
usly approved.

The Glacier approach requires the interaction of four systems
s figure 4.1 shows.

It is possible to argue that industrial relations at Glacier have
one through three phases corresponding to the theory of
rganization prevailing at the time, viz. the classical theory of

organization, the human relations school, and the ta
approach.

Speaking in general terms in the first phase, the managemer
managed and the workers worked. The manager's concept
the worker was derived from two sources: the idea of econom

FIGURE 4.1 *The Glacier System*

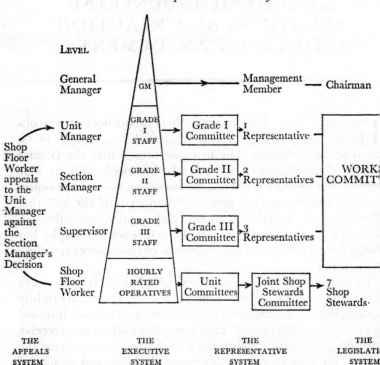

man and the belief that man can be treated as a machine. I
herent in this theory was the idea that the worker was indoler
irresponsible, resistant to change and easily led. The worker
representatives were thought of as being agitators and Cor
munist trouble-makers. Personnel management was unheard
and strikes virtually a curiosity since the management pursu
a policy of benevolent paternalism. Austen Albu[2] in 'Glacie
Experiment in Management' explains how Wilfred Brov
moved his Company into the human relations phase:

Before the last war Glacier Metal was no different from any other engineering company and, during the depression period of 1933, the Amalgamated Engineering Union tried to take advantage of anxiety caused by the introduction of unskilled labour to organise the workers and called a strike. This attempt failed. In 1935 Glacier became a public company and it was at that time that Mr. Wilfred Brown, the present chairman, became responsible for administration and in 1939, managing director.

Brown was disturbed at the state of management-labour relations which he found and which were exacerbated by the strain of expanding under war-time conditions. As he has since written, his views were coloured by his concern '. . . with the apparent dominance of those who owned industry, over the lives of those who worked in it . . . it seemed proper that democracy, the basis of our political institutions, should permeate into industry and form the basis upon which we regulated our working lives also.' (*Can there be industrial democracy?* by Wilfred Brown, Fabian Journal, March 1956.)

In the era of human relations, the main objective of the firm was not 'to get stuff out of the gate' but to provide a social climate where everyone, including the workers, could meet their personal needs. The plant was like a Soviet show plant of the immediate post-war period; the workers were happy to be consulted. The workers' representatives were good strong men, who smoked pipes, felt guilty about being paid for consultative work and were frightened of responsibility. Strikes were anachronisms; things of the past. Everything could be settled at the conference table. The personnel staff included psychologists who were studying to be psycho-analysts. Counselling was of major importance and the method used was the technique of 'working through', 'when all is known, all will be well'.

Finally in the task phase, the mission of the Company becomes the development of the optimal organization. Of course, to develop an optimal organization, it is necessary to consider the human factor. Personnel management consists in getting sanction from the men at least cost to the Company. Defining a person's role becomes the acme of personnel management. A good example of this new philosophy is provided by the fact that the Company required to recruit a new type of personnel specialist, the Company organization officer, which was advertised in *The Times* (20 April 1960) in the following terms: 'The Glacier

Metal Company Ltd., Personnel Division. This Division is being strengthened to implement new concepts of Personnel Management. Applications are sought for two posts at Headquarters in London, immediately subordinate to the Personnel Divisional Manager (PDM). Company Organization Officer. The PDM advised the Managing Director on the structure of roles in the Company. A specialist subordinate is required to assist this work. He will examine work in Production Sales Research, etc. and make recommendations on size of commands, distribution of responsibility, attachment of specialists at various levels, etc. He will also assist in the development of techniques for measuring levels of work, leading to the establishment of a basis for grading and payment. Age range 28–35. High level capacity for conceptual thinking essential. University degree preferred. Experience in such fields as Work Study or Management Consultancy would be an advantage.'

The Company's attitude to representatives has also changed. They can now be criticized, as Wilfred Brown observes on page 203 of *Exploration in Management*. For this purpose a new technique of communication has been invented. It is called 'contracting executive lines'. For example, the General Manager, at some point in a negotiation, may inform the shop stewards that he is going to 'contract executive lines' and address the whole factory. If the stewards complain that they are being bypassed, he informs them, 'I am contracting executive lines. You must change your role from representative to executive.' In 'Negotiations between Managers and Representatives' (Glacier Project Papers) Wilfred Brown explains, 'My meeting with my Extended Command will be an Executive Meeting,[29] held in working hours, and those present will be paid for the period of attendance. I shall then, as the Cross-over Point Manager, issue a Contraction instruction to them to attend. You will be present also, but in your Executive roles, not as Representatives. The rest will not be there as Constituents who elect Representatives, but in their Executive roles. I shall make it clear that the purpose of calling them together is to present my proposals and to have such questions and answers as are required to make them quite clear. As it is an Executive meeting I, as Cross-over Point Manager, have control of it.'

The aim of this chapter is to examine Glacier industrial relations against the changing perspective afforded by the attitudes revealed in these three phases. In particular, two strikes, both of which took place at the Kilmarnock factory of the Glacier Metal Company, in 1957 and in 1962, will be analysed in some detail.

THE 1957 STRIKE

Briefly the details of the strike are that at a meeting of the Works Council on Monday, 4 February 1957, the General Manager announced that 200 workers were shortly to be made redundant owing to a recession in the car industry, and that those declared redundant would be given one week's pay in lieu of notice. The Works Council rather meekly accepted this. But one important department was not represented at the Works Council; the Plant Engineering Department's toolmakers and maintenance men had previously withdrawn from the Works Council. Immediately after the Works Council, the General Manager sent for the A.E.U. shop stewards of the Plant Engineering Department to inform them of the impending redundancy. The A.E.U. shop committee in the tool room objected in no uncertain terms to this intelligence and suggested that the Company should (1) ban all overtime (2) shorten the working week (3) accept 'last in, first out' (4) ensure that each department be treated as a separate unit (5) that all sub-contract work be called in (6) that one month's notice or three weeks' pay be given in lieu of notice (7) that married women with working husbands were to go first. These suggestions the General Manager refused to discuss. As Wilfred Brown pointed out in the *Glasgow Observer* (15 February 1957):

> When the plant department stewards demanded alternative methods of dealing with the redundancy situation, the general manager indicated that he could not seriously discuss these: (1) Because those making the demands had already committed themselves to operate the standing orders procedure, and (2) because a decision had already been taken by the body constitutionally representing all the workers in the factory to operate that procedure.
>
> He pointed out that despite their claim to represent the factory as a whole, the shop stewards of the plant department represented only their own members.

The General Manager would not allow the calling of a mass meeting but suggested that the shop stewards go round the factory and discuss this matter with the men. The shop stewards led a procession through the plant protesting against management's proposals.

At 4.30 p.m. (i.e. during working hours) 150 men met in a nearby hall. This was followed, on Tuesday 5 February, by a meeting of 200 men at 7.45 a.m.; they decided to return to work at 9.30 a.m. When they attempted to return to work, they found that the gates were locked. The General Manager then interviewed the shop stewards and district secretary and informed them that all except the seven shop stewards were to be allowed in at midday. The seven shop stewards were to be suspended for three days. This was extended to four days after a telephone conversation. The men decided to strike and as a first step to picket the gates. The twelve workers on the Works Council resigned and full negotiating authority was vested in the strike committee. On Wednesday 6 February, there was a flood of workers to join the A.E.U. and a meeting decided there would be no violence or interference with vehicles. A mass meeting was held on the Thursday.

Management's attitude, in refusing to discuss the proposals of the Plant Department's stewards, was based on two points. Firstly, management argued that the workers' representatives had already accepted the redundancy agreement passed in 1952, and secondly, the Works Council had already accepted the General Manager's proposals and in their view this was the body which represented all the workers, whereas they spoke only for the Tool Room.

The Managing Director was also on record to the effect that he was willing to discuss the redundancy procedure whenever the representatives sought to amend it, but that this could not be done at the time when it was necessary to apply the procedure and that a Works Council decision which affected everybody could not be changed for the sake of a few. Brown also refuted the charge that the Council was a tool of management and drew attention to the fact that the workers' representatives were all trade unionists, that there had been a 100 per cent return in the ballot, and all decisions of the Works Council require unanimous approval. He further added that the two tool room representatives could have prevented this decision. In his view, the suspension of the shop stewards was a token act of discipline. Finally, he offered to send everyone a copy of the redundancy agreement.

The strike at the factory was settled after nine days on Wednesday, 13 February 1957. A joint statement, on behalf of management, trade union officials and shop stewards, was issued which stated that the redundancy agreement would be redrafted in the following terms: (1) 'last in, first out' (2) consideration to be given to a shorter working week. No mention was made of the suspension of the shop stewards.

The strike produced two interesting incidents. Some of the senior managers met to form a trade union and applied for its registration. The managers' reaction was prompted by their feeling that they were being used as scapegoats by both sides in the dispute. One managerial member of this group claimed that the Company was prepared to recognize the union as a negotiating body. The other interesting event was that the staff, including managers, were asked to do other work including the operating of machines. As it turned out, one personnel officer worked a machine during the strike.

Discussion of the 1957 Strike

A variety of explanations have been offered to explain this strike. On the one hand, it has been argued that the explanation is to be found in the history of the factory which was originally set up as a shadow factory at the beginning of the Second World War. This shadow factory was provided with a skeleton staff on the principle, not unusual at that time, of upgrading those willing to transfer, which meant that setters became foremen, foremen became departmental managers, and departmental managers became general managers. In fact, the expansion was so rapid that many bad appointments were inevitably made; this was especially true for the crucial post of general manager. One of the games favoured by the cynics in the factory, was to see how many ex-general managers could be spotted in the organization chart. These rapid cyclical changes, that is, promotion followed by demotion, had a very bad effect on managerial morale. It is possible to argue that this cynicism to some extent reflected a lack of indoctrination in Glacier philosophy. For that matter, in the mid-'fifties, in the factory it was difficult to find an executive who properly understood the Glacier philosophy; let alone accepted it. Presumably this to some extent is expected to be remedied by the setting up of the Glacier Institute of Management.

Against this view, it has been argued that the true explanation is to be found in the fact that the Kilmarnock factory is 400 miles distant from the London factory and, perhaps more important, that it is located in the penumbra of the Red Clyde. Taking this latter point first, it is certainly true that the Scottish trade unionists have shown a healthy scepticism towards Glacier philosophy. But Brown, with his roots in Scotland and experience of the Labour Party, cannot be wholly unaware of this. Indeed, many Kilmarnock employees feel that it was the absence of Brown and his remoteness from the scene of operation that allowed this leadership vacuum to develop. However, before this strike took place a new General Manager, who had come from a firm of consultants investigating the factory, and who was destined to become the Managing Director of the Company, had been appointed.

Undoubtedly, a proper aetiology of industrial disputes would show that multiple factors have to be taken into consideration in determining causation. Possibly the most important single factor is the economic variable. The Glacier Metal Company is part of the motor-car components industry and, as such, it falls within the most sensitive area of our 'stop-go' economy. At a national level the difficulties in the balance of payments situation are usually remedied by changes in the Government's monetary policy in a belated attempt to curb inflation, which in turn are reflected in a diminished sale of motor cars, which then reduces the demand for production of plain bearings in the Glacier Metal Company. The period 1956–7 was one when the government felt compelled to restrain the economy and this resulted in a definite recession. In fact, in the six months before this strike, the factory had been working short-time. Short-time working tends to create a reservoir of insecurity in a plant. Following this period of short-time working the factory had taken on more than 100 machine operators in spite of personnel advice to the contrary, and this only served to exacerbate difficulties. Nevertheess, when the crisis came in the Works Council, management was able to gain overt acceptance for the standing order on redundancy. In fact, by this time, most of the work people in the plant had lost whatever faith they had ever had in the Glacier System. As the industrial correspondent of the *Glasgow Observer* (15 February 1957) commented, 'Had all the men participated actively or been interested in the council's activities, the management's case would have been truly unanswerable. It would have been a simple issue of breach of contract. As it was, because many regarded the Works Council as a pet idea of the management and little concern of theirs, they did not feel morally bound – whether rightly or wrongly – by the council's decisions. So confronted with a threat of substantial redundancy, it was natural for the more trade-union conscious to think in terms of trade union safeguards. That many have shown lack of interest in the Works Council's affairs is evident from the redundancy procedure orders approved by the council. When redundancy arises it is natural that the management should wish to retain the services of those men they deem to be most useful to the company. On the other hand, the management, under the Works Council's method of procedure, had unfettered powers of selection, so that victimization was theoretically possible. Hence, trade unionists' efforts to achieve certain safeguards, such as the 'last in, first out" principle.'

'The Glacier redundancy procedure was lacking in the customary safeguards. Clause 3 stated:

> The personnel manager will require the manager of each department employing such members to forward him a list of those who are believed to be least entitled to be retained.

'Provision was made for alteration of the lists in discussion with representatives of the men, but there were no agreed principles to which appeal could be made.'

As has been already stated, there was a striking lack of faith and even knowledge of the Glacier system of management among the managers. The weakness of the management's position in accepting a superficial assent of the workers' representatives on the redundancy at the Works Council is demonstrated when it is realized that the strike was settled only after the redundancy agreement was redrafted in favour of 'last in, first out', and a reconsideration of the shorter working week. In essence, the strike achieved nothing positive except that it compelled an agonizing reappraisal of the Glacier system.

THE 1962 STRIKE

This strike at Kilmarnock lasted from 5 to 12 March 1962, and followed the second of two one-day national stoppages, 5 February and 5 March, which were called by the engineering unions in support of a wage increase and shorter working week refused by the Engineering Employers Federation. The strike was extended at Glacier as a direct result of a management directive to section managers about working machines normally operated by operatives in their absence. It was settled by the General Manager withdrawing this directive pending consultations regarding future policy.

In dealing with industrial relations at Glacier it is always as well to remember that Glacier is not a member of the Engineering Employers Federation; but its wages policy is related to the National Award negotiated by this body and the unions. The policy, at present agreed by the Works Council, is that any National Award will be implemented by the Company. Incidentally the Company had, in September 1961, given an increase of 3d. an hour. But earlier in that year (in June) they had refused a request by the Joint Shop Stewards Committee (J.S.S.C.) for a profit-sharing scheme for manual workers. At the same time, the management, in reply to this move, removed the staff bonus by consolidating it in salaries.

Chronology of the Strike

The first one-day national stoppage took place on Monday 5 February 1962. Prior to this, the General Manager (G.M.) called a meeting of the Works Committee and read a statement 'that the managers would, during the strike, be found alternative work (in accordance with company policy) and each would be expected to:

(a) carry out, not only the work of his own role but, in

emergency, to take on the work of other members in the same immediate command.

(*b*) if a supervisor, to operate as is customary, any of the machines subject to his supervisory control.

(*c*) if a manager, to perform in an emergency the work of any member of his immediate or extended command provided he is capable of doing that work.

If he refuses, he is deemed to be on strike without prejudice to his future position.'

The J.S.S.C. warned the General Manager that serious repercussions would result from anyone doing other than his own work. Grade III staff, who were A.E.U. members, pointed out that they had been instructed by their union to observe the one-day stoppage. Members of A.S.S.E.T. had been similarly instructed, and these included some Grade II section managers. Although managers worked machines on 5 February no 'serious repercussions' followed, but strike action did follow the use of a similar procedure on 5 March. The District Secretary of the A.E.U. told the *Kilmarnock Standard* that Glacier management had been warned of what would happen if the practice was repeated on 5 March. None of the Grade III Supervisory staff worked machines during the token strike, and they joined the extended strike. The Grade II staff section managers, who were members of A.S.S.E.T., and some others, did not work machines. On the other hand some of the Grade I staff worked machines. The London factory staged a one-hour token strike in sympathy.

An extraordinary meeting of the Works Council (the first of many) was called by the General Manager on 12 March 1962. He suggested a review of policy on the work to be done during official national stoppages in the following terms:

(*a*) Closure of the factory for all but certain small groups; or

(*b*) Agreement that those not on strike may do urgently required work, on the basis of a prior agreement of the Works Committee that some specified, small proportion of normal output might be obtained; or

(*c*) Agreement that certain jobs vital to future employment should be completed, as agreed to prior to or during the strike with the representatives' committee; or

(*d*) A combination of some or all of these.

At first it appeared that agreement might be had on some form of clause (*c*). But gradually the attitude of the J.S.S.C. began to harden and, after the General Manager made a direct appeal through the loudspeakers to the whole factory on 17 April, the position got worse. The J.S.S.C. claimed that in this speech the General Manager has interpreted the J.S.S.C. to the workers and this was unfair in a broadcast with no questions. To remedy this, the J.S.S.C. asked permission to address the factory, but this was refused.

The J.S.S.C. informed management that national stoppages could be avoided by having an agreement which would anticipate the National Award. Management's reply was that this was not now possible – for one thing their customers would only accept price increases following a national award. At a final meeting on 28 June, attended by union officials, including a representative of A.S.S.E.T., they could find no common ground for a policy governing future national stoppages and there the position remained. The national award was eventually made on 9 July and was implemented by Glacier.

A number of other problems raised by the strike have still not been solved and discussions were carried on with the Grade II staff committee regarding managers operating machines for a considerable time after the strike was settled. On this very issue, a section manager from 'O' unit caused another very short stoppage by operating a machine while he was supposed to be supervising a section in another part of the factory. The result of the matter was that he was reprimanded by the General Manager ostensibly for not being at his post. Incidents of this nature are an inevitable consequence of running against the established mores of the shop floor workers without prior negotiation.

The actions of the Grade II staff committee, at this time, are worth noting. During the strike this committee put down a motion for discussion at Works Committee on 8 March asking for management agreement that section managers would not be required to operate machines except during an unofficial strike. As it turned out, this motion was withdrawn when the meeting took place on 8 March. Nevertheless on 14 June they asked the Works Committee to agree to A.S.S.E.T. becoming a signatory union to the company agreement. The General Manager opposed this on the grounds that A.S.S.E.T. did not rep-

esent all of Grade II (although it did represent a majority).
The General Manager said that a meeting should be arranged
to discuss this question, but the matter was dropped. Subsequently in July, Grade III staff brought up the proposal that
A.S.S.E.T. should become a signatory union, but this was
defeated by Grade II. Grade III staff have also shown signs of
confusion, but are now making attempts to have the clerical staff
organized by the Clerical and Administrative Workers Union.

The 1957 strike may have been an accident–a local affair; the
same cannot be said for the 1962 strike which was virtually a
reaction to a policy decision by the Managing Director in London. In fact, this act of the Managing Director, in ordering the
managers to work machines after the warnings of both local
trade unionists and the personnel manager, was seen by many
shop floor workers as an act of industrial aggression. To the
external observer, it has none of the hallmarks of the scientific
application of task management (or of ostensible Glacier
human relations for that matter), but rather the act of an
aggressive manager. Against this, in the language of the task
specialist, it was argued that this was the only way certain orders
could be completed.

Two points are relevant here. One is that many of the managers were somewhat rusty as machine operators and it was
claimed by the factory stewards that much of the work produced
was of doubtful quality. Secondly, the stewards argued that
since it was a national strike with a political objective, they
would have been perfectly prepared to clear up any small difficulties in production before the official one-day strike began.

Like the 1957 strike, it achieved nothing positive except to
exacerbate management-labour difficulties. In the particular
machine shop, whose unit manager had been most adamant in
pursuing the Managing Director's order, a virtual cold war
existed for a long time. In fact, in the year following the strike,
more than a score of meetings with the stewards in this unit
were held to try and resolve this problem. Among the section
managers in this unit it was still a matter of tremendous importance, 'whether you worked a machine during the strike or not'.
In the factory there seems to be de facto if not de jure recognition
that managers do not operate machines except in certain circumstances, such as training or during an emergency.

GLACIER REVISITED

AN ASSESSMENT OF
GLACIER INDUSTRIAL RELATIONS

Before proceeding to make an assessment of Glacier industria
relations it might be helpful to the reader to keep the followin
paradox in mind, in regard to Glacier theory and Glacie
actualities. Glacier theory is preoccupied with psychological an
political considerations, while Glacier reality is dominated b
economic actualities.

Illustrative of this paradox is the fact that in the immediat
post-war period the engineering industries including the Glacie
Metal Company were preoccupied with problems of productior
Essentially it was a sellers' market. Indeed the Radcliffe Report
(paragraph 20) makes the following comment:

> . . . After 1945 . . . the Engineering Industries were constantl
> troubled by the length of their order books and so far from cor
> tracting, found it necessary to enlarge their productive capacit
> and man power.

Like other engineering companies Glacier was going through
phase of rapid expansion, including the expansion of the wor
force.

In such circumstances, it is not surprising that the Compan
was obsessed with the problems of better relationships on th
shop floor. It is my contention that Glacier's system of manage
ment with its emphasis on joint consultation which evolved i
the immediate post-war period could only have developed in
period concerned with expanding resources including the wor
force. The lack of foreign competition and the operation of
sellers' market gave the impression that marketing problem
were non-existent. Thus, during this period 1945–55, in a sellers
market, economic and marketing considerations were of mini
mal importance. If the economic and marketing logics wer
right, what about the logic of sentiment?

This was an era devoted to the logic of sentiment. Phrases lik
'industrial democracy', and 'industrial justice' were a common
place. The major focus of organization research was joint cor

* Report of the Committee on the Working of the Monetary System
presented to Parliament August 1959.

122

sultation. Three books that typified this period were, *Industrial Democracy at Work* by W. Robson Brown and N. A. Howell-Everson (Pitman, 1950), *Joint Consultation over Thirty Years* by C. Renold (Allen and Unwin, 1950) and *Joint Consultation in British Industry* (Staples Press, 1952). Indeed this latter text, a report on an enquiry undertaken by the National Institute of Industrial Psychology was sponsored by the Human Factors Panel of the Committee on Industrial Productivity which also supported the Glacier research, reported in *Changing Culture of a Factory*. It was only when the Glacier system was exposed to the stresses of the 'stop-go' economy that organizational fatigue became obvious. Indeed both the 1957 and 1962 strikes took place in years when the brakes were being applied to the economy.

While the mechanism of the 'stop-go' economy is not well understood, it follows a set pattern. First there is a boom (1954–1955, 1959–60, 1963–4) in which output rises much faster than productive capacity. At this stage, the production rises make it possible to tolerate fairly reasonable wage increases without too much inflation. The next stage (1955, 1960, 1964) develops when the economy has exploited all the productive capacity to the limit; two consequences follow. On the other hand, further rises in production and productivity are limited; on the other hand shortage of labour causes wages to rise faster than before. This marks the onset of inflation. The Government responds by restricting demand. The next phase (1956–7, 1961) the government applies the brakes more fiercely; the consequence is a recession (1958, 1962–3).

It is, perhaps, significant that the strikes in the Glacier Metal Company took place in 1957 and 1962 and are more or less in phase with the recessions.

Over the last ten years the Company has not only grown in size (net assets in 1952 £2,036,808 and in 1961 £4,556,059) but has also changed its focal centre of interest from production to marketing. It also has found it necessary to raise funds on the open market. This increase in size, with the corresponding increase in the labour force, made it more difficult to apply the principles of human relations which were developed for a much smaller organization. While the Company employed approximately 2,000 people in 1950, it now employs approximately 4,500 people.

The change in function is just as marked. The Glacier Metal Company includes a number of subsidiary companies including Dualloys Limited, Scottish Precision Castings Limited, Glacier Bearings (Proprietary) Limited, Glacier Bearings (New Zealand) Limited, and the Glacier Institute of Management Limited. The sale of Company-built machine tools is a rapidly developing side of the Company's business. Licensees in Germany, France, Italy, Spain, the U.S.A., Japan, Brazil and India are using machinery built by the Company and using techniques developed at Kilmarnock and Alperton (London). Licensee agreements are being negotiated with several other countries and the hope has been expressed that plant will be built for them shortly. The Company is also particularly interested in trading with the Soviet bloc. The chairman's statement to shareholders in 1962 reflects this increased interest in the merchandizing aspect of his Company when he notes:

> The management of the company is conducting a rigorous analysis of our organisation with particular emphasis on speedy delivery, relationship of stocks to turnover, expansion of our sales organisation and the establishment of a closer relationship with export markets.*

This increase in size, coupled with a preoccupation with marketing and the need to raise fresh capital on the open market, has produced a change in Glacier philosophy, representing a switch from human relations management to task management. This can be readily understood in the light of the aforementioned factors and especially when set against the perspective of the unstable British economy.

As has already been noted, the Company has raised funds on the open market and, presumably in order to facilitate this operation, the rate of Ordinary Dividend has been stepped up from $7\frac{1}{2}$ per cent in 1941 to 20 per cent in 1964. This has had effects on the internal organization of the Company. Previously, when the lower rate of $7\frac{1}{2}$ per cent was being paid, the Company was secure against the charge of being only concerned with

* Taken from the Annual Report and Accounts of the Glacier Metal Company 1962 – 'During 1961, as already reported, we undertook (or arranged) two large contracts totalling over £500,000 for the supply of plant to Eastern European countries and we believe that further contracts of this kind are possible in the future.'

1aximizing profits' but, at a rate of 20 per cent Ordinary Divi-
nd, it leaves itself wide open to criticism in this respect.
The level of distributed profits must affect the amount of
oney available for improving employees' wages and conditions
work. Equally important is the effect of dividend rate on their
titudes. An expectation among the employees had been built
) that the Company was vitally concerned with their well-
ing. Jaques has argued in *Changing Culture of a Factory* that the
per cent rate of dividend had helped to maintain an atmos-
ere of democracy in the firm. The lower rate of interest had
en regarded by employees as visible evidence of the Com-
ny's concern both for democracy and their well-being.

TRADE UNION ATTITUDES TO GLACIER

1e Glacier attitude towards unions, particularly as portrayed
Changing Culture of a Factory, seems to be that the unions, or
ore specifically the workers' representatives on the Works
uncil, are reluctant to accept responsibility. This view of
ques warrants closer examination. The basic underlying as-
mption of this approach is that organizational conflict stems
om unconscious and unrecognized motives. The social analyst's
le in this context is to ascribe motive to the parties concerned
a means of explaining observed behaviour. Arguing against
is dangerous practice, it is possible to believe that the stewards
e opposing management because their motives are derived
om consciously-held goals and values.
In Jaques' view this reluctance to accept responsibilities has
e effect of structuring their behaviour in a defensive manner.
1is is particularly true of the interpretation which is placed on
e Weekend Conference (reported in *Changing Culture of a Fac-
y*) at which Brown offered the workers' representatives what
peared to be virtual control of the legislative authority of the
ompany. When the workers' representatives hung back it was
ken to be a symptom of immaturity. But, it might be argued
the other hand, the workers' views are not truly represented.
any representatives share the view of Sir William Carron, ex-
:neral Secretary of the A.E.U., that it is management's duty

to manage and their responsibility to criticize; and in certa
circumstances to advise. Indeed, there is a good deal of ev
dence, particularly during the 1957 and the 1962 strikes, to sho
that Glacier management has not properly understood Briti
working-class culture and has failed to assess what a small de
Glacier has made in the class war that exists between labour a
management. In my opinion, it is possible to argue that th
distrust which shop stewards and trade union officials have
the Glacier System springs ultimately from consciously-he
values. The nub of the matter is that they realize that t
workers' representatives do not have the necessary structu
and sapiental authority to carry through the roles required
them in the Glacier System.

The necessary structural authority could only be conferred
the workers' representatives by Parliamentary Statute or by t
terms of a properly legally defined trust. The former route wou
give the representatives a number of seats on the Board
Directors and the right to decide who filled certain key po
such as the posts of the personnel director and personnel ma
ager. This would require legislation on the West German mod
The right to appoint the personnel specialists would help
increase the sapiential authority of the representatives.

On the debit side of the present arrangements, whereby t
Company has its own social scientist who is held to be co
pletely impartial (he is responsible to the London Works Coun
but is presumably paid by the Company), it must be obvio
that the shop stewards, while they like and respect the soci
scientist, require their own experts to do their staff work. This
precisely the service which union officials can provide for sh
stewards. Generally, Glacier management would prefer not
have to deal with full-time union officials. A good example
union reaction to this view is provided by 'Ice Cold at Glaci
by Robert McCusker,[96] which has the sub-title 'Paternalism pl
Joint Consultation don't change anything', where he questio
the picture of perfect industrial democracy presented by Brov
in *Exploration in Management*. McCusker,[96] an official
A.S.S.E.T., makes the point that

Mr. Brown's theorising overlooks the role of the Trade Union.
the pure theory of his thinking there is no need for trade uni
organisation in his factories.

126

McCusker concludes:

> The theory behind the company's ideas reminds me somewhat of
> the theory of management–trade union relations in Communist
> countries; i.e. we are all working together for the common good
> and thus there can be no differences between us. That may be all
> right in Communist countries, but for Great Britain, under present
> circumstances, it leaves me cold–Glacier cold!

CONCLUSION

Certain criticisms may be levelled against the Glacier system of
industrial relations. The system appears to be predicated on
the assumption of identity of interest between management and
labour. Implicit in this approach seems to be the desire to minimize the role of full-time union officials in plant negotiations. It
is also possible to argue that the system overestimates the average
worker's interest in joint consultation. As might be expected
most workers do not like the principle of 'contraction of executive
lines'. They regard it as a technique for bypassing the shop
steward.

The workers object to the Company's handling of the 1957
redundancy on the following grounds: that a redundancy is
regarded as an example of poor planning by management. In
the period immediately preceding the redundancy, the factory
launched a recruiting programme for approximately 100 machine operators. In any case, with a labour turnover of approximately 25 per cent per annum and a labour force of roughly
1,500, the redundancy would have been avoided by allowing the
labour force to run down over a period of six months. At the
London factory, the Company's personnel department had
handled redundancies in a much more sophisticated manner,
by organizing jobs for those who had been declared redundant.
They also objected to management drawing up the redundancy
list. To the workers, there was a second danger that management would use this opportunity to get rid of 'trouble-makers'.
Fundamentally, most shop stewards believe that they should be
able to consult their constituents about redundancies. This may
mean a mass meeting. If management refuses the opportunity

during working hours, then the workers may exercise their own initiative and call a meeting at their own discretion outside the plant. Once outside the plant, they may elect to stay out.

In general terms the Company ignores, or at least minimizes, the importance of attitudes that employees bring to the factory. These attitudes include: general distrust of management, the belief that when workers go on strike the managers should not operate the machines, the belief that shop floor wage differentials should not be too great.

In fact, wages and conditions at Glacier's Kilmarnock factory, while far from perfect, must be considered good. Wages are high; for the highest paid semi-skilled operative the rate is 8s. per hour (June 1965). Overtime is plentiful; with overtime and the two shift system (two weeks day-shift followed by two weeks night-shift) the average earnings for an operative is approximately £22 per week. This is well above the national average and much higher than the Scottish average. The men are carefully selected. They get an intelligence test (Ravens Matrices), dexterity tests, a medical questionnaire and two interviews. Promotion is 'from within'. Nearly all jobs are advertised within the plant. Labour turnover varies around an average of 25 per cent. No 'clocking in' is required; latecoming is about the same level as in other plants in the area. Induction training is given to newcomers. The Induction course includes the opportunity for the Convenor of the J.S.S.C. to address new starters, who are encouraged to join their trade unions. The Company is rightly renowned for its joint consultative practices. The Convenor of the shop stewards is regarded as having a full-time representative's role; he is provided with an office, telephone and clerical support, is treated with considerable respect and seems to be free to pursue his affairs in his own way. Dismissals are infrequent. There is a well-conceived appeals system which certainly works successfully as far as dismissals are concerned. Payments by results has been replaced by high time rates. Victimization of shop stewards is virtually unknown. Welfare arrangements are good. Canteen facilities are adequate. A part-time medical officer, with the assistance of qualified sisters, runs a well-laid-out medical room.

GLACIER REVISITED

A Glacier Cult?

Where's the rub? If the Glacier books had not been written, there would have been no real basis for criticism. The assessment, so far, has been concerned with actualities; it is when Glacier philosophy is introduced that the difficulties arise.

This change of cultism can be illustrated by considering a critical question from the official catechism. What is a manager? Once the definition has been formulated, then there is no chance of ugly facts destroying it since, in this definition, the manager is held totally responsible for getting his work done. Then, if his operators go on strike, he will operate their machines, with the consequences which have already been discussed. What is relevant is that apparently irrational behaviour can be predicted from a definition which consists ultimately of a set of unverified assumptions. Again, from the same definition, if it is specified that a manager should assess the performances of his subordinates, then he can. In this semantic alchemy, 'should' becomes 'can'; from the normative to the positive. The same discussion could be repeated for the legislative system. Producing an elaborate specification of the function of the Works Council does not change the realities of the situation. The shop stewards accept that the management has the initiating, innovating, executive role and they have advisory and consultative roles. For the stewards, this means they have the right to amend, to know and to withhold support depending on how they see the situation. They do not regard themselves as legislators. At Kilmarnock they have indicated their misgivings by calling the Works Council the Works Committee.

Glacier Industrial Brinkmanship

What are the prospects of industrial relations in the Company? In some ways, conditions are getting better. The 40 hour week and the likely introduction of three weeks' annual holiday for everyone represents a step ahead of the engineering industry in general. But, on the other hand, the Company's economic and social policies are changing. With the rate of Ordinary Dividend trebled in 14 years, the emphasis inevitably must be on the economic at the expense of the human.

As described in Chapter 10, Glacier is emerging as a pocket bureaucracy. Optimal organization, depersonalized strategies, role descriptions, and the 'contraction of executive lines' can hardly be described as the language of job satisfaction. The technique of 'contracting executive lines' is particularly disturbing as it allows the management the initiative to transform a negotiating meeting into an executive meeting. The reshaping of the Company's organization, presumably with the object of 'optimizing it', has already produced serious human consequences. Two illustrations will suffice to illustrate the dysfunctional consequences of optimal organization.

In the Thin Walled Unit, when mechanization of the lines, including transfer machines to link the machine tools, was introduced, the rate of production would have been trebled, but it would have been necessary for the much smaller work group to forgo their communal tea break. Relief for individual operators was to be provided by a slip man. This disruption of the informal group was reinforced by difficulties in this formal organization brought about by management's mooted proposals to dispense with supervisors on these lines and replace them with a higher grade of machine operator. It was only when the situation threatened to turn nasty, and a strike looked probable, that the management moderated these measures.

Again, in 1964, in the Sinter Unit, the management's proposals for a third shift system were so economic that a four-day strike followed which was confined to the Sinter Unit. What is significant about this strike is that it was predictable. (In fact, both the production manager concerned and at least one personnel officer regarded a strike as probable.)

In other words, the management got a better bargain on the shift wage rates by risking and finally accepting a strike. This form of 'industrial brinkmanship' may have short term economic advantages but, in the long term, the cumulative short term human disadvantages may produce important economic dysfunctional consequences.

CHAPTER 5

A WAGE NEGOTIATION

In a progressive and dynamic company such as Glacier, a student of personnel administration might be forgiven for believing that matters of wages determination would be explored and solved using the sophisticated techniques favoured by social scientists. In particular, in Glacier, such a student would wrongly but understandably expect that time-span analysis would be the favoured method. This would be a formidable undertaking and would require the 'time spanning' of a very large number of different hourly paid jobs. In Glacier there are four grades of machine operatives, four grades of process operatives, and a wide variety of supportive shop floor roles such as storeman, inspector, move man, to say nothing of the various craftsmen's jobs. This list of jobs is further complicated by the fact that the definition of the grades of machine and process operative vary from unit to unit. After this mammoth operation these 'scientific results' would be presented to the workers and their representatives and the necessary data passed to the wages department, who would make the necessary arrangements.

In fact, the London factory's Works Council has never accepted that the time-span of discretion should be used as a means of settling questions of payment. Even if they did, questions of practicality would still arise. In the first instance, a very large number of personnel specialists would be required who, after a suitable period of training, would have to study these operator roles which, in any case, are continually changing. The cost of employing these specialists would be substantial, if not prohibitive. Secondly, even if the general principles of time-span were accepted at Glacier, it is doubtful whether this particular technique could decide whether a job was worth 7s. 9d. or 7s. 10d.

In Chapter 6 of *Piecework Abandoned*[28] Brown has analysed the organizational implications of switching from piecework to high time rates for shop floor workers. The principal consequences of this change were: the establishment of full managerial roles (i.e. the recognition of the need to define the section manager), the more precise definition of wage brackets, and the acknowledgement of the need to carry out quarterly wage reviews.

On the issue of the 'full managerial role' Brown quite rightly argues that the abandonment of piecework would place the authority 'to set terms of reference and determine differential rewards' for subordinates squarely on the shoulders of the manager. To fulfil this managerial role Brown argues that the manager *vis-à-vis* his subordinates can be held accountable for:

 (i) Knowing them as individual persons
 (ii) Criticizing them when their work is sub-standard
 (iii) Assessing their work and rewarding them accordingly
 (iv) Arranging their promotion to a higher level when this is warranted
 (v) Firing him from his section when he fails to respond positively after item (ii) has been tried.

Having justified the need to make managerial roles explicit, Brown then examines the need to simplify and define wage brackets. Four wage brackets were instituted for shop floor workers; according to Brown their pay is not related to quantity of work produced but to the level of work to be done and the capacity of the individual. In a footnote on page 78 of *Piecework Abandoned*[28] Brown reserves his position as to how scientific these brackets are, when he observes,

> I wish to emphasize that the descriptions of work in the Wage Bracket standing order referred to are not operational definitions. Elliott Jaques' work on measurement of responsibility provides us with the instrument whereby level of work may be measured. One day, when this is more fully accepted by managers and operators as being valid, we shall be able to employ it to categorize work in its different levels. We shall then have an operational definition of all types of work. In the meantime, it is very important to recognize that using these descriptive categories of work leaves room at all times for argument as to what lies within or without each category.

It is one of the great virtues of Brown's writings that he allows reality to erode away any academic theory of management; in this case, establishment of wage rates will never be the subject of one party defining the level of payment of another unilaterally but will always involve bargaining, testing of the power situation and finally establishment of a contract between two parties which is valid for a limited period. It is entirely to Brown's credit that, excluding pious hopes, he recognizes the reality of this situation.

Assessing Performance – Terms of Reference

Quarterly wage reviews were instituted for the purpose of enabling management to assess the level of work of their operators and as such are an integral power of task management. Brown[28] defines his section managers' terms of reference for making these assessments on pages 79–80 of *Piecework Abandoned*:

(a) Whether or not the operator is in a job involving responsibility consistent with his personal capacity and, if necessary, to change his job or to recommend to the unit manager promotion to a higher level of work elsewhere.

(b) If the operator is in the correct job, the relationship of his total performance and behaviour to the position of his hourly rate relative to the top and bottom of the bracket of pay for the category of work he is performing.

(c) Whether performance is such as to cast doubt on retention by the operator of the job he is doing, and a consideration of other jobs at a lower level which he might more successfully perform or reference of the case to a personnel officer to discover vacancies elsewhere in the factory.

(d) Whether or not the level of responsibility of the work being given to an operator to perform is, in the judgment of the manager, changing. If it seems to be going up, then it has to be recognized that the operator is possibly being promoted without specific recategorization of his work and appropriate action either to increase his rate or recategorize his work, must be taken.

(e) Such matters as future potentiality of the operator, vacancies coming up in the future which he might be able to fill, training needed, etc.

These terms of reference are more important for what they omit than for what they contain. In matters of pay, economic considerations appear to be completely ignored, in theory, if not in practice. The marketing factor which in turn determines the Company's profitability is ignored. The laws of supply and demand relating to labour receive no mention. Apparently, scarcity of a particular type of labour does not affect the wages he will be offered. Again the manager is given no indication as to how he should set about assessing 'the level of work' except that it is not the same as quantity of output. The crucial point is that the fineness of judgment required to make these assessments is completely ignored. The method to be used to justify the fact that an award has *not* been made is not discussed.

The worker's attitude to this unusual system is ignored. Excluding those paid by piecework, most shop floor workers in British industry are paid a flat rate for the job which is sometimes supplemented by a merit payment, which usually, but not always, represents a small proportion of the total rate for the job. A typical merit rate, in my experience, would be 3*d*. an hour. In Glacier, wage rates for operatives working in the same section can differ by as much as 2*s*. per hour. Such differentials conflict with the expectation of most shop floor workers. Nothing is said about changes in wage brackets produced by factory negotiations. 'Going along with National Awards' receives no mention.

CHRONOLOGY OF A GLACIER WAGE NEGOTIATION

On this vital issue of how wages at Glacier are determined, of how they settle 'who gets what?', what are the facts? In fact, wage negotiations at Glacier differ little from those in other companies. To justify this assertion, it is necessary to piece together the facts of a Glacier negotiation. The particular negotiation to be described may be summarized in the following sequence of events. The account begins with a Chief Executive of the Company (one of the overlords interposed between the Managing Director and the General Manager to manage a number of Glacier manufacturing installations) making a general statement on wages to the effect that it is Company policy to go along with National Awards and that wages are to be

comparable or better than those general in the area; a not
unusual expression of good will from the side of management.
Next, the workers submit a claim to management. Management
stalls, then makes a counter offer. As per usual, the workers want
a flat rate increase; and, as might be expected, management's
counter-offer requires a stretching of the wages concertina. Both
bargains will cost approximately the same. Their lack of congruence is recorded in a failure to agree. Now, both sides
escalate one level. Full-time union officials and Company
officials are brought in; the result, again a failure to agree. The
G.M. 'contracts executive lines' and addresses the workers
directly. The shop floor rejects his proposals by ballot; tension is
beginning to build up.

The G.M. sends a letter to all employees, setting out the
Company's case. By now both parties are isolated. The J.S.S.C.
calls a wages meeting. Overtime is banned, and a date fixed for
striking. Communications between the two sides are now by the
informal network. An emergency meeting of the Works Committee is called by management and a compromise favouring
the workers, that has already been agreed in informal meetings,
is ratified. So the merry-go-round is given another push and the
scene is set for a re-enactment of what has gone before.

This ritual warrants more detailed factual analysis, and what
follows is a description of a Glacier wage negotiation. Most of
the material has been taken directly from the minutes of the
Works Committee, with minor amendments to ensure sense and
to remove any reference to particular persons.

A General Statement on Wages

A convenient, if somewhat arbitrary starting point to begin
this chronicle of a Glacier negotiation is the meeting where the
Chief Executive informed the elected representatives that
Company policy was to pay wages comparable to or better than
those general in the area and to go along with National Awards.
Then came 'the writing on the wall' for the shop floor when he
added, 'To avoid the necessity of an overall increase, like the one
recently negotiated, mechanisms would be introduced to keep
brackets under review and preserve trends for the payment of
levels of work; though it was possible there would be variations

in the maintenance of some differentials.' Then came the *quid pro quo*; he referred to an intensive campaign which was being mounted to improve methods of production, and this improved efficiency would be reflected in wage brackets. His next statement hinted at the idea of widening differentials. The General Manager would be coming forward with suggestions for modifying the procedure in connection with brackets, as it was felt that the rigidity of the present system might have inhibited the proper earning capacity of some members. Of course, as might be expected, the managerial prerogative was to be preserved. In this context, this meant that the place of a person in a bracket, and his progress through it, would still be determined by the managerial assessment.

When the T. & G.W.U. representative, who was present at the meeting, raised the not unreasonable question of the possible misuse of a manager's authority when making an assessment, the Chief Executive replied somewhat arbitrarily that 'The person who was paid to know how a subordinate was performing was the best one to make an evaluation and the Appeals System was available to redress grievances'. At this point the factory Convener made the point that while Glacier management encouraged the use of the Appeals System the shop floor members lacked confidence in its efficacy.

The representatives of both the T. & G.W.U. and the A.E.U. supported by the J.S.S.C. then drew attention to the antagonism between management and labour which they felt was engendered by the present complicated wage structure with its wide brackets. Specifically they recommended the abolition of differences in rates paid to operators performing the same job.

The Chief Executive met this criticism by arguing that the bracket in any particular role had to be wide enough to accommodate variations in performance by different operators, and that management was concerned with mobility of labour and the number of jobs that one person could undertake. To maintain stability of employment, in his view it was often necessary to transfer people from one job to another, and the person with greater adaptability should be paid a higher rate. To simplify the complexities of the wages structure, management were considering a system of brackets which would embrace the whole factory instead of individual units as was the case at present.

The Grade I staff representative pointed to the danger of over-simplification in dealing with assessments and went on to argue that in contrast to work of the conveyor-belt type, many jobs in the factory depended on the skill of the operator to control quality and output, and two men on the same job could be of fairly widely differing worth to the Company. In his opinion managers had to exercise considerable judgment in assessing the many factors which decided the rate to be paid.

The question then arose, 'Had a machine operator always the opportunity to extend his technical expertise and thus his earnings?' The General Manager confirmed that the principle of equality of opportunity to acquire further skills would continue to be implemented as long as work was expanding. The General Manager further complicated the matter by observing that 'even at present, there were several people who were at the top of their bracket although they could work only one machine'.

The Convener then referred to the delay experienced by members in regaining the top rate when a bracket ceiling was raised and to the see-sawing of top rates as between machine and process operators. In reply, the Chief Executive said, 'it depended on the level of work being paid for but there would be a case for consideration if the differentials had been over-widened. Final changes in brackets and differentials must be legislated at Works Committee.'

The A.E.U. representative asked if the Company would be prepared to consider separate negotiating machinery, to which the Chief Executive replied that while the present intention was to go along with National Awards he would not rule out the possibility of conversations being held to consider other procedures.

Shop Stewards ask for Clarification

In May 1964, at a meeting of the Works Committee, there was a request that the management member make a full statement to the Works Committee on current Company thinking as regards the elimination of differentials. The Convener opened the discussion by stating that false hopes had been raised in the factory on the question of differentials, and they wished the facts to come from the Works Committee rather than from them. The

General Manager answered that Company thinking as regards the elimination of differentials was precisely the same as before, namely, that it would eliminate differentials *when economic circumstances* permitted. The Convener then queried why a meeting had been called recently, and the General Manager said that it was to allay these false hopes about which they had been speaking, and which were building up to the extent that the Company was bound to step in and say definitely that no dates had been established for the elimination of differentials.

A lengthy discussion followed and the Convener asked the General Manager to read out to the Committee the formal statement which he had made at a recent meeting. The General Manager read out the following statement:

We have noticed that the subject of the differential entitlements which exist between the various grades of Company members is a matter of concern within the representative system and the present Works Committee with difficulty is tackling a number of issues. We recognise the long term need to do work in this area, and to introduce requisite changes as and when economic and other circumstances permit. To this end, Management will carry out an analysis of individual entitlements, what they will cost and what would be the expense involved in introducing these changes. At the present time, however, the Company has added very considerably to its expense level by a number of wage bracket adjustments, the implementation of a National Award, and the introduction of a 40 hour week, and it is planning to introduce certain new policies in salary structures which are likely to add further to our annual expense. In view of these measures it is quite apparent to us that the Company at this time could not possibly support further expense arising from the granting of additional entitlements to any group or groups. We feel that to discuss this matter in Works Committee would naturally give rise to hopes that early changes in entitlement might be expected, and these hopes could not be fulfilled. Although any representative group is, of course, entitled to raise with Management any question of entitlements, we consider that review of the whole subject should be dropped, on the understanding that Management will carry out the analysis mentioned above, and will come forward with proposals when economic circumstances permit.

A WAGE NEGOTIATION

'A Failure to Agree'

At a Works Committee meeting in September 1964, the General Manager gave a short history of the claim made by hourly-rated representatives for increased earnings and longer holidays, as their share of the current prosperity of the Glacier Group. He made it quite clear at the outset that he was not going to enter into any *negotiations* at this meeting, but only reporting on developments to date.

In his view, the present claim for substantially increased earnings was put forward by the J.S.S.C. as a direct consequence of the failure to have the policies specified in the Chief Executive's statement of November 1963 carried out. The members of No. 3 factory felt that, as they had worked to make the present prosperity of the Company possible, they were entitled to reap some of the benefits. The question of comparison with London rates entered into it also, and mention was made of the differentials stated in the Ministry of Labour *Gazette*.

On the third week's holiday with pay, the point was made that this was going to be universal anyhow, and Glacier could anticipate this. The General Manager argued that he could not negotiate this at No. 3 factory alone, but said that this was a matter which would require to be discussed in the Glacier Group as a whole, and that he had passed this request to London.

On the matter of the increase in earnings, the General Manager observed that since this same time, the year previous, very considerable increases had been made–viz. new brackets, 40-hour week, National Award and five quarterly reviews. Cumulatively, this represented an individual average gain of some 17 per cent. Many of these increases were paid out, not only to No. 3 factory, but to others within the Glacier Group–the prosperity had already been shared out. As to the comparison with the London rates, the General Manager pointed out that these rates were negotiated by factory units, and, whereas the rates might be high, the levels of work were also high.

The Convener stuck to his guns and pointed out that, rather than raising the top brackets, the shop floor would prefer to see everyone getting an increase, for then profits would be more evenly shared, and in any case the labour which created the profits was the result of teamwork rather than only the result of the efforts of machine operatives at the top of their respective brackets. He went on to say that, while the method of determining wages seemed to be acceptable in London, it had always been a bone of contention at Kilmarnock; similarly, London had differing views on how to deal with the possibility of a redundancy situation. In his view, it seemed that the London way of thinking did not appear to coincide with the wishes of personnel at Kilmarnock.

The minutes of the Works Committee recorded the rather doleful statement, 'The matter rests at the present time (September 1964) in a formal "Failure to agree", and negotiations would continue when the situation permitted.'

A Ban on Overtime

At a meeting on 10 December 1964, the General Manager said that *he had been told* that there was a ban on overtime effective as from 9 December, and that, unless a demand for an overall wage increase by 11 January 1965 were conceded, a withdrawal of labour would take place on that day. Comment was invited. Grade III considered that the present situation was a most regrettable one. Grade II had not discussed the matter, and had no comment to offer. But what about this unilateral action the shop floor proper had taken? If junior and middle management representatives had nothing to say on this vital point, then the senior management spokesman had.

The Grade I staff representative expressed concern at the breakdown in constitutional methods, and asked why it had not been possible for proposals for the change of the present policies to be made by J.S.S.C. without resorting to the use of power; he was also seriously disturbed about the effect which this dispute would have on the present security of employment and on the future expansion of the factory.

The General Manager stated that he had already discussed the formation of a working party to consider various aspects of Glacier payment policy with which the hourly rated members disagreed, and he was now somewhat apprehensive in case it should be felt that this working party would be considered as a possible means of providing a solution to the present dispute.

On this point he advised the meeting that, if this was in fact the feeling, he would consider it necessary to withdraw from the present discussions. The Convener agreed that this might initially have been the case, but not now that the shop floor personnel realized that the dispute would have to be resolved by other means.

The General Manager then pointed out that the working party should operate within defined terms of reference. Against this view the Convener argued that they would have little scope for putting forward their views if in fact they were restricted to discussing existing policies. To meet this difficulty the General Manager conceded that alternative methods of payment could be put forward for discussion. The General Manager then issued a warning. In his view the situation could be reached, however, where the proposals were such that, although he was capable of showing their impracticability, other members of the working party would still wish to pursue them; if this were the case, it might be necessary to discontinue the discussions. The Convener accepted this point and returned the compliment by noting that either party in the discussions would be free, of course, to withdraw if in fact the situation became completely unacceptable to them. The Convener further stated that this dislike of the present Glacier policy on wages and assessment had been made known quite frequently during previous wage demands, as in each case the workers had asked for an overall wage increase.

Management's Proposals

While the workers' claim for an overall increase of 2d. per hour had been rejected, management were, however, prepared to have a look at the rates paid in all units with a view to raising the brackets, with a resultant reassessment. But the shop floor view was that a situation could then arise that differentials would be created where none previously existed (e.g. the 'B' unit top rate could end up 1d. higher than that in the other machining units, while in the Sinter unit it would end up rather less).

To test out the practical implications of management's offer, a trial run was carried out, using 'N' unit as the sample. While the following figures were the outcome of the 'N' unit survey, it could be taken that a similar adjustment would take place throughout the other units.

TABLE 5.1 MANAGEMENT'S PROPOSALS

Brackets	Old Rate	Proposed New Rate
Training	6/0·3 – 6/3·45	6/0·3 – 6/4
B	6/3·98 – 6/7·13	6/4½ – 6/8
I	6/7·65 – 7/1·95	6/8½ – 7/4
II	7/2·48 – 7/9·30	7/4½ – 8/–

This would mean in effect that:

22·5 per cent of the workers would get 3d.
45 per cent of the workers would get 2d.
17 per cent of the workers would get 1d.
15·5 per cent of the workers would get 0.

The management then took the initiative and sent a letter to all hourly paid workers. In this letter, the General Manager set out the Company's case for differential payment for different levels.

The Workers' Case

To the workers, the nub of the matter was: the management wanted to stretch the concertina of wage brackets wider; the workers wanted a flat rate increase for all of 2d. per hour. It is as well to understand that basically what the workers were rejecting is the idea that section managers are capable of making an objective assessment of a worker's worth. In other words, to their mind the management's discretion is not only too great but badly exercised.

The facts are that before the dispute the operators were paid from 6s. to 7s. 9d. (excluding decimals). Movement through the training grade and Grade B was more or less automatic; this amounted to 8d. an hour. But this still left management's margin of discretion 1s. 1d. an hour. The vast majority of the operatives felt that they would never reach the maximum. In one shop, only 25 out of 400 operators had reached the top of the Grade I

vage bracket, i.e. 7s. 9d. per hour. If the management's proposals were accepted, the differential would be 6s. 1d. to 8s., i.e.
a widening of the differential. In the trial run, management's
proposals would have the effect of reducing the number of operatives at the maximum from 25 to 9.

One of the oddest points of this negotiation was the fact that
while, at one stage, in the shop stewards' committee there was
a slight majority in favour of accepting management proposals,
yet when it was put to the workers directly in the shops – 1,000
voted against accepting management's proposals and 200 voted
for acceptance of them. Fundamentally, the workers lacked
confidence in the ability of section managers to assess their performance, a doubt shared by some of the managers as the following extract from a Company memorandum on 'The Assessment
of Hourly Rated Members' shows: 'This task of assessment and
its communication is one of the most difficult aspects of managerial responsibility and not unnaturally there is a desire on
the part of some mamagers to ease the burden by seeking some
simple device which avoids the necessity for making careful
analytical appraisals of individual performance and attainment.
Hence the demand for a yardstick or formula which can be in-
discriminately applied. In some quarters there is a growing
desire for the elimination of differential rates and the establishment of a fixed rate for each job category. This feeling is supported by some managers who are overwhelmed by the difficulty
of making objective individual assessments.'

But supposing the worker is wrongly assessed, the fault can be
redressed by appeal. But can it? Is this view widely shared on
the shop floor?

The Shop Stewards' View of the Appeals System

In general, to the minds of the stewards the Appeals System
was held to work well except for those appeals concerned with
wages. But, unfortunately, as one shop steward wryly observed,
'95 per cent of the appeals are concerned with wages'. 'On
wages, the appeal could go either way', as another steward put
it. 'They win 50 per cent of the time, and we win the other 50
per cent.' Such comments reflect basically 'the hit or miss'
nature of wage assessments.

On the Appeals System, the stewards' comments are instruc
tive.

A senior steward: 'Management thinks the Appeals System
is great, but we don't agree.'

A steward: 'The Appeals System is all right in theory but it
doesn't work in practice. We don't always expect justice, but
we do expect fairness. Whether we like it or not we have to work
under the Appeals System.'

Another steward: 'We are satisfied with the Appeals System
in all appeals except those concerning wages. The Appeals Sys
tem on wages does not work because the wages of an operative
are based on reports by section managers, and as the reports
and recommendations can be, and often are, over-ruled by unit
managers, appeals on matters of wages are almost bound to fail.
It is mainly for this reason that we prefer flat overall increase
in pay.'

A senior steward: 'The Appeals System in matters other than
wages works well. For instance, Glacier has a good record as far
as dismissals are concerned. There is no instant dismissal because
of the Appeals System. On the other hand the Appeals System is
not conducive to instant action on the part of management.'

The Compromise

After the ritual of negotiation has been gone through – i.e.
first the proposal, then the counter-proposal, followed by the
recording of 'a failure to agree', then the bringing up of the
managerial heavy artillery from London with the stewards
reinforced by union officials, again a failure to agree, followed
by a ban on overtime (with a date fixed to strike), and both
sides isolated with only informal contacts, then the *compromise*
begins to emerge. At first reading the terms of the compromise are
not quite obvious. Reading the minutes of the Works Committee
would give an outside observer the impression that manage
ment's proposals had been accepted in their entirety. But what
of the question of assimilation? Assimilation refers to the method
of determining the point where particular individuals will be
placed in the new brackets. Instead of the sacred management
principle of 'the right of a manager to assess a subordinate and
reward him accordingly' which had held up the negotiation

the following rules of assimilation were proposed (according to the report of a personnel officer):

1. All workers would get a minimum increase–equal to the amount by which the bottom of the bracket had moved.
2. Except in very special circumstances, those at the top of the bracket would move to the top of the new bracket.

In essence, this meant for each worker a proportionate shift from the old bracket to the new bracket. In addition, a working party was to be set up to examine the assessment system.

Some Comments on this Wage Negotiation

It is interesting to note that the *Company Policy* as specified by a Chief Executive of the Company was 'to pay wages comparable with or better than those in the area and to go along with National Awards'. But in his view, the manager's assessment of the level of work done by the operative was still the vital function in deciding the actual rate to be paid. A curious argument was used to demonstrate this factor, viz. 'The person who was paid to know how a subordinate was performing was the best one to make an evaluation'. In determining where an operative should be placed within a wage bracket, the mobility and the number of machines which they could operate were to be taken into consideration. But, apparently, 'two men on the same job could be of fairly widely differing worth to the Company.'

On the other hand the workers would prefer the removal of differentials. To the Convener of shop stewards, it was the group rather than the most highly skilled operative who made the Company prosperous. Therefore, to his mind, a flat rate increase for all workers was appropriate. But management believed that the appeals system would take care of any injustices produced by these assessments. As has already been pointed out the stewards had very little confidence in the fairness of appeals against wage assessments.

The most significant point to emerge from the study of this negotiation is the fact that the stewards could take unilateral action and declare a ban on overtime and fix a date for striking without first following the constitutional procedure of raising such a proposal at the Works Committee.

Being realists, the stewards knew that it would be virtually impossible to get the Works Committee to agree to a ban on overtime since the General Manager (like all members of the Works Committee) has the power to veto any proposal.

On communications, Glacier management has loaded the scales in its own favour, by instituting the principle of 'contracting executive lines'. One of the stewards interviewed described this technique in these words:

> Management is in the habit of by-passing workers' representatives and speaking direct to workers. Instances have occurred when workers have been told to 'down tools' and go to a meeting when management will speak to them, alternatively the workers may go home. At a meeting of this type when the Convener asked permission to address the workers as well, he was refused permission and told that he had his own opportunities to speak to the men.
>
> The Tannoy system has been used by management to make statements to the workers collectively. Sometimes when management calls a meeting of all workers they make statements when no questions are allowed.
>
> Even when questions are allowed the representatives find this embarrassing because workers may be of the opinion that such questions will not have been given due consideration by the representative committee.

'PIECEWORK ABANDONED' RECONSIDERED

Summarizing the advantages to be gained from the abandoning of piecework Brown[28] notes–'release of managerial time from concern with bonus, made possible increased attention to the real production problems of tooling, machines, flow of work, training of operators, reduction of scrap etc.'

But empirical studies of the section manager's behaviour (reported in Chapter 7) showed that during some periods, he could spend up to 20 per cent of his time on personnel work, mainly on assessments of operators. Brown[28] also argues that, 'Responsibility for the assessment of the appropriate level of pay for each individual operator can be placed squarely on the shoulders of their managers. Because they have hour-to-hour contact with operators, they are in a better position to judge performance and pay of operators instead of leaving such important matters to the variations arising from time study of samples of work'; and he further argues that this will cause a 'decrease in feelings of hostility and suspicion between managers and representatives. On this very point the above account of a Glacier negotiation illustrates to what extent such feelings of hostility have been allayed.

The critical question is—'Has piecework really been abandoned?' Strictly speaking, the answer must be 'Yes', but something rather similar to piecework has emerged. Now, something worse seems to have developed for instead of the work study officer measuring the job with the aid of a stop watch, the manager assesses not only the quantity and the quality of the work, but also the personality characteristics of his operators. Evidence on this very point is afforded by the Company memorandum on assessment which notes that:

> When a manager is making an assessment there are two groups of questions which he needs to ask himself.

1(a) Has this member acquired additional skills of which I am making consistent use?

(b) Have I assigned additional responsibilities to him since the last assessment? e.g., training other operators, deputising functions, etc. etc.

2(a) How well is he doing his job—*is the quality of his work up to standard—is his rate of output satisfactory?* Is he improving, if so—*by how much?*

(b) Does he use his initiative in organizing his own work? Am I confident in his ability to work without constant supervision?

(c) Is his personal behaviour acceptable? Is he *co-operative and helpful?* Does he fit in well with other members of the section —if not, why not? Is his timekeeping and attendance record satisfactory?

From the section manager's point of view, the above criteria represent an assessment of the manager himself. In other words, the rating tells you as much about the rater as it tells you about the ratee. For this reason, section managers dislike the process of assessment and in my experience are certainly not unaware of the practical difficulties of this system.

The crux of the matter is that abandoning piecework maximizes management's discretion, while circumscribing not only the operator's behaviour (in terms of quantity and quality of work) but also his attitude ('Is he co-operative and helpful?'). It can come as no surprise to the experienced line manager to know that in one unit at least, on one occasion the workers asked for piecework to be restored. In general terms, the bracket range is too wide, the assessments too frequent, the margins at review too tight, the temptation to settle old scores too great, the basis of assessment too complex, the number of appeals too numerous, the time for assessment too consuming, and the resulting differentials too wide.

Surely the Glacier executive ought to be wondering whether the Company is not too introverted in its approach to the problems of wage negotiation. Perhaps the Fawley Experiment has some relevance here. In this experiment, William Allen, the American Managing Director of Emerson Consultants Limited recommended a 'productivity package deal'. This meant the workers were offered wage increases of up to 40 per cent. In return, they had to give up certain defined practices, limit demarcation and accept shift working. Esso also agreed to a policy of 'no redundancy'.

It might be argued that the increase in earnings would be too great for Glacier to bear. Yet, according to the General Manager's letter to the workers, they had had a 17 per cent increase in earnings in just slightly over a year. Thus, it would seem possible and, indeed, desirable for Glacier eighteen months before the compromise was reached to have offered the workers a 'productivity package deal' with a 20 per cent increase in earnings as their offer to them. But with strings. In return the management could have negotiated the details of the following:

(a) A shift system for the Sinter Plant.
(b) The mechanization of the Thin Walled Unit.
(c) The introduction of a higher grade of machine operative.
(d) A better arrangement of overtime.
(e) Better deployment of the supervisors.
(f) Acceptance of the Company Policy Document.

Perhaps it is as well to point out that item (a) caused a four day strike when it was introduced and item (*b*) took the factory to the brink of one.

Of course, every stage would require to be bargained out as it was at Fawley. This would involve discussions between the management, shop stewards and union officials. But, as Allan Flanders[47] in *Fawley Productivity Agreements* pointed out, in detailing the agreements and discussing the lessons to be drawn from them, the onus for taking the initiative must be with management. As Flanders stresses, the unions constitute the permanent opposition; their function is to react; management must propose and initiate.

CONCLUSION

Wage negotiations at Glacier follow a pattern, not atypical in British industry, and usually involve a test of strength. To the outsider the approach seems essentially irrational especially in the long term, and the management usually seeks short term advantages; in cold war terms the process looks like 'industrial brinkmanship'.

But the workers lack confidence in the Appeals System in regard to rates and would prefer flat rate increases as opposed to a system which requires assessment by a manager. Basically this is because they believe that the wage differentials are too great. On the other side of the fence the management leaves itself open to the charge of being too introverted. Perhaps the productivity package deal might have some application in Glacier.

Finally, this wage negotiation illustrates just how task oriented the Company's approach to industrial relations has become. It certainly seems to me that the question of retaining the workers' goodwill seems relatively unimportant compared with the short term advantages of giving the minimum increase in wages. As an ex-Glacier manager put it, 'Supposing we do have an odd strike. Provided they are brief, we will still win in terms of task effectiveness.' The critical question here is how do you measure ineffectiveness? How do you measure the work that is *not* done?

PART III

THE GLACIER SECTION MANAGER

CHAPTER 6

THE GLACIER SECTION MANAGER—
AN INTERFIRM COMPARISON

O ne of Glacier's most striking and intriguing innovations has
been the creation of the role of section manager, which was
invented to do something positive about 'the break in the executive system' which inevitably arises at the fissure between management and labour and which Glacier met by injecting some
managerial authority into the traditional foreman role. This
crude and oversimplified explanation of the section manager
role is only a first sighting on what is a very complex role with a
very complicated history. To try and unravel some of these
complexities it was decided to devote a major part of this research to the problem of evaluating this role. This problem was
tackled from two angles. In the first instance, an interfirm comparison was carried out in regard to this role by questionnaires
and interviewing; this involved 21 firms. Secondly, an observational study using activity sampling was made of four section
managers.

Any attempt at an objective appraisal of the role of section
manager must take cognizance of its peculiar history. Up to
1944, the lower levels of Glacier organization were complicated
by the existence of a multitude of supervisory roles: chargehand,
leading hand, setter, supervisor and assistant foreman. In an
effort to clarify this complex and bewildering situation, the
terms chargehand, leading hand, supervisor, were abolished
and each production shop was divided into a number of small
machine sections with a *section supervisor* in 'full managerial command' of each. The *section supervisor*'s role also carried the responsibility for doing any machine setting required and for
supervising closely the work of any operator where this was

necessary. The sections were quite small, ranging from about six operators to a maximum of fifteen.

A group of from three to seven sections was under the charge either of an assistant foreman (in the case of a department with a superintendent in charge) or a foreman (where there was no superintendent in the department). Thus, in theory, operators were responsible to the section supervisors, their managers, and *on paper* the section supervisors had the job of selecting, disciplining, assessing and, if necessary, discharging operators. Perhaps it is just as well to point out that there is little doubt that these section supervisors had sanction from 'high up' to take command.

FIGURE 6.1. THE '1944' SOLUTION TO THE PROBLEM
AT THE FOOT OF THE EXECUTIVE SYSTEM

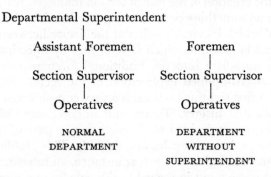

The 1944 changes had been introduced for a number of reasons: for a start turnover of supervisory staff was very high and there was a lack of effective management, as Brown notes on page 180 of *Exploration in Management*:

> The fact was that, after five years' experience of running an engineering company during a war, I had come to realize that managers were not in command of events. Some of the more obvious indices to me of the extent to which a situation is, or is not, under control in a factory is the discipline at stopping and starting time, tidiness and care of machinery. (While these are not necessarily the most important in their effect, they are the most obvious to higher management.) I found that carefully thought out orders and instructions on these questions had no effect. You could be in the shops at twenty minutes before stopping time and see men closing down work. If you got hold of the foreman and told him to stop that happening, he would blame his charge hand

or setter. They would blame it on the men, or on general indiscipline in the country, or on anything they could think up. Apparently, nobody was really prepared to take command and to give instructions.

The existence of production difficulties arising from tooling that was correct from an engineer's angle but, when used in production, proved to be unsatisfactory and was complicating matters. There were also a large number of problems about individual pay rates. Not unexpectedly disciplinary problems were arising due to the lack of clarity about responsibility and authority.

The 1944 changes which required this introduction of the *section supervisor* were only a limited success partly because the members of a particular section were continually changing. This being so the section supervisors could not properly assess their subordinates when wage reviews came round. The nature of the work was such that the section supervisor was too heavily engaged in trouble shooting and setting to spend sufficient time on planning. Understandably the operators regarded the foreman as their manager and to complicate matters further many of the foremen were not acting as managers.

THE SECTION MANAGER CONCEPT

In 1953, Elliott Jaques suggested that the clarification of the *section supervisor*'s role would go far to heal 'the split at the bottom of the executive chain'. According to Brown[26]–'Dr. Jaques went on to point out: that the precise responsibility and authority of section supervisors was the most strongly felt and widely raised problem met in the analysis of the Company organization'.

In the light of Jaques' analysis, it was decided to abolish the titles section supervisor, assistant foreman, foreman and superintendent, and to use the terms supervisor, section manager and unit manager.

In *Exploration in Management* Brown lists some of the inadequacies of the 1953 solution; some supervisors were behaving almost as managers, while others were working full time as setters. As might have been expected, some section managers were failing to take up their managerial role.

One of the advantages of the Glacier system lies in its pro
vision of an official language. The 'specification for the job'
starts by explaining 'to whom this section manager is account
able' (the unit manager) and 'who his subordinates and col
leagues are'. Having settled this, the duties of the section manage
are spelt out in terms of tasks. The resources available to achiev
these tasks are analysed into programming, technical and per
sonnel elements. All of this latter material is considered unde
the broad heading of Prescriptions.

FIGURE 6.2

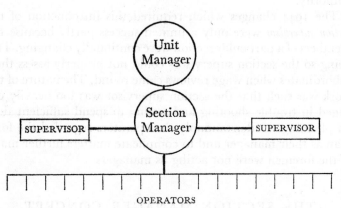

According to the official job description the section manager'
job is managerial in the full sense—he carries responsibilities fo
engaging his operators and supervisors, setting standards fo
them and ensuring that standards are met, and assessing an
rewarding his subordinates with wages appropriate to the wor
they are doing. He is responsible for training his subordinate
and ensuring that they have the skills needed to get his wor
done; for planning his production to meet his current and for
ward load; and for deploying his men and machines in the mos
effective way. Line-shop activity is characterized by sudde
changes in demand which must be coped with by equally rapi
changes in plans to meet the new demands. The section manage
is responsible for maintaining a high level of technical efficienc
on his lines. He must continuously make decisions about pro
duction methods, interpreting manufacturing instructions wher
necessary. Although the development of production methods i

normally the work of the production engineers, the manager has to see that the best possible methods are being used in production. He must meet standards of efficient operation set by his unit manager. His duties include the requisitioning of supplies and services needed to maintain his machines.

The section manager is responsible for establishing adequate relations with his colleagues, with other section managers, and with staff specialists of his unit manager. He must be able to contact and use the services of inspectors, personnel specialists, works engineers, the tool room, and other staff in an effective manner. He must be able to work with representatives so that problems that arise are dealt with quickly and decisively. He has to carry out all his activities in conformity with established Company and factory policy. He is responsible for establishing and maintaining in his section safe standards of work and a high standard of cleanliness and tidiness.

LEVELS OF SUPERVISION

Any attempt to summarize the research in this field is complicated by problems of terminology. A very wide variety of terms are in use to describe those persons below the level of management when there is responsibility for planning and organizing the work of others. The National Institute of Industrial Psychology's[107] *The Foreman* (Staples, 1957) suggests four levels:

Level A is intended to include the most senior supervisors, usually bearing some such title as Shop Superintendent, General Foreman or Senior Foreman.

Level B includes the men and women who are probably most generally in mind when the terms 'Foreman' or 'Forewoman' are used, although here again there is a wide range of titles.

Level C covers the Assistant Foreman, Junior Foreman and those who are normally responsible to a level B supervisor but who are themselves engaged almost entirely in supervisory rather than operative work.

Level D is intended to include the 'working' supervisor, the Chargehand or Leading Hand who is normally an operative but who carries some specific supervisory responsibility for which he is separately rewarded.

In my view the Glacier section manager, as proposed by Brown, corresponds to Level B.

In Scotland it is generally accepted that foremen have a critical role to play being management's representatives face-to-face with the workers. By their styles and standards of behaviour, they determine the attitudes of workers to their work and to the objectives of the firm as a whole.

While the importance of the human aspect of foremanship is gaining increasing recognition, it is still necessary for the foreman to have a considerable degree of technical skill. The traditional archetype of the old time foreman 'decked out' with bowler hat, gold watch and abundant self-confidence, has all but disappeared. The foreman of the 'sixties does not have anything like the same standing; all too often he does not 'know where he stands' and, more important, nor do those who are subordinate to him. There are three main reasons for this. For a start, the increased technical complexity of work is such that to occupy the position which the foreman of fifty years ago held, his modern counterpart would require an impossibly wide range of detailed technical and managerial knowledge. As a consequence of this demand, specialists have had to be introduced and this has complicated the situation. Secondly, some of this loss of stature must be attributed to the better educated operative, who is more aware of his political and social rights. Finally, the basis of the old time supervisor's discipline – fear – has largely disappeared.

Vertical relationships in this case refer to the relations between foremen and management above and their subordinates below. Between 1954 and 1956 the National Institute of Industrial Psychology[107] (N.I.I.P.) conducted an investigation into the work of the supervisor. One interesting finding that emerged from these studies was that the foremen attached more importance to relations with senior management apparently because they presented more problems. On their relations with the shop floor, the foremen seemed to be surprisingly unconcerned.

According to the N.I.I.P. studies, little emphasis was placed on the problem of enforcing discipline. In general terms, it appeared as if the workers understood the role of the foreman and automatically accepted his authority. Presumably a great deal of this sprang from the fact that foremen had been in their

present positions for a number of years and so had their subordinates.

All of the firms studied operated incentive schemes. It does
not seem to be generally realized that the kind of supervision
exercised in a firm operating an incentive bonus scheme is quite
different from that required in a firm paying time rates. Operatives on an incentive bonus scheme largely control their own
activities. When levels of output are fixed, either by management-labour agreement or by the informal mandates of the
group, the most important function of the foreman is to ensure
an adequate supply of work or, in its absence, to arrange lieu
payments and to 'tune in' the other specialists involved in the
working of the bonus system.

ABANDONING PIECEWORK AND
MANAGERIAL ROLES

At this point in the discussion it is relevant to consider if there
was any relationship in Glacier between abandoning piecework
and the introduction of the section manager concept. In *Piecework Abandoned*, Brown[28] gives an account of how Glacier dis-
pensed with various wage incentive schemes. Piecework in
the Foundry was abolished on 23 June 1949. Again, in June
1957, payments by result was abolished in the Thin Wall
Department of the London factory. Brown notes that the Kilmarnock factory had eliminated wage incentive schemes alto-
gether by 1953. It is worth remembering that Jaques proposed
in 1953 the institution of the section manager's role. Brown[28]
notes on page 80 of *Piecework Abandoned*:

> These, then, are the three more important organizational implica-
> tions of giving up wage incentive schemes:
>
> (a) Fuller institution of real managerial roles on the shop floor.
> (b) Categorization of all types of work in the factory and the
>   attachment to each category of explicitly stated and pub-
>   lished wage brackets and,
> (c) The working out of a formalized process of quarterly reviews
>   of the work and personal capacity of each operator by his
>   manager.

This reinforced the earlier detected need for more effective management if time clocks are abandoned. As Brown[28] remarks 'It would seem that if a company desires to get rid of the practice of clocking, then it may well be necessary first to arrange organization so as to be sure that consistent lack of good timekeeping on the part of any individual will be noticed and assessed by a manager with the requisite authority to deal with it.'

In other words, in a piecework situation, shop floor workers carry an organizational as well as an operative role; they have a greater share of the initiative than would be the case in a properly organized time rate situation; in piecework the norms of output have already been fixed by the workers themselves as in the Hawthorne Experiment. In such circumstances, there is less need for the efficient foremen to be production oriented. Being task centred cannot improve productivity and may only serve to alienate the workers. Thus where piecework is practised efficient supervision is likely to consist of placing greater emphasis on human relation skills.

While it is widely recognized by management consultants that plants on time rates can usually be made more productive by installing piecework, the question then arises how further increases in productivity can be obtained while the workers retain the 'right' to fix the norms of output. Given this perspective, it can be readily recognized that there comes a stage in the evolution towards a more efficient organization when it is desirable to abandon piecework.

For example, in Glacier's factories as they became semi automated, a piecework system could have been a distinct disadvantage to management. As production became more mechanized through the introduction of faster machines linked by transfer machines, the existence of piecework and its corresponding attitudes (that norms of output are specified and enforced by the primary working group) could have made management's task very much more difficult. In one unit at Kilmarnock, when the production workers realized that the new lines would increase productivity by a factor of 3, they expressed the desire to have a piecework system reintroduced.

Even more basic is the question—who is more capable of managing? The managers or the workers? The modern managerial society is predicated on the principles that some individual.

are more capable of managing than others and that the quality of the manager is frequently the most important single factor determining the productivity of the work force.

On the other hand, the foreman regards his relations with higher management as being more important and more trouble-some. The explanation for this seems to be that it is senior management who specifies the organization and conditions of work of the operatives, as well as defining the foreman's actual duties and the limits of his rights and authority. In addition, they determine the efficiency of the organization from the top down to the point where the foreman is vitally concerned. The extent to which he is able to do his work efficiently must depend to a very considerable extent on how management functions are carried out at various levels of the organization.

But managers are also important to him in a less formal way. In any organization and within any system of planning, however rigid in theory, specialist or functional managers have to consult with line managers and supervisors and line managers have to consider alternative lines of action and make decisions. In other words, there is a considerable amount of what might be called informal management activity in all organizations, more in some than in others. The official duties and rights and status of the foreman then are determined by the formal organization, but his actual freedom of action and his real participation in management may be determined largely by his relations with managers.

In the first of these N.I.I.P.[107] studies, personal relations between foremen and managers were affected by the fact that managers tended to move from one position to another while foremen remained in one position. Another major reason for this was that managers–line and specialist–had tended to take over functions which had originally been the prerogative of the fore-men.

RESULTS OF THE POSTAL QUESTIONNAIRE

The questionnaire, shown in Appendix I, was completed for 21 firms who together employed over 1,000 foremen. These firms were placed in three categories: light engineering, heavy engin-eering, and a miscellaneous group, which included a number of food processing firms. The aspects covered by the survey were classified under three broad headings—functions, fringe benefits, and salaries.

TABLE 6.1. SALARIES OF FO

Type of Industry	No. of Company	No. of Foremen	Lowest Salary £	Highest Salary £	600 – 675	675 – 750	750 – 825	8 9
	1	54	900	1350	–	–	–	
	3	22	826	1275	–	–	–	
LIGHT	5	31	600	1425	1	2	3	
ENGINEERING	6	50	600	975	9	15	12	1
	7	29	900	1425	–	–	–	
	8	16	675	1050	–	2	3	
	20	35	750	1050	–	–	2	2
		237			10	19	20	4
	4	25	825	1050	–	–	–	
	9	185	900	1275	–	–	–	
	10	54	675	1275	–	1	–	
HEAVY	13	7	975	1050	–	–	–	
ENGINEERING	15	47	750	1050	–	–	4	1
	17	16	750	1200	–	–	1	
	14	477	975	1125	–	–	–	
	21	3	750	825	–	–	3	
		814			–	1	8	3
	11	34	600	900	2	12	11	
	12	16	600	975	1	–	4	
MISCELLANEOUS	16	14	*No information*		*Board restricted infor*			
(Food Processing	18	9	825	1350	–	–	–	
etc.)	19	20	750	1425	–	–	1	
	22	44	750	900	–	–	11	
					3	12	27	4
	Light Engineering				10	19	20	
	Heavy Engineering				–	1	8	
	Miscellaneous				3	12	27	
	TOTAL				13	32	55	1

Nearly all of the firms in the survey stressed that the foremar is held accountable for the quantity and quality of products and for ensuring that they are produced on time at the right price all within the framework of the company policy or departmenta schedule. This survey confirmed that foremen are held account able for maximizing the safety of their operatives. They are als required to requisition maintenance when it is required.

Regarding the right to hire—in the light and heavy engineer

ing industries the majority of foremen played a limited part in the choice of subordinates, but only half of the foremen in the miscellaneous category enjoyed this privilege. Generally speak-

IN THE WEST OF SCOTLAND

50	1125	1200	1275	1350	Mean	Standard Deviation	Median	Q.1	Q.3
25	1200	1275	1350	1425	£	£	£	£	£
5	13	10	5	—	1137	NA	1081	966	1163
4	7	2	—	—	1066	112	1087	966	1163
4	2	3	1	2	1049	195	900	825	1076
—	—	—	—	—	722	88	759	693	837
3	1	1	—	1	1082	72	1077	1033	1085
—	—	—	—	—	862	105	857	800	900
—	—	—	—	—	898	46	880	848	922
9	23	16	6	3					
—	—	—	—	—	941	NA	950	—	—
—	15	14	—	—	1152	50	1170	1106	1221
—	3	1	—	—	982	106	962	925	1103
—	—	—	—	—	1012	NA	1044	—	—
—	—	—	—	—	894	NA	906	858	944
—	1	—	—	—	932	146	946	889	1006
—	—	—	—	—	1042	NA	NA	NA	NA
—	—	—	—	—	787	NA	NA	NA	NA
2	19	15	—	—					
—	—	—	—	—	787	NA	770	715	829
—	—	—	—	—	862	NA	875	806	975
Board restricted information					—	—	—	—	—
1	—	—	1	—	982	75	944	916	972
2	1	1	3	1	1042	147	958	916	1200
—	—	—	—	—	832	NA	775	—	—
3	1	1	4	1					
9	23	16	6	3	968	177	952	842	1103
2	19	15	—	—	1063	71	1016	986	1045
3	1	1	4	1	869	132	866	794	906
4	43	32	10	4	985	133	1005	919	1048

ing foremen in this latter group seemed to have little authority or status. Secondly, approximately one-third of the foremen in engineering determined wage increase for subordinates; this right was exercised by one-sixth in the miscellaneous group.

In general it may be concluded that the foremen in the engineering industries carried a wider range of managerial duties and consequently enjoyed higher status than their counterparts in the miscellaneous section.

In all firms surveyed the foremen were able to participate in a contributory pension scheme, and in all but three a non-contributory sick benefit scheme was in operation. While profit sharing was found in only three firms, eight others had some form of non-production bonus for foremen. Though a few foremen enjoyed twenty-eight days' annual holidays most had to content themselves with twenty-one days. None of the firms questioned provided rent-free housing for their foremen; but five did offer some form of subsidized accommodation.

The other outstanding feature was the universal provision of sports and family recreational facilities in the heavy engineering industry. This may be explained in some cases by the location of this type of industry; whole towns and villages have grown up around the works.

TABLE 6.2

Type of Industry	Lowest Salary £	Highest Salary £	Average Salary £
Light engineering	600	1,425	968
Heavy engineering	675	1,275	1,063
Miscellaneous	600	1,425	869
Total	600	1,425	985

One of the main objects of the investigation was to determine the salaries paid to foremen in the West of Scotland. Table 6.2 presents an analysis of the salary data relating to the foremen surveyed.

According to the survey most foremen are paid salaries which fall within clearly defined limits, but these limits may or may not be known to the man himself. In the light engineering industry the foreman takes four years on the average to move from the bottom to the top of the scale. The length of time

TABLE 6.3

Type of Industry	Do so regularly
Light engineering	14%
Heavy engineering	22%
Miscellaneous	16%

taken by those in the other two industrial categories varies considerably and may be anywhere from 2½ to 10 years or more. Table 6.3 answers the question: 'can subordinates earn more than their foreman?' In other words, the facts are at variance with the widely held view that shop floor workers usually earn more than their foremen.

GENERAL CONCLUSIONS

From an overall point of view the survey reveals that foremen in the light and heavy engineering industries carry out approximately the same functions. Their levels of salary are comparable, the average for heavy engineering being slightly above that for light engineering, but with the range between the lowest and the highest salaries greater in the light engineering group.

One significant point that should be made is that salary increases, and presumably promotion within the grade, appears to be more 'planned' in light engineering, judging by the fact that all the firms in this category questioned were able to estimate the length of time that the 'average' foreman would take to go from the bottom to the top of the scale.

Foremen in the miscellaneous group have limited duties compared with their engineering counterparts. Their salaries are markedly lower and the only area in which they 'score' is in the provision of free protective clothing and the like.

It can, therefore, be concluded from the evidence produced by the questionnaire that the status of foremen in the light and

TABLE 6.4. A SALARY COMPARISON

	Industry	Lowest Salary £	Highest Salary £	Average Salary £
Great Britain 1958	Engineering	785	1,250	974
	Miscellaneous	598	935	754
Scotland 1961	Light engineering	600	1,425	968
	Heavy engineering	675	1,275	1,063
	Miscellaneous	600	1,425	869

heavy engineering industries is higher than that of their counter-parts employed in the firms included in the miscellaneous group.

Some comparison may be made with an investigation into the pay of foremen made by the Institute of Personnel Management in 1958. Table 6.4 gives the details of the comparison. However, it should be remembered that the 1958 I.P.M. Survey was conducted on a country-wide basis, while the 1961 investigation was conducted entirely in the West of Scotland.

It would appear from the survey that most engineering foremen were earning on the average, at the time of the survey, approximately £1,000 per annum and some may earn as much as £1,350 per annum. Referring to the comparison with the I.P.M. Survey 1958, and assuming that the salaries of the British

TABLE 6.5. ANALYSIS OF THE LABOUR FORCE OF THE P: FOR THE FORE1

No. of Company	Type of Company	Total Labour Force	No. of Staff	N. Work
3		1590	333	12
5		571	108	4
6	LIGHT	1009	290	7
7	ENGINEERING	973	368	6
8		240	45	1
1		1492	423	10
20		800	166	6
		6681	1733	49
4		686	214	4
9		3989	731	32
10	HEAVY	2060	495	15
13	ENGINEERING	650	290	3
15		3109	1084	20
17		575	209	3
14		11300	3800	75
21		99	15	
		22468	6838	155
11		700	103	5
12		800	45	7
16	MISCELLANEOUS	1085	165	9
18		130	37	
19		492	114	3
22		2036	573	14
		3243	1037	42

foremen have been rising at a conservative 5 per cent per annum, it may be inferred that while Scottish foremen are slightly worse off than their English counterparts, it is not so marked as is sometimes claimed. It is also interesting to record that the difference is probably greatest at the bottom of the distribution and least at the top.

The survey confirms that the foreman is in a transitional stage in his development, that he is slightly more affluent than many people believe him to be, that his role is changing to include that of co-ordinator of specialists in the primary working area, and that educational qualifications will become more important in choosing foremen.

| | D Showing Spans of Authority and Titles used | | |
| | DIATE Superior | | |

of isors	No. of Workers to each Supervisor	Title of Supervisor	Position held by Supervisor's Immediate Superior
	57	Foreman	Superintendent
	15	Foreman	Head Foreman
	14	Foreman	Manager
	21	Line Manager	Project Manager
	13	—	—
	19	Section Manager	Unit Manager
	18	Foreman	Superintendent
	20		
	19	Group Foreman	Shop Superintendent
	17	Head Foreman	Manager
	29	Foreman	Shop Manager
	51	Foreman	Works Manager
	43	Foreman	Superintendent
	22	Foreman	Assistant Superintendent
	15	Junior } Senior } Foremen	Junior Superintendent
	28	Foreman	Works Manager
	19		
	17	Foreman	Departmental Manager
	50	Foreman	Assistant Production Manager
	65	Departmental Foreman	Assistant Production Manager
	10	Mill Manager	Director
	19	Title varies	Title varies
	33	Foreman	Departmental Manager
	31		

FIGURE 6.3. PART OF THE ORGANIZATION CHART OF THREE
COMPANIES (NOS. XIII, XIV AND II)
SHOWING THE POSITION OCCUPIED BY THE FOREMAN

COMPANY XIII   Heavy Engineering   (600 employees)
   Departmental Structure
      Superintendent
          |
       Foreman   Present maximum salary 1,030 p.a.
          |
      Charge Hand   Present maximum salary £998 p.a.
          |
       Operators

COMPANY XIV   Heavy Engineering
   Departmental Structure
                 Superintendent
                       |
             Junior Superintendent   Minimum salary
                       | £1,200 p.a.

   Time Study   Production Planning
                                         Maximum salary
                  Senior Foremen   £1,125
                                          (Monthly Staff)

   Tool Progress
   Engineering
                       |
              Junior Foremen   Maximum salary
                       | £1,050
                   Operators   (Weekly Staff)

COMPANY II   Light Engineering   (1,650 employees)
   Departmental Structure
      Department Head   Minimum salary £1,450 p.a.
          |
       Foreman   Salary range £1,000–£1,275 p.a.
          |
   Assistant Foreman   Range £800–£900 p.a.
          |
      Charge Hand   Range £600–£750 p.a.
          |
       Operative

MATERIAL BASED ON
PERSONAL INTERVIEWS

To define the role of the foreman more accurately a number of personal interviews with personnel managers were conducted. In the interests of brevity only one full report of an interview is included.

Company II

In this particular firm, female employees outnumber males by two to one but supervision is almost totally male. This is not unusual in British industry as is the fact that it is possible for the foreman to become a departmental head without acquiring any further formal qualifications. Promotion depends largely on personal attributes. The present level of educational requirements is a Higher National Certificate–this is required on account of the technical nature of the company's products.

On the vital managerial right to hire and fire, the authority to determine who his subordinate shall be is almost completely denied the foreman. So far as selection is concerned the Departmental Head acts in conjunction with the Personnel Department and only consults the foreman as a matter for confirmation (not approval) in isolated instances. Dismissal of an employee is again a matter of higher decision and does not fall within the discretionary sphere of the foreman. Recommendations from foremen would, however, be taken into account.

The foreman does not set standards of quality or quantity in his section; these are predetermined and he is responsible for ensuring that they are attained. His production targets are also determined from above and it is extremely unusual for such a target to be questioned by a foreman. For the foremen and subordinate supervisors there is no form of profit sharing but a Christmas bonus, roughly equivalent to a month's salary, is paid at the option of the management. It is most unusual for hourly paid operatives to earn more than foremen and is only possible in cases of exceptional overtime which occurs rarely.

The foreman discharges an important function in the sphere of training. Although there is a training school which provides basic training by the analytical method, he is responsible for the application of these basic principles and for the introduction of recruits to the actual work situation in an appropriate manner. He also decides if any worker is in need of 'refresher training'. Generally speaking this level of supervision is not required to discharge any part of the personnel function; queries of a personal nature are almost invariably referred to the personnel department. But he does represent a level in the appeal procedure, albeit a relatively insignificant one.

Apart from the annual bonus mentioned above, other non-financial benefits are standard: three weeks' paid leave, sickness benefit based on service, and contributory pension scheme.

From information given by this company it would appear that the role of the foreman is in a period of transition. Insistence on a Higher National Certificate is a recent innovation and the salary range (comfortably above the average for the area) should provide sufficient incentive for men of this level of achievement to seek employment with the firm. The degree of responsibility is not, however, consistent with the level of remuneration, since a number of functions, especially personnel, considered to be outside the foreman's discretion, should fall within it. For this reason it is assumed that a revision of responsibilities is intended: at present the foreman does not co-ordinate any of the specialist services like time study and production planning and unless there is a contraction in the present chain of command he is unlikely to be given any chance to determine the selection of personnel subordinate to him. From the point of view of promotion the emphasis is on the technical qualifications; the personnel aspect of the work situation is beyond his immediate control. This presents something of an anomaly in view of the high rate of pay and the calibre of personnel employed. But that may soon change as the company evolves more efficient policies.

The Foremen and Specialists

According to this survey, the main difficulty of the foremen arose from the impact of specialists on the traditional sovereignty of the foreman's command. These specialists, if they are to function properly, require access to the primary working group.

In the primary working group, communication is usually on a

ace-to-face basis and involves frequent interaction among its members which has the effect of developing very strong group oyalties. The primary working group is usually made up of a group of shop floor workers under a supervisor. It has been widely recognized by psychologists since the Bank Wiring Room Experiment of the Hawthorne Studies that informal groups exist

FIGURE 6.4. PART OF THE ORGANIZATION CHART OF THREE
COMPANIES (NOS. III, IX, XII)
SHOWING THE POSITION OCCUPIED BY THE FOREMAN

COMPANY III   Light Engineering   (1,600 employees)
Departmental Structure
Superintendent   Minimum salary £1,400 p.a.

Foreman   Salary range £850–£1,350 p.a.

Operative Charge Hand

Setting Operators   Operators (Ordinary)

COMPANY IX   Heavy Engineering
Departmental Structure
Departmental Manager   Minimum salary £1,500 p.a.

Assistant Dept. Manager   Salary range £1,300–£1,500 p.a.

Head Foreman   Maximum salary £1,275 p.a.

Assistant Foreman   Maximum salary £975 p.a.

Operatives

COMPANY XII   Manufacturing   (800 employees)
(Non-Engineering)
Departmental Structure
Production Manager

Assistant Production Manager Salary range £1,000–£1,750 p.a.

Foreman   Salary range £750–£1,000 p.a.

Operatives

within the primary working group. Efficient production man
agement requires that specialists gain access to the primar
working group. This represents a conflict of interest an
authorities. The role of the foreman must be in part, in suc
circumstances, the co-ordinator of specialists in the primar
working group. Not all firms in the survey seem equally aliv
to the consequences of this change in role, which would b
facilitated by training the foreman in human relations an
communications as well as giving him appreciation courses i
the work of the various specialists.

The conflict for the foreman can be mitigated by 'putting th
monkey on the other fellow's shoulders' as American Civil Ser
vants describe the technique of returning a projected anxiety t
its originator. At Glacier an elegant solution to this problem ha
been achieved by re-organizing the specialists so that they ar
executively responsible to the unit manager. In this way th
functional specialist is put in the two-boss situation and the fore
man is 'taken off the hook' to some extent.

In Glacier, as has already been mentioned, the *foreman* ha
been abolished and the role of *section manager* created. If th
careers of the section managers are examined, then it will b
seen that most of them joined the Company as machine operator
and attained their present positions via the position of *supervisor*

If reference is made to the official 'specification for the role
of section manager, the picture that is presented is one of a ful
magerial appointment. The crucial question 'Does the sec
tion manager manage?' is fully discussed at the end of th
present chapter, but anticipating the conclusions of this dis
cussion, it is possible to assert that in the general terms, th
answer must be a reserved 'No'. It is easier to understand wha
has happened to the section manager's role if it is regarded a
more of a semantic transformation rather than as an actua
organizational change. The trouble is that the creation of th
section manager role has taken place in an organizationa
vacuum. More specifically the organizational implications of th
institution of this new role have neither been anticipated no
realized. *The crux of the matter is that the section manager is in
adequately supported technically in terms of setters and trouble shooter*
*clerically in terms of clerks, and on personnel matters in terms of the uni
personnel officer.*

THE GLACIER SECTION MANAGER

SOME COMMENTS ON THE ROLE OF
SECTION MANAGER

At this stage, it might be considered appropriate to make some *editorial* comment on the Glacier section manager. The word 'editorial' is used advisedly to draw the reader's attention to the argument that 'behavioural facts' are inevitably contaminated with value, and that social scientists ought to have a formal signal to indicate that they are stepping into an editorial role where questions of interpretation of fact arise, where problems of semantics manifest themselves and where questions of value judgments arise. The basic question is, 'Is the section manager role a good idea?' Impossible to answer, but it is possible to list advantages and disadvantages, starting with the pros.

The Advantages of the Section Manager Role

Glacier policy, which in terms of levels of organization, has been to reduce the number of layers to five, is in itself entirely laudable. As Brown notes on page 38 of *Exploration in Management*, 'Five ranks seem appropriate, because this is the maximum number of roles which, in any line of authority, span the system from Managing Director at the top to operative or clerical worker at the bottom.'

To implement this excellent policy, the role of the section manager was created as the first level of management. Theoretically, by reducing the number of stations or filters in the system these arrangements should improve communication within the organization. But, inevitably, as every experienced line manager knows, certain difficulties arise in relation to fitting in specialists to this 'set up'. Brown alludes to this difficulty when he notes on page 39 of *Exploration in Management*:

> We know that most of the half-rank role positions are to be found in the specialist commands, embracing engineers, metallurgists, accounts, production control personnel, etc; though there are a few examples in operational (line) management.

Thus figure 6.5 indicates only the ideal but not the actual. This ideal picture is complicated by the existence of these 'half

173

rank roles'. Worse still, recent changes in the upper echelons of Glacier have had the effect of introducing another rank between the General Manager and the Managing Director. These 'overlords' have been introduced to control new groupings of factories, service stations and warehouses. So there is nothing magic in the number five after all.

FIGURE 6.5. DIAGRAM OF THE FIVE
GLACIER LEVELS

Managing Director
|
General Manager
|
Unit Manager
|
Section Manager
|
Operators

Again, the Company's claim to have organized the section manager's span of authority so that he has a relatively small number of subordinates is entirely to Glacier's credit. The present survey showed that the section manager had an average of 19 operators in his section. But according to the survey this was by no means exceptional. The average for the seven light engineering firms surveyed was 20, and in three of these firms the foreman supervised fewer operatives.

One tremendous advantage of Glacier organization has been the fusing of line and functional management. The problem of tuning in specialists has been solved, by attaching to the unit manager, a production engineer and a production controller. The supreme advantage of this solution lies in the fact that it avoids the main pitfalls of remotely based specialists swarming into the primary work group with all the consequent upsets which frequently produced a situation where the machine operators had more than one boss; or at least they were in a position where they could receive instructions from not only their line superiors but also from production engineering staff, programming staff and work study officers; this could in some circumstances put the operator 'on the spot' by presenting him with conflicting and ambiguous orders.

Of course, removing a complication at one level inevitably produces a complication elsewhere. In this case, while the machine operators basically have only one boss in this pattern of organization, the specialists, on the other hand, find themselves with two bosses. For example, the production controller is *executively* responsible to the unit manager and *technically* responsible to the factory programming manager.

Theoretically at least, Glacier is only too well aware of the inadequacies of the section manager role. One way of strengthening this role would be to make more effective use of personnel specialists at unit level.

To this end the Company has been experimenting since the mid-'fifties, with the idea of introducing at Kilmarnock a unit personnel officer into this pattern of organization. A personnel specialist, operating within the unit itself, could be of tremendous assistance to the section manager. It seems strange that the Company having willed the end is unable or unwilling to will the means. Two possible explanations suggest themselves for this state of affairs. One is that the Company has not the necessary financial resources to implement this policy; the other is that the Company does not believe that there are many personnel officers available who could carry this role.

What about the level of remuneration for section managers? A section manager is rewarded with a good salary, by foreman standards; in the salary survey, only one company bettered Glacier for approximately the same role. It may be only a co-incidence, but this particular company which paid higher salaries than Glacier was the only firm in Scotland which had a higher proportion of its supervisors members of A.S.S.E.T. and according to the local union official, it pursued a policy which was very task oriented.

Turning now to the disadvantages of this role, it is perhaps just as well to point out that the disadvantages which are listed below are not inherent in the type of organization that Glacier has developed to carry out the work to be done, but rather arise from the way the role has been exploited. In my opinion, the tasks are too great for the role taking into consideration the personnel recruited for this position. The task loading on all members of the Glacier organization is very considerable. Ample evidence of this strain was afforded during interviews with Glacier executives at all levels in the organization. Nearly all the interviewees were in agreement that too much was expected of section managers. At present, section managers lack adequate training to enable them to carry out their designated roles effectively. The recruitment of personnel to fill this role is faulty; for it is mainly internal, from operators on the shop floor ultimately. This means, in effect, the person doing the job of section manager is likely to be operating at the upper limit of his abilities, intellectual, technical, social and above all managerial.

An important consequence of this is that promotion beyond section manager to unit manager is rare, and unfortunately is frequently followed by demotion. Understandably in such circumstances, ambition for further promotion is uncommon among section managers. Recently the Company has been recruiting some better qualified candidates to this role—mostly men with Ordinary National Certificates.

But the turnover among these better qualified candidates is fairly high; especially after they have had some executive experience with Glacier. The survey confirmed that Glacier was not the only company facing this problem. In the long run, especially in the post-Robbins phase, British industry will be compelled to follow the practice of certain American companies and recruit university graduates for the role of foreman. Yet another disadvantage of this role is to be seen in the fact that Glacier policies sometimes have the effect of putting the section managers 'on the spot'. For example, the Company policy of ordering section managers to operate machines during National Strikes. As might have been predicted this has had the effect of making the section managers choose between their loyalties to the management or to the union. The result has been that most section managers (85 per cent) have become members of A.S.S.E.T.

Life for Glacier section managers has been complicated by the failure of the Company to solve the problem of the supervisor. Theoretically, the supervisor is supposed to be a staff assistant to the section manager: in fact, in many cases he is little more than a higher grade of machine operator. If the supervisor was trained for his assignment, particularly that part of his work that helps to relieve the section manager of the technical part of his role, then the section manager could function more efficiently as a manager. Putting it another way, joining the 'section manager' to the 'supervisor' by a horizontal line instead of a vertical line in the organization charts does *not* transform their respective roles or interrelationships.

In my opinion, comparatively few section managers understand the Glacier System. Discussing organizational problems with them, one is continually astonished at their ignorance of Company policy. Even such elementary information as the Company policy on appointments does not have wide currency in their ranks.

DOES THE SECTION MANAGER MANAGE?

Glacier's section manager concept raises one critical question, 'Does he manage?' What is at stake on this issue is whether the Glacier system has in fact succeeded in injecting some managerial authority into the traditional foreman role. What does the verb 'to manage' mean? Historically, 'to manage' has very wide connotations, and in some circumstances means to cope or the ability to get by; or again it can mean to succeed; other meanings include to take care of something; yet another meaning is to control; and 'managing' can even mean meddlesome. A more frequently encountered definition of 'managing' emphasizing its human implications is the aphorism 'managing is the art of getting results through people'. Yet another definition defines managing as the process of making decisions usually on the basis of inadequate information.

But it is not enough to say that managing is making decisions because everybody makes decisions. A better starting point is provided by defining managing as the process of making decisions which require for their achievement the co-ordination of the activities of a number of people; this concept implies the existence of an authority system where the superordinate has the entitlement to command and to expect and require obedience'. The traditional concept of authority has its basis in the idea that the superordinate has the right to command, the subordinate has the duty to obey. But the right to command does not necessarily infer the capacity to command. In *A Methectic Theory of Social Organisation*, T. T. Paterson[112] has defined management as, 'The process of ordering and co-ordinating functions, and the persons fulfilling these functions, in an enterprise'.

What is at stake in the question 'Does the section manager manage?' This question can be examined from three different aspects; in terms of authority exercised, in terms of behaviour displayed, and the manner in which the role and the role behaviour of the section manager is perceived. In terms of authority has the section manager the right to hire and fire, to discipline and reward his subordinates? In regard to hiring, he has the opportunity to select applicants who have been screened by the personnel officer. Regarding firing, he has the right to remove an operator from his own section, but not 'to fire' him from the Company. The operative then becomes available for employment in any other part of the plant. In my experience section managers usually consulted with a personnel officer before 'firing' an operative. In any case, it is possible for the 'fired' subordinate to appeal. Few if any section managers relish this business of firing.

Can the section manager reward his subordinates? This question is discussed in detail in Chapter 5. In general terms, he carries through a review of the wages of his operators every three months. These assessments, which are vetted by his superior, the unit manager, are a continual source of friction and lead to a large number of appeals; and according to the stewards 50 per cent of these appeals are allowed. In other words, the section manager is regarded by shop floor personnel as having limited and circumscribed authority to reward their efforts, partly because actual assessments are vetted by his unit manager, but mainly because machine operatives, when they are given an adverse assessment, frequently appeal to the unit manager. If the section manager had the authority and financial resources to honour the system set out in the Company policies on wages, he would be carrying a proper managerial role. But what the shop floor worker is in fact doing is escalating this issue to where management begins in Glacier, i.e. at unit manager level.

THE GLACIER SECTION MANAGER

Behaviour and Perception of the Section Manager

Anticipating Chapter 7 findings it is possible to say that in general terms the behaviour of section managers reveals a preoccupation with either programming or technical aspects of the job. What is being asserted is that the section managers were so heavily engaged finding out what had to be done and getting it done, including sometimes doing it themselves, that they could not engage in important management functions such as training. It was precisely this inability to routinize and automate such functions which stopped them from carrying out a managerial role.

How is the section manager's role perceived? The operators do not regard him as management. The first line of management, as far as they are concerned, is at unit manager level. It is not uncommon to hear personnel officers referring to the unit manager as the 'definitive manager'. In interviews many of the shop stewards went further, to emphasize that in their view 'You only get management when you have to deal with the General Manager'.

'Does he have appropriate management qualifications such as the Management Diploma?' The answer in the main must be NO.

'Are his earnings such that he feels it is in his social and economic interest to identify with management?' With a salary of £1,500 per annum, this is just possible. In terms of conditions, he is at a distinct disadvantage, as he does not have a proper office or any real clerical assistance. Most of them take their tea and meals in the 'Workers' canteen' at the same time as shop floor personnel. The unit managers, on the other hand, have lunch at a different time in the 'Staff recess' with the General Manager.

'What are his intentions in terms of career?' This question is worth asking if only because from research in social psychology we know that behaviour and attitudes adjust to what is regarded as appropriate to the individual's conception of his terminal role. The basic question is, 'Are section managers tied to supervisory roles, or do they see themselves at some future date in management proper?' As has already been stated, most of these section managers lack any kind of formal qualifications and, as such, most are content with their present posts. In effect, they are more concerned with stabilizing their positions than with improving them. This explains why such a substantial majority of their number have joined A.S.S.E.T. Thus they lack the motivation to improve their status. This inadequate motivation results from the failure to develop their managerial potential. Behaviour and attitudes always develop in anticipation of intention. Nothing substantial can be achieved in terms of attitudes and behaviour unless the section manager finds the sense of identification with management that flows from a sharing of ideals, beliefs and expectations. Austen Albu,[2] writing about the section managers' difficulties, points out that,

> Some surprise is expressed by works committee members that they find it easier to come to agreement with Grade I representatives than with those of the other two Grades. This, however, is a common experience. It is always easier for top management to see the point of view of the workers on the shop floor than for those caught in the middle of the sandwich. It was therefore to be expected that those who feel the crunch of the system most should be the section managers. It is they who find the greatest difficulty in understanding their roles and who feel that the system undermines their authority. For instance, it may take three months to discharge a worker, in spite of the fact that they are supposed to be fully responsible for those under their command. Brown recognises this problem in the book (*Exploration in Management*) in which he describes his idea in a section entitled: 'Split at the bottom of the executive chain'. It arises partly out of the fact that, whereas other managers have time for consultation as part of their jobs, the operators who are the section managers' subordinates are tied to their machines and the section managers themselves must spend most of their time in the shops. Whatever may be said about the executive and discretionary content of their role, the production workers are the only ones who only receive and do not give orders and whose resentment of authority is consequently greatest. On this the Glacier theory of work has so far nothing to say.

CHAPTER 7

THE STUDY OF THE
SECTION MANAGER'S BEHAVIOUR
BY ACTIVITY SAMPLING

What does the section manager do? How does he allocate his time to different functions? In particular, how much time does he spend on programming, technical and personnel work? With whom does he interact? Answers to such questions would be of great assistance in deciding how the Glacier system of management works in practice. The absence of hard information in Glacier publications concerning the behaviour of the section manager leaves Brown and Jaques open to the charge of theory building in an empirical vacuum.

The purpose of this chapter is to compare the official picture of this role with the portrait of the section manager derived from behavioural data. The principal source of information concerning the official picture of the section manager is the Company's written job description of this role, which is replete with all the terminology of a full managerial position. This material was supplemented by the evidence produced in interviews with the unit manager, section managers themselves and members of the personnel department.

It was proposed to study the behaviour of four section managers at the Kilmarnock factory of the Glacier Metal Company. Before the study could be initiated it was necessary to gain the approval of the General Manager of the factory, the unit manager, and the section managers concerned. It is understandable that, when approval was being sought, the section managers who were to be the subjects of the study showed some reluctance in the first instance. It was only after they had been reassured that the investigation would not make serious inroads on their managerial tasks, or if it did that the position would be reviewed, that they gave their assent. When the project was under way the section managers were extremely helpful and co-operative in every respect.

Having gained acceptance and won the approval of the section managers it was necessary to make a preliminary analysis of the section managers' work by interviewing various Company officials. Following this, a record form was designed. In designing this form, it was necessary to keep in mind the kind of behaviour being studied, and how to describe and measure it. Without such guides, it would be impossible to select what to record from among the many possible observations that could be made.

FIGURE 7.1. *The Formal Organization of the Wrapped Bushes Unit*

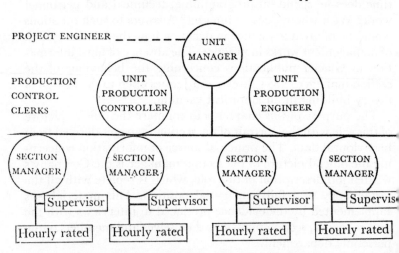

At this stage it was considered advisable to carry out a pilot study. The aims of the pilot study were: to establish and verify the categories to which the elements of the work of the section manager could be assigned; to estimate roughly the percentage of time spent on each of these categories; and to determine the practical number of random observations that could be made during any eight-hour shift. Activity sampling technique requires instantaneous observations to be made at random times which are determined by the use of random numbers translated into clock times. From the pilot study it was possible to determine the required number of observations, assuming error limits of 2 per cent at the 95 per cent level of confidence. The number of observations required was found to be 2,500. In fact, 2,800 observations were made over the three-week period.

The investigation was conducted in the unit making wrapped bushes at the Kilmarnock factory of the Glacier Metal Company. In the unit there were 200 men employed in two shifts, day and night. The shop was divided into sections. The unit manager (U.M.) had two staff officers, a unit engineer (U.E.) and a unit production controller (U.P.C.). Four section managers were studied in this investigation.

It was decided to conduct a pilot investigation into how different individuals perceived the role of section manager. Implicit in this approach is the view that the cognitions of the individual are selectively organized. There are two main kinds of determinant: stimulus factors and personal factors. By stimulus factors are meant those factors which derive from the nature of the external stimulus object. Personal factors are those which derive from the characteristics of perceiving individuals. A questionnaire was developed to highlight the personal factor in the perception of the section manager's role. The questionnaire consisted of twenty statements, each covering an incident in the work of the section manager. These events or incidents were a representative sample drawn from the pilot study. The testees were asked to allocate ten points between the three categories programming, personnel, and technical. Examples of the incidents included:

	Program-ming	Person-nel	Tech-nical
(1) Present on shop floor with own supervisor, discussing deployment of machines and operatives in own section.			
(4) Completing schedules of production figures, deleting from list jobs which have been completed, and adding new work which has reached section.			

	Program-ming	Person-nel	Tech-nical
(13) Discussing with shop steward his objection to your supervisor setting a machine on your own instructions.			
(4) Writing notes for night-shift section manager and giving details of the day's production, stating requirements in terms of priorities for the night shift, in order that the following day's shift programme can be followed through.			
(15) Discussing with inspector the rejection of a batch and convincing him that it is in fact within the accepted tolerance, so that it is passed by inspection for dispatch.			
(19) In canteen with other section managers, after unit manager's meeting.			

The 't' test at the 0·05 level was used as a test of significance. From these tests it would seem that the unit manager, the section managers, and the supervisors perceived the role of the section manager in more or less the same way. However, the machine operators, in their perception of the work of the section manager, appeared to overstress the personnel aspects and understress the programming aspects. These data will provide a contrast against the behaviouristic data at a later stage in the study. (A fuller account of this study is given in Appendix III.)

TABLE 7.1

Role	N	Programming	Personnel	Technical
Unit manager	1	41	45	14
Section manager	10	46	38	16
Supervisors	4	45	38	17
Machine operators	5	36	50	14
Unit engineer	1	44	31	25

Three different types of section are to be found in this unit: initiating sections, where batches to be manufactured are 'started'; machining sections whose functions are facing, plating, machining, slitting and chamfering; and a self-contained section producing thrust washers.

The unit manager, following the Glacier system, described the section manager's work under the headings programming, personnel and technical. He estimated the proportions of time allocated to each of these functions to be 25, $62\frac{1}{2}$ and $12\frac{1}{2}$ per cent (i.e. $\frac{1}{4}$, $\frac{5}{8}$ and $\frac{1}{8}$) respectively.

With reference to the programming function he pointed out that the programme is issued three weeks in advance. A number of load meetings are required to fulfil the programming function; these include a fortnightly meeting with the general manager of the factory. There is also a daily meeting with the unit manager, the unit production controller, and the unit engineer, where the load for the day is defined. Batch production is used with 750 batches on the floor at any time.

According to the unit manager his personnel work embraced three activities: assessment, reward on the basis of assessment, and training. Taking assessment first, he stated that there is a quarterly assessment of each worker, but noted that the section manager is, in fact, carrying out this assessment daily and hourly. The section manager specifies standards for quality, output, excessive scrap etc., and ensures that these standards are being kept. On reward of operatives, the section manager has guidance criteria, within which he uses his personal discretion. The section manager is held accountable for training his operatives.

On the technical aspect of the job he noted that the section manager is held accountable for ensuring the maintenance and repair of equipment. He is not held responsible for a machine breaking down, but he is held responsible for the length of time taken to repair the machine.

At 7.30 a.m. the section manager checks machinery and obtains a note of any absentees from the supervisor. Then he makes a review of the work completed on the previous day. Next, he tours the section while the men are setting up, to ensure that there is an adequate supply of work. This is followed by a tour of other sections to discover what work he should receive, and when. From 10 to 10.30 a.m. he sits in with other section

185

managers, the unit production controller and the unit enginee at the unit manager's load meeting. The tea-break follows which should last 15 minutes but in fact may go on unti 11 a.m. The unit manager recognized that valuable discussion may take place at this canteen meeting. Between 11 and 12.30 when the section managers have lunch, they carry on with their supervisory duties.

AN ANALYSIS OF ACTIVITIES AND INTERACTIONS

It will be seen from table 7.1 that the section managers spen approximately two-thirds of their time in contact with persons This compares with Burns' study, where the executives spent 8(per cent of their work time talking;[30] or with Stogdill and Shartle,[142] whose 470 naval officers spent 60 per cent of their time in contact with persons. It is easy to understand why 'skil in communicating' is usually included in the list of desirable qualities for foremen. It is also worth noting the small propor- tion of time taken up by the section managers in personal matters. This is not unusual. It is also worthy of note that the observers do take up some of the time of the managers being studied.

TABLE 7.2. PERCENTAGE ANALYSIS OF THE TIME OF THE SECTION MANAGERS ACCORDING TO THE RANK OF PERSON

Section	Alone	Superiors	Peers	Subordinates	Personal	Observers	Unclassified
Initiating	33	18	20	20	5	2	2
Machining (1)	33	10	18	34	2	0	3
Machining (2)	27	10	21	39	1	0	2
Self-contained	36	15·5	20·5	21	3	$\frac{1}{2}$	$3\frac{1}{2}$
AVERAGE	33	13	20	28	3	$\frac{1}{2}$	$2\frac{1}{2}$

From table 7.2 it can be seen that the analysis of interaction is almost identical for the two machining section managers, and for the managers of the Initiating and Self-contained sections respectively. The Machining section managers studied were in fact doing identical work–i.e. supplying machining function as a service to other sections–whereas the managers of the Initiating and Self-contained sections were performing functions rather similar to each other, which necessitated greater contact with the unit manager. This would seem to vindicate Brown's view on the relation of organization to work:

> Effective organization is a function of the work to be done and the resources and techniques available to do it. Thus changes in methods of production bring about changes in the number of work roles, in the distribution of work between roles and in their relationship one to another. Failure to make explicit acknowledgement of this relationship between work and organization gives rise to non-valid assumptions, e.g. that optimum organization is a function of the personalities involved, that is a matter connected with the personal style and arbitrary decision of the chief executive. . . . Our observations lead us to accept that optimum organization must be derived from an analysis of the work to be done and the techniques and resources available. (Brown,[26] 1960.)

Joan Woodward[157] in her 'Management and Technology' has also argued that technology is a major determinant of industrial behaviour.

Table 7.2 also shows that approximately one-third of the total interaction time is devoted to peers. Dubin[41] (1962) has drawn attention to the lack of reference in the literature to 'the horizontal dimension of organization and the volume of business that is transacted among peers to keep the organization going'. Indeed, it is probably among organizational equals that much of the real co-ordination of work flow and operations take place, in what Dubin[42] (1958) has called the non-formal behaviour system: 'The non-formal behaviour system is the arena in which the organization is made to work by supplementing the formal procedures, rules, etc.'

Elliott Jaques[65] (1951) has drawn attention to the need for 'informal activity' to make policy completely explicit. 'There remains always a residue of unrecognized and unidentified aspects of the culture of concern.' Much of this informal behaviour takes place at the section managers' tea-break which is timed to follow the unit manager's meeting. Recognizing this need for informal contact, the unit manager allows the tea meeting to run well beyond its prescribed time.

TABLE 7.3. PERCENTAGE OF SECTION MANAGERS'
TOTAL INTERACTION TIME
SPENT WITH PEOPLE OF VARIOUS RANKS

Section	Superiors	Peers	Subordinates
Initiating	30	35	35
Machining (1)	16	29	55
Machining (2)	14	30	56
Self-contained	27	36	37
AVERAGE	22	32	46

The data in table 7.3 may be compared with the analysis of the table of interactions. Again, it will be noted that, in the case of the Machining section managers, who are performing identical functions, the distribution of their time by location is very similar. At first sight these figures would appear to give little support to the theme of individual styles of leadership. On the other hand, if the data were analysed on a daily basis for each manager, there might be a significant variety in the life of the section manager, owing to the different 'mixes' of the same work content through time. Weiss[149] (1956), in his study of the activities of research administrators, and Burns,[30] in his study of executives, have presented data to support the view that there may be a rhythm of 'content mix'.

On this question of personal style, the unit manager, referring to the work of M1 and M2, noted that the proportion of their time in the Production Engineering department was identical (18 per cent) showing that their jobs were of equivalent technical difficulty. On the other hand, M1 spent 17 per cent of his time in his office and 10 per cent in other sections, while M2 spent 11 per cent of his time in his office and 17 per cent of his time in other sections. M1, according to the unit manager, sat in his office waiting for work to come to him while M2 went into other sections looking for work.

In the case of the I manager and S.C. manager who spent 14 and 9 per cent of their time respectively in other sections, the unit manager explained this as being due to the fact that the work went from the Initiating section to three other sections, i.e. the Plating sections and the two Machining sections, while the Self-contained section work went only to the Plating section.

Table 7.5 shows that the section manager's job is primarily a programming job (half his time); technical work takes up a quarter of his time; and personnel work just over a tenth of his time. The emphasis on programming is understandable since the section manager's job is to find out what his section is required to do (the programme), make sure that the raw material or semi-finished work is moving towards his section, check that the work is moving through the section, rearrange priorities in the light of changing demands and operating circumstances, and ensure that the finished components leave his section. The technical aspect is concerned with the optimal use and maintenance of plant and equipment.

The personnel aspect is mainly concerned with manning, overtime, wages and assessing and reviewing operators, safety, and complaints.

Table 7.6 shows that the various studies referred to are in broad agreement. Four different studies confirm that most of the foremen's work with other people is devoted to close details

TABLE 7.4. PERCENTAGE DISTRIBUTION OF SECTION MANAGERS' TIME BY LOCATION

Section	Own section Floor	Own section Office	Other sections	Production and Engineering Dept. PE office	Production and Engineering Dept. Shop manager's office	Production and Engineering Dept. Other shops	Outside unit Canteen	Total
Initiating	50		14	24			12	100
	21	29	9		15	6	6	100
Machining (1)	62		10	18			10	100
	45	17	10	8	10	3	7	100
Machining (2)	53		17	18			12	100
	42	11	17	11	7	4	8	100
Self-contained	54		9	28			9	100
	28	26	9	14	14	3	6	100
AVERAGE	54		12	24			10	100

of work. The three areas, technical, programming, and personnel, account for between 63 and 89 per cent of all activities.

A picture of the section manager can be built up from this
study. He spends two-thirds of his time with other persons—a
fifth of his time with his unit manager, a third with his colleagues, and just under half with his subordinates.

TABLE 7.5. PERCENTAGE DISTRIBUTION OF SECTION
MANAGERS' TIME BY FUNCTION

Section	Tech-nical	Program-ming	Personnel	Personal	Section manager's meeting	Holi-days	Total
Initiating	22	45	20	4	5	4	100
Machining (1)	26	55	8	4	7	–	100
Machining (2)	35	45	11	1	8	–	100
Self-contained	22	58	8	4	6	2	100
AVERAGE	26	51	12	3	7	1	100

The unit manager meets him mostly at the morning meeting.
A great deal of informal rearranging of work takes place,
especially at the rather extended tea-break with his fellows in
the morning. He spends half of his time on the shop floor, a
quarter in the Production and Engineering department, and the
balance in other sections or outside the unit. His work is mainly
programming (a half), followed by technical (a quarter), and

TABLE 7.6. COMPARISON WITH OTHER STUDIES

Area of operating responsibility	4 Glacier section managers	12 high effective GEC foremen	12 low effective GEC foremen	56 auto assembly plant foremen	Radio Corp of America foremen
Technical	26	20	14	34·5	
Programming	51	30	40	34·5	78
Personnel	12	23	12	13·2	
Other	11	37	34	17·8	22
Method	Activity sampling	Observa-tion	Observa-tion	Observa-tion	Self-recording
Source		Ponder[120] (1958)	Ponder[120] (1958)	Guest[52] (1956)	Zinck[159] (1958)

includes only a little personnel work (a tenth). Compared with other studies, this study shows that he spends more time on the close details of work. In a phrase, he is a 'task specialist'.

TABLE 7.7. PERCENTAGE ESTIMATES BY VARIOUS
MANAGERS OF HOW THE SECTION MANAGERS USED
THEIR TIME
(*Actual times are in brackets*)

Aspect	Unit Manager	Personnel Manager	SC	M1	M2	Average of actual time
Alone	12½	40	15 (36)	40 (33)	8 (27)	33
With others	87½	60	85 (64)	60 (67)	92 (73)	67
Superiors	10	20	5 (27)	10 (16)	10 (14)	22
Peers	15	40	10 (36)	50 (29)	25 (30)	32
Subordinates	75	40	85 (37)	40 (37)	65 (56)	46
Technical	12½	25	30 (22)	30 (26)	20 (35)	26
Programming	25	60	60 (58)	50 (55)	65 (45)	51
Personnel	62½	15	10 (8)	20 (8)	15 (11)	12
Unclassified			(12)	(11)	(9)	(11)

The unit manager, the personnel managers and three section managers (the section manager of the Initiating Section left the company soon after the observation study was completed) were invited to estimate how much time they spent with others, how they distributed their time between technical, programming and personnel work. There were wide discrepancies between the estimates and the actual distributions, as one would have expected. The most accurate overall estimate was made by the personnel manager and the most divergent overall estimate by the unit manager. In the case of the unit manager, he grossly over-estimated the personnel work–62½ per cent against an actual of 12 per cent. The unit manager regarded the personnel aspect of the section manager's work as extremely important. Certainly his emphasis of the personnel function was supported by the fact that the more efficient section manager spent twice as much time on personnel as the least efficient section manager. (The question of efficiency of the section manager is discussed in more detail later in this chapter.) Undoubtedly a great deal of personnel work by the section managers was required if the unit was to improve its efficiency. Again, the personnel aspect was over-estimated by the section managers. On the other hand, the estimates on both technical and programming were reasonably accurate.

TABLE 7.8. ANALYSIS OF THE PERSONNEL WORK
OF THE SECTION MANAGER

Description of the Event	Percentage of Total
(a) Manning the line	58·0
(b) Arranging overtime	15·7
(c) Assessing and reviewing operators	5·3
(d) Arranging for operators to work during holiday	1·6
(e) Wages administration	6·3
(f) Accident and safety records	1·6
(g) Handling complaints with the Shop Steward	1·6
Undefined	
TOTAL	100·0

The amount of time spent on the personnel aspect of the section manager's work varied from 8 to 20 per cent. Because of the importance attached by Glacier to this managerial function, it was decided to make a more accurate determination. To achieve this, the section managers were invited to give a fuller account of each personnel event during the second half of the study. The distribution of these personnel events is shown in table 7.8. It is important to note that no wage review took place during this study and this may have had the effect of reducing the amount of time spent on personnel matters.

TABLE 7.9. THE UNIT MANAGER'S ESTIMATE OF
THE SECTION MANAGER'S EFFICIENCY

'Sheer Task Efficiency'	'Human Efficiency'
I	M_1
SC	M_2
M_2	SC
M_1	I

When the unit manager was invited to rank the section managers in terms of efficiency, he spontaneously divided this criterion into 'Sheer Task Efficiency' and 'Human Efficiency'. The unit manager's concept of 'Sheer Task Efficiency' referred in his words 'to the capacity to get the job done, to figure out what comes next. It demanded above all a cold calculating logic which would enable plans to be worked out and their implications considered.' The unit manager described 'Human Efficiency' as 'being approachable, interested in your men, easy to talk to and not too harsh.'

The unit manager drew attention to the fact that the Initiating manager had more academic training that the other section managers. In fact, while not a graduate, he had two years of higher education. The unit manager further added that an important reason for his success was the analytical bite of his intellect. The Initiating manager left the company 'for promotion' soon after this part of the research was completed. Of late, the Company policy has been to appoint better educated personnel to the job of section manager. His ranking of the section managers on these two categories represents an inverse relation. Yet the Initiating manager spent 20 per cent of his time on personnel work compared with 9 per cent on personnel by the other section managers. This reinforces the view that a good deal of personnel activity is task directed. Again, this inverse relationship between the task aspect and the human aspect is supportive of Fiedler's[46] hypothesis that the psychologically distant manager or task specialist who is remote and reserved in dealing with his subordinates, is the more efficient.

The four section managers on the average spent 12 per cent on personnel work. But the most efficient executive devoted 20 per cent of his time to it. While any comparison must be viewed with caution this accords with the findings of an American study[120] which has shown that the more efficient foreman gives approximately a quarter of his time to this aspect of management, while the less efficient foreman gives only half as much time to personnel. In Ponder's[120] study 12 'High Effective' foremen were compared with 12 'Low Effective' foremen; his data which was based on observation showed that the 'High Effective' foreman spent 23 per cent of his time on personnel matters while his 'Low Effective' colleague spent only 12 per cent on the same activity. While Ponder's results are in broad agreement with the findings of the present research, such a comparison must be viewed with some caution. The reservation arises in relation to the uncertainty regarding the way in which the term 'personnel' was defined.

If this personnel aspect itself is analysed further, then it will be seen that the larger part of it is concerned simply with task elements, i.e. getting the job done.

THE NATURE OF THE SECTION MANAGER'S PERSONNEL WORK

The most interesting point about this analysis of the personnel work of the section manager is the fact that it contains no evidence of training activity. Yet, most textbooks on management are insistent that the line executive not only ought to train, but does train. A good illustration of this unrealistic attitude by an academic to executives doing training is provided by Mason Haire[56] in *Psychology in Management* (p. 123) where he notes:

> The Line Superior Must Train
> Because of these problems the line superior must do the training, not only do we find that he is doing the training all day and every day, but he is the appropriate person to do it. Because he controls so many of the values within the group, because he is a part of the culture of the group, and because of the isolation of the staff man from the culture and authority of the group, the responsibility falls on the line superior. Since he is the one who possesses these characteristics, he is the person in a position to do the training. Because of the meaning of his role as a leader, it is his proper function. He must continually shape the behaviour of his subordinates to create a situation in which they can help him to get the job done.

Yet the facts are at variance with this exhortation to production managers to train. Training in this context refers to the *conscious* effort of the section managers to instruct his operatives in the techniques of operating and setting machines. By this definition, the section managers in this study did *not* train. On the other hand, inevitably, training does take place. Some of the section manager's activities inevitably spill over into training. For example, he spends time trouble shooting, i.e. clearing stoppages on machines. A natural consequence of trouble shooting must be to provide the operator with insights into operating and setting skills. But a machine operator acquires most of his technical skill by 'sitting next to Billy'. In other words, the training process is largely informal, unplanned and dependent upon peer relationships. The conspicuous absence of any reference to training will be noted in the self-recording exercise conducted by the Initiating manager. What is specially significant about this lack of reference to training is the fact that training is not regarded as a preferred activity which ought to be the subject of recording. The official job description of the section manager refers to his training responsibilities but the data of his behaviour provides convincing evidence of the gap between exhortation and actuality.

Another item which takes up a microscopic amount of the section manager's time is 'handling complaints with the shop steward'. Again, the empirical data challenges the popular picture of the relationship between the shop steward and his immediate boss. Notwithstanding the popular idea of the production managers being slowly strangled into inactivity by the shop steward, the facts show that there is scarcely any contact between them.

The most important single personnel activity of these executives was 'manning the line'. What is involved here is ensuring that there is a correct distribution of skills and men between the day and night shifts. It also necessitated 'borrowing operators' from other sections. The personnel officer had some difficulty in accepting that so much of the line personnel work was related to 'manning the line'. 'Arranging overtime' is closely related to 'manning the line' and is next in order of importance. Union agreements allow one man to work 30 hours a month overtime, but the men were in fact working overtime at a rate of between 36 and 40 hours per man per month. Overtime was a problem in the factory and figures frequently in the minutes of the Works Committee, as the following extract shows:

> Members of the council agreed that the whole question was worth discussing and the Management Member said that he anticipated that the current situation of increased load would continue until the shutdown and the current policy was to have 10% overtime throughout the factory. Considering planning overtime it was

Management's policy that this should be worked on Tuesday and Thursday evenings, Saturday morning and Sunday, in this order. The Management Member felt that Saturday and Sunday overtime working should be non-working days except for panic situations, maintenance work etc.

The Joint Shop Stewards Committee pointed out that overtime was voluntary, and it was left to individuals. As the Convenor observed, 'Management have the right to state when overtime is necessary, but individuals have also the right to refuse if they do not desire to work overtime'.

The General Manager pointed out that if hourly-rated members did not wish overtime, the management must achieve the task assigned without overtime, but this would have an adverse effect on the future load position, and a redundancy situation would arise when the load fell.

The Grade I staff representative drew attention to the fact that in National Agreements the figure which is normally quoted for overtime is 30 hours per month. They further argued that when people were engaged to work in the factory, it was to be pointed out to them that a certain amount of overtime was necessary and members would be expected to work overtime. 'It is appreciated that members are occasionally unable to work overtime, but if overtime is consistently refused, management would consider a member much less acceptable within the factory as an individual who was prepared to work overtime when required.'

The Company was using overtime work to meet increased demands for production, while insuring against the dangers of a possible redundancy, if demand should diminish. The workers, on the other hand, were selling their overtime labour at the highest premium, i.e. for sale on Saturday and more especially on Sunday with its double rates. Thus getting men to work on weekday nights involved a fair amount of persuasion and a significant amount of time.

Assessing and reviewing operators takes only a twentieth of his time. A review of the operators' rates of pay takes place every three months. On such occasions, the amount of line personnel work increases substantially. What is significant here is that the section manager is continually involved in the activities of assessment and review according to our data. This assessment of operators' work had been causing difficulties as the following extract from a Company memo shows:

> There is evidence that managers are experiencing difficulty in determining how to position correctly their hourly rated members within their respective wage brackets. . . . The question is often asked as to why we should now be running into difficulty when for years rate reviews have been conducted with the minimum amount of acrimony and disturbance. A number of answers suggest themselves. Until eighteen months ago wage rates reviews were conducted only twice a year—they now take place at quarterly intervals. Despite the fact that when the change took place management asserted that there was no intention of disbursing more money in the form of rate increases over a twelve month period it is apparent that many people have a persistent expectation that they should receive an increase on the occasion of each review. If no increase is awarded the member feels that his manager must be dissatisfied with his performance and that he has fallen from grace. Furthermore, during the last two years there has been no labour turnover amongst those who have established themselves in the factory with the result that people who have been steadily advancing through their wage brackets now find their heads pressing against the ceiling and their managers displaying greater reluctance to allow them to break through into higher brackets.

Arranging work during the holiday takes a minute fraction of the section manager's time and refers to the seeking of contracts to work during the factory annual shut-down. Wage administration, which takes up a twentieth of his personnel time, requires the section manager collecting the pay slips from the wages office on the Wednesday, their issue to the operators who check them for accuracy, and the actual collection, issue and receipting of the pay on the Thursday. In relation to accidents and safety work, the section manager does not engage in any positive measures, but is concerned only with the administrative recording of the event after the damage has been done.

THE PERSONNEL MANAGER'S PICTURE OF THE SECTION MANAGER

The personnel manager had drawn up a list of selection criteria for section managers. These included:

1. Knowledge of the Company.
2. Enough maturity to lead 18–65 year olds.
3. Decisive.
4. Even-tempered.
5. Capacity to inspire confidence.
6. Capacity to plan six months ahead.
7. Capacity to carry through Company policy in himself and to BE it.
8. Capacity to be definite, tenacious, resourceful and ingenious.
9. Capacity to make quick and sound judgments.
10. Capacity, by habits and disposition, to set standards on maintenance, orderliness and cleanliness.
11. Capacity to appraise and report on the job situation in total or in part at any time.

It was decided to see how others perceived the role of the section manager. To achieve this a test was constructed, as I have already stated, which included a number of items, descriptive of the work of the section manager, such as 'Discussing with a shop steward his objections to the setting of a machine by a supervisor on your instructions'. Ten points were to be allocated between programming, technical and personnel. A full account of this test is given in Appendix III. From these tests it would seem that the unit manager and the section manager are in broad agreement on their perception of the section manager's job. However, the machine operators, in their perception of their boss's behaviour, emphasized the personnel at the expense of the programming aspect.

It is not only among machine operators that there is a preference for a more 'personnel conscious' boss; executives seem to have the same type of need as the following study suggests. V. F. Wilson[156] in an article entitled 'Some Personality Characteristics of Industrial Executives' invited 20 executives on a course to 'choose the man whom you consider to be the best executive you have "been under" at any time, anywhere. Write a sketch of that person in about fifty words, making clear why he impressed you so.'

Twenty-nine separate ideas were recorded. Those most frequently expressed pictured an executive thus: 'He is a man who gives reasons for his orders, welcomes advice and ideas from his staff, and is interested in his subordinates; who sets a good example; who is honest, sincere, determined and courageous; who is personally likeable, courteous and pleasant; who gives encouragement and praise; and who has high technical ability.'

One of the most interesting features of this research was the fact that both machine operatives and the unit manager had a strongly expressed preference for a personnel-oriented section manager. This comment requires some amplification. To my mind, the unit manager and machine operative would attach different meanings to the concept personnel. For the machine operative, the term would have a definite human relations connotation whereas for the unit manager the central notion of personnel would be related to the idea of effective human resource planning. This observation suggests the following generalization in regard to the relation between personnel and level of hierarchy, viz. shop floor workers prefer human relations; management prefers good human resource planning; and top management (such as Wilfred Brown) prefer optimal organization where the factor of personality is minimal.

Another interesting fact to emerge from this research was the general belief of the section managers who regarded themselves as essentially operating in an almost exclusively vertical plane in regard to communications with relatively little horizontal activity. The section managers appeared to think of themselves as heavily engaged in issuing orders to shop floor operatives with scarcely any contact with their boss or fellow section managers. But the behavioural data show that a good deal of his time is spent in horizontal communication where organizational logic is prime and the principle of reciprocity the order of the day. This lateral activity with its lack of hierarchy is heavily dependent on a balance of favours being established where the meeting of a request from a fellow section manager builds up an expectation of the compliment being returned at a later stage. It is just this *quid pro quo* activity that enables organizations to function properly.

But perhaps the most significant single conclusion to emerge from this behavioural study of the section manager is the structuring effect of technology which, on the face of it, appears to be the principal determinant of what he does.

To test the accuracy of the activity sampling technique, it was decided to compare the results from three different phases of an observational study. The subject of this study was an initiating section manager. This depended upon comparison of the results of the main study which used an activity sampling procedure with the results of a pilot study, which also used activity sampling with a self-recording study. The three studies were in broad agreement as table 7.10 shows; the section manager spent half his time in programming, one-fifth in both technical and personnel work and one-twentieth on personal matters. It was thought that good agreement would be achieved if the comparison was made by referring to the data by location or person contacted. This was, in fact, so. On the other hand, it was felt that a comparison based on function would show more variation. Table 7.10 shows the comparison by function. Under the heading technical there is good agreement in all three studies. There is good agreement between the pilot study and the self-recording study. Under personnel, it is striking that the self-recording study shows the section manager as spending nearly one-third of his time in this way. Both the pilot study and the main study put the figure for this activity at nearer one-fifth.

TABLE 7.10. COMPARISON OF THE DATA COLLECTED BY TWO DIFFERENT METHODS ON A MANAGER AT DIFFERENT TIMES

Type of Study	Pilot Study Activity Sampling	Self-Recording Study	Main Study Activity Sampling
Month	November	February	March
Period	1 week	2 weeks	3 weeks
Technical	27	24	22
Programming	39	39	50
Personnel	22	31	20
Personal	6	6	8
With observers	6	—	—
TOTAL	100%	100%	100%

The selection of the episode is also important, e.g. if the study was carried out either when a wage review was on or when a recruiting blitz was on, then personnel proportion would presumably rise sharply.

The consistency of observation between two observers was assessed. Two observers studied the same section manager on alternate days. The results are shown in table 7.11. Again, it will be seen that agreement was best as far as technical was concerned and worst in relation to personnel.

It is appropriate to ask what special virtue flows from using an elaborate technique like activity sampling as a means of studying executive behaviour. It has to be thought of primarily

TABLE 7.11. COMPARISON OF THE RECORDING
OF THE BEHAVIOUR OF A MACHINING MANAGER
BY TWO DIFFERENT OBSERVERS

	Observer (1)	Observer (2)	Average of (1)+(2)
Technical	28	25	26
Programming	53	57	55
Personnel	5	10	8
Section Manager's meeting	8	6	7
Personal	6	2	4
TOTAL	100%	100%	100%

as a diagnostic technique. Many of the senior managers and even the section managers themselves seemed to have a very vague idea of what section managers did. Behaviouristic studies of this type provide the necessary data to enable the work of the executive to be more efficiently planned, facilitate his selection and training and spotlight any weaknesses in his behaviour.

A SYNOPTIC PICTURE OF THE SECTION MANAGER

The most important single conclusion that emerges from this behavioural study of the section manager relates to the fact that all the evidence argues in favour of viewing the section manager as a foreman. This evidence may be summarized thus:

(a) The behavioural data relating to the section manager is in broad agreement with the empirical studies of foreman behaviour by Ponder, Guest and Zinck. Their categories are basically the same as those employed in this research.

(b) The section managers are so busy getting the job done that they have very little time left to engage in certain aspects of the managerial function, such as personnel and training.

(c) If their interaction time is analysed, it will be seen that nearly half of their time is spent with subordinates mostly with machine operatives. A similar pattern of communication was found in the case of the Thin Wall section managers reported in table 8.5 of Chapter 8. Thin Wall section managers spent more than three-quarters of their interaction time with subordinates; most of this time was spent with operatives in technical work such as trouble shooting and setting.

What is being asserted is that this is primarily the behaviour expected of a foreman. The work of a *manager*'s immediate subordinates must be so organized that with a properly defined policy, proper delegation and appropriate training, it is possible to routinize how their tasks will be handled. When these conditions are met, the manager is free to deal with exceptions to his policy and to prepare for innovations. This routinization will also enable him to do more personnel work.

The section manager's superior, the unit manager, is clearly of managerial rank in the sense that he limits his contacts with his subordinates. He has very little contact with his section managers except for the daily load meeting. His principal contact with his shop stewards was at a regular meeting with them. On the other hand the section managers had very little contact with the stewards. The concept of the unit manager as the *definitive* manager appeared to be widely held.

The portrait of the section manager that emerges from this study shows that he spends a very large proportion of his time talking, and that much of this conversing is with other section managers and functional specialists at the same level. A great deal of this horizontal communication takes place at an extended tea break which follows the daily programme loading conference with their boss, the unit manager. In fact, the problem of pro-gramming takes up most of his time. What is striking about this preoccupation with programming is the fact that it reveals that the underlying problem of this unit is too many batches on the floor at any given time, and all of them requiring a considerable number of operations. In other words, the complexity of the task is the main determinant of what they do.

When section managers doing identical work were compared, it was obvious that personal factors did not greatly influence how they distributed their time. This was true whether the analysis was by place, person or function. When their superior saw this data, he was able to explain the residual differences in personal terms. For example, by referring to the analysis by place, he argued that the figures supported his belief that one manager preferred waiting in the office for problems to come to him whereas the other manager left his office to seek them out.

Personnel work took only a small proportion of their time. Most of this activity in any case was 'task loaded', e.g. manning the line. Nevertheless in terms of efficiency, the most effective section manager devoted twice as much time to personnel work as the average section manager. What comes first is not clear. Being efficient in programming and technical work frees him for personnel activities, or, more likely, effective 'task loaded' personnel work increases his efficiency in the other two areas. In any case, the difficulty of deciding between these alternatives is further complicated by the personality factor. The efficient section manager, as well as having had a more extensive educational background than his colleagues who were the sub-jects of this research, impressed the observers as being very intelligent with a highly integrated personality. In any case, he left the Company soon after this particular piece of research in this unit was completed. It is possible to argue that with better educated personnel to fill this role, his actual work would have approximated more closely to Brown's theoretical definition of this role. The training aspect is virtually non-existent.

In their idealized picture of the section manager both the unit manager and the machine operator portray him as preoccupied with personnel matters. Presumably subordinates always prefer personnel oriented superiors. While all the line managers, in-cluding the unit manager, made wild estimates of what the section managers did, the personnel manager's estimate was very near the mark.

A point of caution is required as to the degree of generality that may be attached to these results. Studies of one manager were made on three different occasions. The amount of time devoted to the personnel function varies widely. For example, when a quarterly review is imminent, the section manager is heavily involved in personnel assessment. This question of assessments is fully discussed in Chapter 5, entitled 'A Wage Negotiation'.

Here the difficulty is ultimately theoretical. In the official glossary, taken from *Exploration in Management*,

> Managerial authority is defined as 'the minimal authority attached to a managerial role which has to do with the control of work by subordinates, i.e. that a manager must have subordinate roles into which he can appoint members, from which he can remove them, and within which he can set terms of reference and determine differential rewards'.

By defining the manager in this way, that he can determine differential rewards for his subordinates, does not solve anything. In the last analysis definitions are arbitrary and represent a set of arbitrary assumptions. In fact, as pointed out in Chapter 5, 'A Wage Negotiation', section managers lack this capability, lack confidence in their ability to judge or justify their assessments. In essence, the Glacier concept of the section manager is not fully supported by the empirical evidence and should be amended accordingly.

SUMMARY

1. The nature of the task is the principal determinant structuring the behaviour of the section managers.
2. As a corollary, personal factors are of limited significance in determining his behaviour.
3. The section manager is heavily occupied in communicating; much of this is in the horizontal dimension.
4. His personnel activities are limited:
   (a) most of it is task oriented.

(*b*) none of this time is consciously devoted to training.

(*c*) assessments for wage reviews can consume much of his time.

5. The effective manager spends more time on personnel than his less effective colleagues. But this is 'task loaded' personnel work.

6. Both the unit manager and the shop floor workers would prefer section managers to devote more of their time to personnel.

7. The theoretical description of the section manager in *Exploration in Management* is not supported by the facts.

PART IV

THE GLACIER SUPERVISOR
AND GLACIER MEETINGS

AN EMPIRICAL EXAMINATION
OF THE BEHAVIOUR OF THE
GLACIER SUPERVISOR

The greatest single difficulty in reporting this part of the research flows from the problem of defining the role of supervisor. The literature of supervision is replete with terms indicative of the ambivalence inherent in the role of supervisor. The language which reveals what Wilfred Brown calls the 'split at the bottom of the executive chain' includes such terms as the 'man in the middle', 'marginal men', 'the manager in no man's land', and 'master and victim of double talk'. Sandwiched from below by an expanding democracy and from above by a diminishing but penetrating autocracy, the supervisor finds himself in a very difficult position.

Thus finding himself placed on the boundary between the middle management system and the workers' shop floor system induces a certain degree of ambivalence in the role of the supervisor. This ambivalence arises from the fact that the members of these two different systems have different expectations of the supervisor's role-behaviour. Certainly the supervisor is the most maligned and least understood of all members of the organization.

The etymology of the term does not take one very far towards solving this enigma. The term 'supervise' is derived from *super* (over) and *videre* (to see), and is defined as to oversee; to superintend; to inspect; to direct and control. Certain observations may be made about the supervisor: His discretionary powers are restricted compared with management. Examination of the literature reveals that many supervisors experience feelings of

isolation, particularly in their relations with middle management. This feeling of isolation is reinforced by a lack of appropriate station, privilege, hours of work and fringe benefits. As
many practising managers have discovered from experience, he
is confused by company policies which, in theory, aim to
identify him with the executive structure but which, in practice,
allow him to be treated as a senior operative. Not surprisingly
the ambivalence inherent in the role of the supervisor is such that
he sometimes identifies with the operators and sometimes with
the management.

BROWN'S VIEW OF THE SITUATION AT THE BOTTOM OF THE EXECUTIVE SYSTEM

In *Exploration in Management* Brown explains how the whole
executive system is dependent for its efficiency on the co-
operation that exists at the bottom. In his historical review of
Company thinking about supervisors, he explains how the titles
charge-hand, leading hand, setter, assistant foreman, foreman
and superintendent were abolished and replaced by the terms
supervisor, section manager and unit manager.

FIGURE 8.1. *The Official Glacier Picture of the
Situation at the bottom of the Executive System*

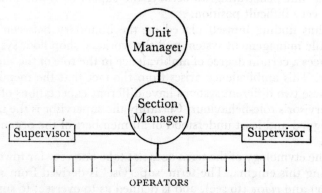

This reorganization, at least in theory, gave full managerial
status to the section managers with the supervisors as some kind
of staff assistant to them. The Policy Document defines a supervisor as 'A member who assists his manager by assigning approp-

riate work to those members of his manager's immediate command allocated to him, and seeing that this work gets done'.

The Relation between the Section Manager, Supervisor and Operator

T. T. Paterson[112] in *A Methectic Theory of Social Organisation* has suggested a more fundamental and useful way of discussing the relationship between the section manager, the supervisor and the operatives. Following Paterson's approach, the relationship may be presented in the following manner.

FIGURE 8.2. *The Triad showing the Relationship between the Section Manager, the Supervisor and the Operative*

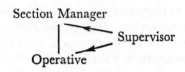

Referring to figure 8.2 – a section manager may say to a supervisor[112] 'One of your functions, for which you are responsible to me, is to see that the operative fulfils his function which I have assigned to him. To do so you have the right to give him orders but I retain the right to punish him if he fails.' That is, the section manager delegates to the supervisor 'the right to command (authorises him) but not the right to enforce obedience (does not empower him). (The most typical example is the triad of the officer, sergeant and private. The commissioned officer is authorised and empowered, the non-commissioned officer is authorised but not empowered.)'

Since the section manager 'assigns the function and since the operative must have freedom of operations in order to be responsible for his function', the supervisor 'will be limited to giving orders on operations which are specific to or entailed in function, that is, operations which, of necessity, must be performed, either to fulfil the function or to co-ordinate the function with other functions.'

In Paterson's terms, the supervisor 'cannot use the categorical imperative but he can give an order to the operative which implies, "You must do this or else the" section manager "will punish you". That is to say, since the order concerns operations specific to function, it must be obeyed. It is a proper order and is therefore right. However, the operative is not perfectly obliged to obey for he may consider obedience to these orders might bring about failure to fulfil his function, and punishment by the manager would ensue, the operative being responsible to the manager. He is expected as of right, but not obliged, to obey.'

Since the supervisor 'is authorised but not empowered the relation between supervisor and operative is not responsibility. The operative reports to the supervisor (as a private to a sergeant) but only the manager can punish (as only a commissioned officer).' Without this type of analysis, 'the split at the bottom of the executive system' is further complicated by the creation of an additional managerial role implied by the terms 'allocated to him, and seeing that this work gets done'. (Definition of the supervisor given in the Policy Document.)

For those lacking direct experience of the Glacier system, the best approximation, if such is required, is to regard the section manager as a foreman who has, according to Brown, managerial authority, and the supervisor as something between an assistant foreman and a machine setter. These are only rough guides, particularly in the latter case. The object of this exercise is to furnish a more objective description of the role of the Glacier supervisor.

When the Tavistock team began to investigate 'the split at the bottom of the executive system', they reported deep-seated resistance by both management and the operatives to any attempts to resolve these difficulties. The key problem is to distinguish the supervisory role from the managerial role. Any attempt to define the role of supervisor is complicated by the fact that the term 'supervisor' is used extensively in other contexts to refer to a variety of different appointments, some of which occur in the upper echelon of management. In the more exact terminology of Glacier, the role of the supervisor exist only on the shop floor.

Wilfred Brown[26] argues that:

> the whole economy of the factory depends ultimately on the production work on the shop floor. Therefore, the consequence of any stoppage on the shop floor by even a single operator is that a part of the cost of plant, building, services and the entire organisation

of the company ceases to be recovered from the market; for all expense is recovered by including a portion of it in each item of production which is sold.

Thus, to minimize the absence of an operator from his machine, a series of roles has been created. For this purpose, according to Brown,[26] the supervisor has the following duties:

1. To find out what work is coming forward for each machine.
2. To discover which work has priority.
3. To make certain that a specific type of work is within the capacity of the operator and his machine.
4. To arrange a study of a particular job to improve output and quality.
5. To organize running repairs to the machines.
6. To improve methods of production and to overcome *ad hoc* difficulties.
7. To discuss quality and finish with the inspector when difficulties arise.
8. To check the availability of tools for the next job.

In developing the supervisor's role in this way Wilfred Brown[26] argues that,

the essential basis of the supervisor's work arises from the need to have somebody available to do that component of the production job which the machine operator is unable to do without stopping his machine.

or again

the supervisor is essentially an 'off-the-machine direct producer of the product'.

Having dealt with this work of the supervisor which arises because of the nature of production work, Brown now considers the further work, which the section manager would otherwise do if the supervisor was not available. These additional tasks, which free the section manager for a larger command, include:

9. Allocating work and ensuring that it gets done.
10. Appointing tasks between machine operators.
11. Assessing operators' performance and conduct.
12. Reporting this assessment to the Section Manager.
13. Training operators.

At the beginning of 1964, the General Manager invited the writer to help in clarifying the role of the supervisor in the Thin Wall Unit of the Kilmarnock factory. The Thin Wall Unit, N Unit as it is known in the factory, is concerned with the manufacture of bearings which are used in the assembly of motor-car engines and are commonly referred to as 'big end bearings' by car enthusiasts. Production of these components is inevitably required on a very large scale; to achieve this a considerable measure of mechanization has been introduced. This has been achieved by the introduction of magazine-fed machines, linked by transfer machinery. A number of machine tools capable of working at 2,000 pieces per hour have been linked together in this way.

The manufacture of these bearings requires the backing of low friction linings to very long strips of steel by a complex metallurgical process. This is carried out in the Sinter Unit. These very large rolls of strip are then taken to the Thin Wall Unit. The first process consists of slicing the strip into pieces, which in turn are bent into semi-circular cylinders by a series of machine operations. The sections which were the subject of this research then perform a series of operations which include drilling an oil hole, cutting an oil groove, boring the surface of the bearings to a specified standard and cutting a locating nick. All of these operations are subject to very high standards of accuracy. After this process, the bearings are given an electroplated finish.

Four grades of machine operatives are employed in the Unit as in other parts of the factory. These consist of an A grade, or training grade; a B grade which is achieved at the end of three months if the trainee is considered satisfactory; a grade I and finally a grade II. The men work two shifts, one a normal day shift and the other a night shift (except on Friday, when a back shift is substituted). The average earnings of the operators is approximately £22 per week. The standard of recruitment of these machine operators is very high. They are interviewed by the personnel officer, then by the section manager where they are going to work, and medically examined; and recently they have also been required to take a Raven's Matrices intelligence test and dexterity tests. While officially they are described as semi-skilled, they have, after a period in the factory, a considerable measure of technical competence. The most popular union is the A.E.U. followed by the T. & G.W.U., but though it is nearly 100 per cent union organized, the factory is not a closed shop. The Joint Shop Stewards Committee is made up of 20 members from the A.E.U., five from the T. & G.W.U., one from the E.T.U. (Electrical Trades Union) and one from the F.W.U. (Foundry Workers Union). All machine operators are classified as hourly rated employees.

The supervisors who are the subjects of this study are members of Grade III (b) staff and have a basic wage paid weekly for a forty hour week with payment for overtime. The maximum salary for section managers, part of Grade II staff, is slightly in excess of £1,500 per annum.

The introduction of mechanization in the Thin Wall Unit has given rise to a number of problems, which affected two related groups of employees, the operators and the supervisors. The introduction of transfer machines and the speeding-up of the machines from 600 pieces an hour to 2,000 pieces an hour per machine, had produced a situation where inevitably:

1. The Company was looking for longer runs free from the interruptions of tea breaks and lunch breaks, to be achieved by staggered breaks and the use of 'slip men' as standbys.
2. A smaller number of operators per line would be required. To facilitate this development a higher grade of operator would be required to act as a patrol man.

When these proposals were considered by management and the operators, a fairly sharp reaction of anxiety was experienced by both the operators and the supervisors. In the case of the operators, seeing the very large increase in the productivity of the machines, there was a demand to return to piece rates, and the selling of their overtime at the highest premium. On this latter point, this involved a preference for Saturday and Sunday work, particularly for the Sunday with its double rate. On the other hand the supervisors said that there would be fewer operators to supervise and that inevitably, if a higher grade of operator were created, then this would be a threat to their position.

The Works Committee has been occupied from time to time with the problem of defining the role of the supervisor, as the following item taken from November 1962 minutes of theWorks Committee shows.

At this meeting the Joint Shop Stewards Committee made the point that although they had made their views well known on previous occasions, supervisors were still doing work which to their mind ought to be done by hourly rated members. They referred particularly to N Unit where, although there were hourly rated members capable of setting machines, supervisors were spending sometimes a whole shift setting one machine after another, and hourly rated members were thereby deprived of experience in doing this kind of work. The stewards further argued that a supervisor's role was to see that the work coming off the machines was up to the customer's standards and where an operator was having trouble in setting or running a machine to assist him in eliminating snags. The stewards also drew attention to the fact that 'there were criteria in existence which called for hourly rated members to be able to set machines before they reached the higher grade in the bracket and where possible they wanted the men to be trained to do this'. The stewards had raised the matter at the Works Committee in the hope that the situation could be prevented from deteriorating.

By way of answer to these comments the General Manager pointed out that the job of the unit and section managers was to achieve the task set in the most economical manner consistent with quality and delivery, and this would not be accomplished if supervisors were used in the role of hourly rated members. The General Manager went on to say that 'there were special problems, probably not fully understood at shop floor level, in N Unit at the present time. The rate of production was not at a satisfactory level with the result that on two occasions, promises to one of our largest customers that by an agreed date we would be out of arrears with them had not been kept. A third promise had been made for a deadline on 26 November and to achieve the necessary output it may have been considered necessary to use supervisors to set machines. To increase the labour force would only be a temporary remedy and would involve redundancies when the rate of output improved.' The General Manager had given the unit managers an estimate of the work to be done next year and the indications were that the N Unit manager would have to organize training.

BEHAVIOUR OF THE GLACIER SUPERVISOR

Grade III staff representation* said that nothing of these matters had been reported to their Committee by the supervisors and until they had discussed it with them they were not able to comment.

Joint Shop Stewards Committee concluded by saying that if the practice continued it could cause serious unrest.

ANALYSIS OF THE SUPERVISOR'S BEHAVIOUR

The aim of this study was to produce an objective record of the behaviour of eight supervisors in the Thin Wall Unit of the Kilmarnock factory of the Glacier Metal Company. The method used was the technique of activity sampling which depends upon observations being made of the behaviour of the subjects at randomly determined times. During the three weeks that this study lasted, 6,000 observations were made. Data was collected on where the supervisors spent their time, with whom they interacted and the activities in which they engaged. Secondly, it is intended to compare the official role description of the supervisor with the portrait of him that becomes available from the empirical evidence of activity analysis.

The Thin Wall Unit is under a single roof on the same floor and there is easy access from one part to another. Thus, little use is made of the telephone or written communication for exchange of information within the unit. The building housing the administrative staff of the factory is nearby.

The supervisor apparently spent nearly all of his time within the Unit mainly in his own section. What is significant here is that the supervisor is rarely to be found in either the Production Engineering Department (PED) or other sections. The PED contains the Unit programming and the production engineering staff. It is in the PED that he would get any programming data he required, or find the blueprints related to his work. His absence from other sections reveals that he is not involved in seeing what work is coming forward.

* Supervisors are members of Grade III staff.

FIGURE 8.3. PLAN SHOWING THE LAYOUT OF THE THIN WALL UNIT
(*Not to scale*)

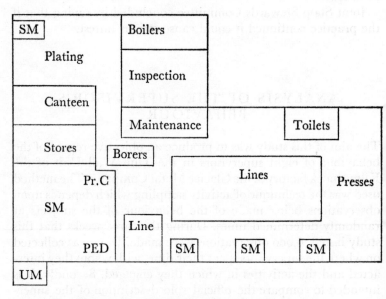

SM   = Section Manager's Office
UM   = Unit Manager's Office
Pr.C = Production Controller's Office
PED = Production Engineering Department

TABLE 8.1. PERCENTAGE DISTRIBUTION OF THE SUPERVISOR'S TIME BY LOCATION

In his own section	84%
In other sections	1%
Production Engineering Department	2·6%
Stores (P.E.D.)	2·6%
Canteen	5·8%
Outside 'N' Unit	4%
TOTAL	100%

218

Table 8.2 shows that supervisors spend nearly two-thirds of their time at work in contact with others. Most of this time is spent in contact with his operators. Lateral contacts with supervisors of other sections, as the data in location would suggest, are relatively infrequent. The supervisor and section manager are together for nearly a tenth of their working day.

TABLE 8.2. ANALYSIS OF TIME SPENT IN CONTACT
WITH OTHERS
Percent analysis of the time spent with others, according to the rank
of person

Alone	37·5%
With the Unit Manager	0·5%
With Section Manager	9·8%
With other Supervisors	4·7%
With operatives	42·0%
With engineers	1·5%
With others (storemen, fitters, electricians)	4 %
TOTAL	100·0%

Table 8.3 displays the distribution of time spent in personal contact; therefore it does not include the time spent alone. The term 'superior' in the case of the section managers refers mainly to the unit manager but also includes the General Manager with whom they have little contact; 'peers' refer mainly to other section managers and to the unit production controller and the unit engineers; and subordinates refer to supervisors and operators.

In the case of the supervisors, 'superiors' refer to the unit manager and section manager; 'peers' refer to other supervisors; and 'subordinates' refer to machine operators and other hourly rated employees such as fitters.

In the Thin Wall Unit the pattern of communication is very similar for section managers and supervisors. In essence most of the communication follows a vertical route with a small amount of lateral communication which is approximately the same at both levels. On the other hand, the section managers in the Wrapped Bushes Unit spent nearly a third of their time in contact with peers.

TABLE 8.3. ANALYSIS OF INTERACTION DATA
Comparison of Section Managers' and Supervisors' total time with people of different ranks

Ranking of Person with whom interacting	Thin Wall Unit		Wrapped Bushes Unit
	Section Managers	Supervisors	Section Manager
Number	2	8	4
Superiors	11·9	18·9	22
Peers	11·6	7·5	32
Subordinates	76·5	73·6	46
TOTAL	100·0	100·0	100

The explanation for this difference in the rate of horizontal communication between the two Units becomes obvious when the difference between their respective tasks is considered. In the Bushes Unit, with 750 batches on the floor at any given time and a through-put time of 13 weeks, programming is the main activity of the section managers. The number and nature of the tasks demanded a sophisticated production scheduling apparatus which the factory had not yet developed. In other words the demands of production were so complex that they could not be made explicit in terms of exclusively vertical instructions, and a considerable measure of lateral contact with other section managers, the production controller and the unit engineers is required to make explicit what had priority on the programme and where it was. Whereas in the Thin Wall Unit, with very much longer runs, and a high degree of mechanization, programming takes up a relatively small amount of time; thus, contacts with peers is comparatively less frequent.

To what extent is it possible to generalize from these results it is impossible to say with any assurance. Indeed, how far these results are typical of this kind of industrial concern is uncertain. There is a tendency in the literature of communication to generalize from a study of this type; to produce propositions which are assumed to be valid in every executive area irrespective of the nature of the industry or the sophistication of the management.

The behaviour of the supervisors was recorded on a special

form. In this context, the description 'technical' refers to the setting and operating of machines, trouble shooting, advising or training operators and also includes inspection.

Ascertaining what comes next, where it is, what tools are required, getting 'the work' to the right stations, briefing the operators on particular tasks, are all included in the term 'programming'. It also refers to the process of ensuring that 'the work' is moving at a satisfactory rate down the line. While in official 'Glacier Speak' all these operations are known as programming, the supervisors described the actual process of ensuring that 'the work' flows down the line as production. This has presumably developed because of the necessity of having a special term to distinguish what they regard as the most important activity, the machining of the product on the lines, from the planning of production, programming. 'Personnel' refers to matters concerned with the arranging of overtime and payment of wages, but could include selection, assessment of performance etc. In fact, none of these latter activities were observed in this study of the supervisor.

TABLE 8.5. COMPARISON BETWEEN SECTION MANAGERS'
AND SUPERVISORS' BEHAVIOUR BY FUNCTION

Rank	Number	Technical	Programming	Personnel	Personal
Section Manager	2	50·5	27·5	17·5	4·5
Supervisor	8	70·2	17·6	3·7	8·5

The supervisor spends most of his time on technical work with programming and personnel work taking very little of his time whereas the section manager's main activity is technical work (a half of his time), followed by programming (a quarter of his time) and then personnel (a sixth of his time).

If the technical element of the supervisor's job is subjected to closer analysis, then the importance of 'trouble shooting' as an activity becomes manifest. 'Trouble shooting' refers to the process of clearing a stoppage on a machine. In a study of this type, it is easy to decide when 'trouble shooting' is the appropriate activity to record, as it is evidenced by the piling up of bearings at the entrance to the magazine which is used to feed the machines. Technically qualified engineers frown on the encouragement of 'trouble shooting' as they regard it as a symptom of bad technical organization. They argue that it represents first-aid action which deals with effects rather than causes.

It is possible to argue that the supervisors lack the requisite technical knowledge to 'trouble shoot' effectively. Certainly, the supervisor must be so conversant with the technical details of the job that he is able to diagnose difficulties and is capable of taking appropriate action. Above all, he must be able to distinguish between the problems which he can tackle himself and those that require the skill of the production engineer. It is on this latter point that the supervisor tends to be over-sanguine. At the other end of the scale, the difficulty could be of the simplest order, e.g. swarf or metal cuttings blocking the machine. Some of the supervisors attribute this to the mental state of the operator who, they argued, falls into a state verging on a hypnotic trance induced by the machine's motions. The operators, on the other hand, believe that they do not have enough time to clean the machines. A great deal of 'trouble shooting' could be avoided if the operators were suitably trained.

TABLE 8.6. THE TECHNICAL ASPECT OF THE SUPERVISOR'S JOB

Trouble shooting	53·25%
Setting	19·25%
Inspection	14·25%
Advising	13·25%
Training	Nil
TOTAL	100%

The amount of time the supervisor of our study spends on training is nil. Closely allied to training is advising. Advising is the briefing of an operator on what he has to do, including the sequence of technical operations. While the supervisors never describe this activity as training, it must inevitably cover, to some extent, the same ground.

The supervisors spend a seventh of their 'technical' time on inspection. In their own estimate, the supervisors reckoned that this activity took up half of their time. This reflects the importance which the supervisor attaches to this part of his work. It is here that he makes a significant contribution to the quality of the product. The sequence of events goes like this. The machine operator is required to bring the 'first off' to the supervisor who examines it. If he is satisfied, he signs the job card which allows the operator to machine the component in quantity. In some circumstances a 'first off' may be sent to inspection as well. A period of thirty minutes may elapse before the piece is checked. If the piece is rejected then as many as 500 components may be scrapped. Thus, by his decision on quality, the supervisor feels that he is making a significant contribution to the manufacture of the Company's product.

The supervisor spends nearly a fifth of his 'technical' time on the setting of machines. As has been observed, he spends no time on the training of operators. This is in spite of a clear injunction in the Company's description of the supervisor's job where it says 'that the supervisor will be responsible for . . . and training new operators and ensuring that established operators according to their potential are given adequate guidance and training'.

From interviews with supervisors, it is clear that the reasons for the failure of the supervisors to engage in training include:

1. The supervisors have no special training in the technique of job instruction.
2. They generally prefer doing to supervising.
3. They live from emergency to emergency, from crisis to crisis and work under considerable pressure.
4. A natural fear that the higher grade of machine operators represent a threat to the tenure of their position if they acquire further technical competence. This has been re-inforced by the possibility of a higher grade of machine operator being created by management.

Just under a sixth of the supervisor's time is devoted to programming. Programming/loading, which takes up more than a quarter of this time, is how the supervisor finds out 'what job comes next'. This question of priority is settled by consulting a display board in the production control section which contains details of the load prepared by the unit production controller. Armed with this information, the supervisor can now draw the appropriate job cards, material requisition forms and lay-out cards. From this, he can work out which machines and tools are required for the operators to achieve this task.

Next, he briefs the operators. Briefing also refers to the section manager passing programming information to the supervisors. Both aspects take only a twentieth of the supervisor's total programming time. The supervisor having put his operators in the picture, the programme must be transformed into a production actuality on the machines. This involves identifying batches and organizing their transfer to the appropriate work stations for machining. The supervisor must ensure that the components move smoothly from machine to machine. This part of his work is referred to as 'production' by the supervisors and denotes the programming of work which is done within the section. A third of his total programming time is given to production.

TABLE 8.7. PROGRAMMING ASPECT OF THE SUPERVISOR'S JOB
Analysis of the programming content of the Supervisor's work

Programming/Loading	26·4%
Briefing	5·5%
Production	29·2%
Task pricing	1·4%
Task performance	37·5%
TOTAL	100·0%

When the work has been produced, the supervisor must reconcile the amount of work done against the load by counting the bearings and ensuring that his tally agrees with the number specified on the batch card. This activity, known as task performance, requires a third of his programming time. Finally, the supervisor records the time to complete the batch. This takes a microscopic portion of his time.

An extremely small proportion of the supervisor's time is taken up by personnel work. Most of this is concerned with the arranging of overtime or is related to the payment of wages.

COMPOSITE PICTURE OF A SUPERVISOR

A summary picture of the supervisor's behaviour emerges from the above data. Most of his work is technical, and is mostly devoted to 'trouble shooting', but also includes sizeable elements of setting, inspecting and advising but surprisingly does not include any training whatsoever. Next, in order of importance, comes programming, which includes finding out what work is next in line and working out the tooling and material implications; secondly, making sure the pieces to be machined are moved to their correct stations and that the work flows through the section, and finally checking that the number of components produced agrees with the figure in the batch record. Personnel work takes up very little of his time.

If his pattern of communications is examined, it will be seen that in the case of the supervisor, it follows a vertical route with a small amount of lateral communication. Most of this vertical activity is downwardly directed, supporting the view that the supervisors are so heavily occupied getting the job done that they have very little time to spend with either their superiors or colleagues.

THE OFFICIAL ROLE DESCRIPTION
OF THE SUPERVISOR

The accepted account of his work is given in the vacancy notice which is used to advertise supervisory posts in the Thin Wall Unit of the factory. 'The Supervisors will ordinarily be assigned to a particular line on which they will be required to supervise, within the terms of Company Policy, members of the Section Manager's command assigned to them, in the manufacture of bearings.

'The Supervisors will be accountable to the Section Managers for ensuring that the work flow is maintained, that the necessary materials are available as required, that the best use of space given to them by their manager is obtained, that quality and delivery targets are met and, generally, that standards set by their managers are maintained.

'The supervisors will be responsible for allocating work, and giving directions to operators on behalf of the Section Manager; for assessing the work of the Manager's subordinates and making appropriate recommendations to the Manager; for maintaining day to day discipline and morale, and for training new operators and ensuring that established operators, according to their potential, are given adequate guidance and training.

'Flexibility is required to deal with changes in the operators assigned to them, and in changes from one line to another, or between day shift and night shift.

'The authority of supervisors lies not so much in any formally allocated authority, as in their own personal ability to deal with people and get the best out of them. They must realise the limits of their authority and, working as they will be in close relationships with other supervisors and operators, they must have the ability to work with them in helping their Manager to maintain an effective working team.'

The above role description implies, not unnaturally, that this role contains a large supervisory element. Reference in particular to paragraph four of this description where it argues that the supervisor is responsible '. . . for maintaining day to day discipline and morale, and for training new operators' seems particularly inappropriate in the light of the empirical evidence. If reference is made to the last paragraph of the above description it will be readily seen that there is a failure to recognize the difficult position in which the supervisor finds himself in relationship to the question of authority.

T. T. Paterson[112] has analysed the sources of authority and has developed the subject of Methectics which he defines as 'the study of participation in group life in terms of bestowed and adopted roles'. In this scheme five forms of authority are recognized depending upon the purpose of the group and the organization of its functions. These five forms are structural, sapiential, moral, charismatic, and personal. Structural authority refers to the right springing from ultimately legal contract which is 'vested in an office' in an organization and therefore in the manager holding that post. Structural authority enables a manager to organize and control the work of his subordinates and to operate effectively requires obedience from them as a matter of routine generally without challenge. In some circumstances, structural authority may be thought of as identical with line authority.

The rediscovery of hierarchy in modern thinking about business organizations derives its utility from the consideration that people come to work with the idea that they are going to be subject to authority and that their first reaction will be to comply with instructions and furthermore that acting in this way makes them feel comfortable, provided that neither their sense of logic nor moral sensibilities are outraged.

Sapiential authority is the entitlement or right to be heard by virtue of knowledge or expertise. 'It is wrong to assume that when an individual is vested with structural authority that he is necessarily vested with sapiential authority.'[112]

For example, the personnel manager has sapiential authority insofar as he has the necessary knowledge of behavioural science, industrial relations and so on which he can use to improve the efficiency of the organization.

'Moral authority is the entitlement to control and direct by reason of "rightness" or "goodness" in action according to the contractual system (ethos) of the enterprise.'[112] Managers often seek moral authority by emphasizing the rightness of the proposals which they are advancing. The structural authority of the 'fair and just' manager will always be backed up by moral authority. Charismatic authority, beloved by both witch doctors and old fashioned country doctors, is the right to command and direct by reason of grace. Some managers attempt to assume charismatic authority when they adopt the role of father figure and develop an aura of omnipotence and omniscience. Personal authority is the right to command or lead by virtue of the fittingness of personality with the purpose of the enterprise.

Let us now return to the role description of the supervisor with a view to assessing what kind of authority he is assumed to have. Of the five kinds of authority specified by Paterson, the supervisor can have only that which is designated personal authority, the weakest. He may not have even that; lacking structural authority because of the failure of the organization to make his position explicit, devoid of sapiential authority in the sense that he does not have an adequate technical background, and with scant chance of developing moral authority because of the marginal position which he occupies (finding himself at the boundary between management and labour), the supervisor finds himself in a very weak position as far as exercising any form of authority.

Let us now examine the selection criteria at present used in the factory.

227

1. Must be Line Shop skilled, and know machine work in detail.
2. Ability to gain personal respect and to get work done on personal ability and authority.
3. Definite, tenacious and resourceful.
4. Ingenious.
5. Adaptable.
6. Capacity to be, as it were, part of the section manager and be able to work in close relationship with him. Thus demanding absolute loyalty and the ability to accept the manager's judgment as his own even though, in the first instance, he may not have agreed with him.
7. Linking with the last, capacity to know each individual whom he supervises.
8. To anticipate each individual's training need and to provide for each individual's training taking into account the circumstances operating at any time.
9. Capacity to appraise and to report on the job situation at any time.
10. Patience and tolerance.
11. By habits and disposition, ability to set standards of orderliness and cleanliness.
12. Capacity to plan, at least two weeks ahead, and be able to anticipate difficulties.

FOUR CRITICISMS OF THE SELECTION CRITERIA FOR SUPERVISORS

Four criticisms may be made of this list of selection criteria. First of all, it repeats the emphasis on personal authority. This contrasts oddly with the statement from Brown's *credo* that optimal organization is *not* a function of personality. Secondly, it stresses the training aspect of his job. The analysis of the activities of the supervisor shows that the training function takes up none of his time. Thirdly, item 6 refers to the need for 'absolute loyalty' to his section manager. In the light of studies such as Roethlisberger's and Dickson's at Hawthorne, 'absolute loyalty' to his section manager would surely rank as a disqualification. Finally the use of terms such as 'definite, tenacious, resourceful, and adaptable', and 'ingenuity, patience and tolerance' shows an underlying acceptance of the trait approach to leadership. This requires further elaboration.

The trait approach to leadership which is concerned with the identification of the characteristics of leaders has proved disappointing. A survey by Bird[16] of the literature prior to 1940 included a list of personality traits that distinguish leaders from non-leaders. Only five per cent of the 'discovered traits' were common to four or more investigations. A later survey by Stogdill[141] confirms this picture. Typical of the traits that appear in such lists are decisive, determined, acceptable, honest, courageous, keen, patient and pious. This approach continues to be used, not because it assists in analysing the concept of leadership, but because it expresses a deep and popular belief about how leaders should behave. Research in social psychology suggests that a more 'situational' approach is required.[79]

The inadequacy of the role description of the supervisor and its lack of congruence with the behavioural data supplied from activity sampling lead naturally to the development of inappropriate trait descriptions which are then used as selection criteria. This type of failure arises inevitably when the personnel executive carries through the selection process in a compartment isolated from the realities of the situation. Personnel managers tend to be desk bound, play down the technical aspects of supervisory roles and very rarely have the necessary training and experience to go out on to the shop floor and make systematic inquiries concerning the role to be filled. An empirical examination of the supervisor's role in the Thin Wall Unit shows, without doubt, that as it is presently constituted the technical element is of supreme importance. What is required here is a reorganization of the role relations of the supervisor with a clearer and more explicit definition of his functions; and adequate training, plus technical and managerial support, is required if the supervisor is to develop a more effective role.

CHAPTER 9

GLACIER MEETINGS

One of the most puzzling paradoxes to emerge from Glacier writings is the fact that, at the beginning of the project, the Company seemed 'to manage by committees', then suddenly management was by the command meeting.

A major focus of Glacier research in the 'forties was the committee, in particular how to make the Works Council more effective; the focus in the 'sixties is the command meeting, in particular to develop a procedure within which management can spell out policy and make instructions explicit. This chapter is concerned with an empirical study of two kinds of Glacier meetings: Works committee and the command meeting. The study of the Works Committee analyses the interactions at one meeting. This chapter is concerned with demonstrating Glacier's confusion in regard to the concepts of authority and responsibility and their failure to recognize both the significance of commitment developed through participation and the relevance of the principles of group dynamics. The other study is that of a command meeting. The analysis of these data reveals how the task-centred command meeting is eroded by human problems and the complexities of its tasks (which it fails to solve); and how an informal group is evolved to resolve these difficulties. The general conclusion of this chapter emphasizes the need for the theoretical specification of the nature of meetings to be reconciled with the behavioural data of these encounters.

To ensure their survival and maximize their effectiveness, organizations require the establishment and utilization of efficient communication systems. In organizations, policies and instructions flow downwards and percolate to the lower reaches of the organization and reports, criticisms and information flow back up the line; as the transmission of the latter data (and feelings) is filtered by each executive level as they move upwards, the information, in fact, received by top management tends to be distorted and present a favourable, or at least uncritical, picture of the communicating subordinates.

This matrix of communication, or network of communicating channels or more simply 'networks', is usually associated with the concept of organizational structure. Social psychologists such as Bavelas[12] have shown that the speed and accuracy of communication are both related to the structure of the network. Organizations achieve their effectiveness by defining roles and specifying the method of linkage between role holders. The critical question is what factors promote efficient communication? In this context, efficiency may refer to speed, accuracy, lack of ambiguity, flexibility or adaptability. Research findings such as those of Bavelas suggest that it is not possible to have all of these and at the same time maintain high morale. The organization may have to choose between those factors which facilitate task effectiveness and those that promote human satisfaction. The restriction of the free flow of information is precisely what favours co-ordination; but it has the disadvantage of inhibiting innovation and invention. The vital issue is to decide what is the optimal level of structure to achieve the best balance between task effectiveness and human satisfaction and, within task effectiveness, to get the desired mix of co-ordination and innovation.

It is clear that group commitment, based on discussion where members feel free to contribute (and at the best have contributed towards solving the problem and at the worst have exercised their right to be heard), has a better chance of providing a basis for co-ordinated action.

GLACIER DEFINITIONS OF COMMAND MEETING AND THE COMMITTEE

Before proceeding further in the theoretical analysis of communications in organizations, it is necessary to examine the Glacier concept of the committee and command meeting. According to Brown and Jaques,[29] 'The most widespread perceptions about true committees are that they carry corporate responsibility. That is to say that in the last analysis a committee makes its decisions on the basis of a majority vote of its members. They are both quite firm on the way in which a committee can be identified and they go on to say that they will 'use this perception as the single property which separates committees from non-committees'.

Brown and Jaques then tackle the question of who is to be held responsible for a committee decision and they point out, 'At law, corporate responsibility involves the notion that if a committee decides by a majority to take a particular action, the minority who voted against that action are, nevertheless, equally responsible with the majority unless they resign from the committee and thus dissociate themselves from the action. In other words, the responsibility is truly corporate and not vested in individual members of the committee.'

The essence of a committee lies in the acceptance of corporate responsibility of the members.

Having defined the committee, the Glacier theorists then turn their attention to the command meeting. 'We use this term (the command meeting) to refer to a situation when a manager meets with his team of immediate subordinates. It is commonplace for managers to refer to such meetings as committee meetings but it is clear, if the structure of such meetings is examined, that *they do not carry corporate responsibility* and are, therefore, not committees. One of the effects of lack of clarity about the real structure of these meetings is that those present cannot be clear about the role in which they are contributing to the discussion. In the manager-subordinate relationship, it is a requisite responsibility of the subordinate to state his view of the policies which he would favour so far as his own executive command is concerned. It is for the manager in charge of the command which is meeting, to concern himself with the wider frame of reference and to decide what policies to set, taking into account the views of his subordinates.'

The Dynamics of Discussion Leading

Nearly all executives and many trade unionists pride themselves in their innate skill in human relations, especially interviewing, instructing and discussion leading. Most training courses emphasize the logical aspects of discussion leading by defining the responsibilities of the leader. These include:

1. to direct the group's thinking in an orderly fashion,
2. to present the problem correctly and clarify it so that the participants can discuss it intelligently.
3. to follow the discussion and keep it on track in a gracious manner.
4. to summarize the discussion at appropriate periods.

But a different approach has been suggested by the findings of group dynamics. Group dynamics is a field of inquiry dedicated to extending knowledge about the nature of groups, the laws of their development, and their interrelations with individuals, other groups, and larger institutions. This latter aspect relating to interaction of the group with the institutions spills over into the subject of sociology.

The group dynamics approach assumes that a group has two problems, a logical problem and a human problem. To deal with these problems the group usually throws up two individuals who have been designated by Bales[8] the task specialist and the human relations specialist and whose functions have been described as 'work' and 'non-work' respectively. He finds that in the operation of problem solving groups the individual who is judged by others to have the 'best ideas' is not generally the 'best liked'. It is the former who is usually referred to as the 'task specialist' and the latter as the 'human relations specialist'. The group usually try to find leaders to fill these roles. It is wrong to think that a good committee is made up of one leader and a number of followers.

The members must evolve a solution that is psychologically acceptable and logical to boot. In the language of many American experts on group dynamics the logical problem is described as the public agenda. The human problems which affect the group are described as the hidden agenda.[77] In a pamphlet called *Understanding How Groups Work*[3] it is explained in this way:

> Hidden agendas are neither better nor worse than surface agendas. Rather they represent all of the individual and the group problems that differ from the surface group job and therefore may get in the way of the orderly solving of the surface agenda. They may be

conscious or unconscious for the member or for the group. They are not to be blamed or damned.

Burying them does little good. Pretending that they, like country cousins, are unrelated to the group is equally ineffective. They are important, because they concern the group, and something needs to be done about them. The answer may be to solve them or to shelve them.

Groups, fortunately, can work on both agenda levels at the same time. As a rule the task specialist cannot get going with the 'work' until the human relations specialist has done some 'non-work', i.e. the group must de-tense itself by releasing some of its social or emotional forces. This may be achieved by discussing football, sex, 'clowning or perhaps simply by the chairman telling a joke against himself'. Some groups never manage to get off the ground; in many cases because they fail to do the necessary non-work.

Brown regards non-work as largely a waste of time and effort, as he observes in *Exploration in Management*:

> Time is often wasted unwittingly in meetings by discursive comment on issues which are not requisitely the business of that particular meeting. There is need for managers to teach subordinates how to get through the work of such meetings with speed, by sticking to the requisite problems of those present.

Phases of the Problem

R. F. Bales[8] has suggested that the group moves through three phases in solving the problem. These are clarification ('What is it?'), evaluation ('How do we feel about it?') and finally control ('What shall we do about it?').

In practice, according to Bales, it is best to start with the facts. This should be done even where the facts are thought to be well known; a brief synopsis of the situation is rarely a waste of time. As Bales[7] points out in 'In Conference':

> In an environment barren of consensus, only a fact can survive; and where there is hostility, even facts find a slim foothold. But a rich background of common facts lays the development of common inferences and sentiments, and out of these common decisions can grow. No decision rests on 'facts' alone, but there is no better starting point. To start the decision-making process at any other

point is to multiply the risk of a vicious circle of disagreement—and at no saving of time in the long run.

If the phases of clarification and evaluation are not gone through properly, attempts at control will meet with resistance. Frustration may be created. This may cause backtracking to the earlier phases. Tackling the 'work' and 'non-work' aspects simultaneously may produce anxieties and tensions which will impair the solidarity of the group. This danger will grow as the group passes from the relatively less demanding problems of clarification, which is mainly intellectual in content, to the problems of evaluation, and it will become greatest on the problem of control.

Bales[8] recommends that the best procedure is to go through the phases of clarification, evaluation and then control. Care should be taken to lay the ground work before proceeding to specific suggestions. This falls in the third phase.

Paterson[116] has analysed the process of decision making into four stages:

(1) He examines the evidence, that is to say, information available on the situation which requires action.
(2) He then concludes that action could, should or must be taken, or not; that is to say, he uses sapiential authority in the hypothetical imperative of the injunction. He has not yet decided to take action, it is merely a conclusion good, not good, or bad, that action be taken.
(3) On the basis of this second-stage exercise of sapiential authority he decides that action will be taken or not. It is proper and so right that action be taken.
(4) Having concluded and decided it would be good and right to take action he decides what action to take.

A discussion group which is working properly moves through these four phases. There is a basic congruence between the theorizing of Paterson and the empirical findings of Bales. For Paterson stages (1) and (2) provide the logical basis for his two types of conferences: informative and conclusive; stages (3) and (4) correspond to his two types of committees: directive and executive. Paterson makes the point that 'a committee always includes a conference', which presupposes the use of sapiential authority.

AN ANALYSIS OF
ONE GLACIER COMMAND MEETING

One of the virtues of employing an observational research tech
nique such as activity sampling which was the method used in
the study of the behaviour of the section managers in the
Wrapped Bushes Unit is that it is possible to ascertain exactly
how much of their working time these managers spent alone and
how much with others. Table 9.1 presents a breakdown of how
these four section managers spent their work time. If this data
is examined on a weekly basis, this means that for just under two
days he is on his own, but it also means that they spend just over
three days per week in contact with other people. On two of
these 'interacting days' they interact with only one other person
the other 'interacting day' is spent in meetings (including in
formal meetings such as canteen tea breaks). That they should
spend about one fifth of their time in meetings highlights the
need to examine this type of encounter more closely.

TABLE 9.1. PERCENT TIME SPENT AT MEETINGS BY
FOUR SECTION MANAGERS (WRAPPED BUSHES UNIT)

Section Manager	Initiating Manager	Machining Manager	Machining Manager	Self-Contained Manager
Distribution of time	I	M_1	M_2	SC
Alone	33	33	27	36
Formal meetings	14	13	10	17
Canteen	5	6	8	6
With individuals	41	46	54	38
Personal etc.	7	2	1	3
	100	100	100	100

This data was collected during the research reported in Chapter 7

These meetings were of two types, formal and informal. The
formal meetings were mainly devoted to production scheduling
This daily production or load meeting represents an example of
a Glacier command meeting. After the load meeting, all the
participants, except the unit manager, meet informally in the
canteen.

The purpose of the load meeting which the unit production controller and the unit engineer attend is to review the load position. It usually begins at 9.45 a.m. and lasts for a half to three-quarters of an hour. In Glacier terms the managers present are 'in role' and they believe themselves to be constantly in a 'review situation' as they put it. The 'review situation' is a phrase which makes them conscious of the structural relationship between them. Generally, in Glacier, executives seem to be very self-conscious about the manager-subordinate relationship.

On day 1 the section managers present the production estimates for the day; on day 2 they produce production figures for the previous day. The unit manager with his two staff officers co-ordinates these estimates in relation to the unit's load.

Any necessary adjustments are made to accommodate urgent batches accepted by the unit manager in addition to the normal weekly load. Quality and costing are also important topics at this meeting. At these meetings, the Initiating Section managers are the key men. The other section managers may be regarded as performing a service to them. In that part of the meeting designated 'any other business', a wide range of topics may be raised, e.g. technical problems regarding tooling, absenteeism, anticipated changes in the load, unit manning policy, safety footwear, policy in regard to unit shop stewards etc.

The section managers who attended these load meetings made it quite clear that with regard to the category 'any other business' that no opportunity is given to speak 'out of role'. What is being emphasized is that the unit manager himself may have no contact with the section managers in a situation structured in such a way that they are both 'out of role'. But the canteen meeting following the load meeting seemed to provide an opportunity for the section managers to step 'out of role'. To confirm and assess the significance of this canteen meeting, a special study was made of this informal meeting.

The length of the canteen meeting is significant. It is formally of ten to fifteen minutes' duration but may in fact and often is extended to thirty minutes. From observing this meeting it was concluded that the conversation was mainly concerned with work rather than with leisure. The section managers and the two staff officers 'step out of role' to discuss the broader aspects of work matters such as unit load deficiencies of programming, and management training courses. A certain amount of discussion may take place on individual problems carried over from the unit manager's meeting. But this is unusual – such problems are usually held over until the managers concerned are back 'in role'.

When this point of view was expressed to the unit manager regarding the function of these two meetings, his comments were instructive. He accepted that the function of the load meeting where his subordinates were in role was to get their 'marching orders'. The canteen meeting, on the other hand, was where his staff officers, the unit production controller and the unit engineer could explain 'what the hell' the old 'so and so' had in mind.

The personnel manager regarded the extension of the morning canteen meeting by the section managers as a failure on the part of the unit manager to conduct his command meeting efficiently. The General Manager, on the other hand, saw it as a consequence of the programming complications inevitable with 750 batches on the floor at any time. To his mind this difficulty was exacerbated by the dualism of the role of the unit engineer who is responsible for both production engineering and technical development work. The latter is technically more interesting but the production engineering aspects of his role have a more immediate pay-off in terms of production. Thus the personnel manager saw the problem as a personal difficulty of the unit manager while the General Manager saw it as an organizational difficulty, the tasks specified by the factory programming manager being too numerous, coupled with a failure to resolve the dualism inherent in the unit engineer's role.

These two meetings, the command meeting and the informal meeting in the canteen, may be thought of as one meeting which had been convened in two different places. In other words the command meeting in the unit manager's office is adjourned and then resumed in the canteen; the only person who does not take part in the second meeting is the unit manager. This 'combined meeting' represents an unusual solution to the dilemma of balancing 'task' and 'human' problems. The unit manager's concentration on the task gives rise to disturbances in the relations between the section managers, and these human relations difficulties must be solved if they are to continue to work successfully on the problem of task co-ordination.

Two mechanisms have been evolved to cope with this dilemma: differentiation of time (task work followed by human relations work, or work then non-work) and differentiation of roles (the task specialist and the human relations specialist). Both mechanisms are involved in this compound meeting. The unit manager is the task specialist, spelling out the load for the department but giving his subordinates little scope for stepping out of role. In his own words, in the command meeting the section managers were getting 'their marching orders'.

In the canteen phase the staff officers, the production engineer and production controller, assume the roles of the human relations specialists who explain (in the unit manager's words) 'what the hell the old so and so has in mind'. This mild and jocular self-critical comment by the unit manager is precisely the semantic stuff required to transform a task situation into a human relations situation. Thus the unit manager by pursuing Glacier dogma on the command meeting has created a situation where not only the business could not be transacted properly (i.e. reducing task effectiveness) but also had managed to make his subordinates feel anxious (i.e. low in human relations) so that they felt that they were unable to help the department sort out production priorities. To meet these difficulties the production specialists were forced into human relations roles.

This analysis illustrates the dysfunctional consequences of an over-rigid application of the concept of the command meeting. The unit manager felt constrained by Glacier dogma to behave in a manner which was inappropriate in terms of problem solving.

These empirical findings challenge the efficiency of the command meeting and give a reminder that the more pronounced hierarchical differences in status are, the less effective it will perform. E. P. Torrance's[146] comments in 'Function of Expressed Disagreement in Small Group Processes' are relevant, where he argues that effectiveness in aircrews is directly related to the ability of the aircrew to tolerate disagreement.

In a study of aircrew effectiveness in combat over Korea, we found that the more effective crews in comparison with the less effective crews and crews which did not get into combat were characterized by greater tolerance of disagreement. Several studies support the contention that the more effective groups are characterized by greater participation, initially wider divergence of expressed judgment, and greater acceptance of decisions.

Torrance[146] makes this recommendation to management:

> First, management needs to accept the fact that task-orientated disagreement is almost always 'good'. You have been long conditioned to believe that it is 'bad'. Parents become quite disturbed if their children argue or fight. Teachers, managers, and supervisors behave similarly. You may be afraid that you are 'playing with fire'. 'What if somebody blows up? What will the higher ups think? Will I lose the respect of my subordinates by letting them disagree with me?' Perhaps you are neglecting to recognise the fundamental difference between task-orientated and person-orientated disagreement. Or, you may be too prone to assume that all differences of opinion are a threat to managerial control.

Torrance's findings challenge Brown's basic premises that a meeting between a manager and his immediate subordinates (the command meeting) is improved in effectiveness by being more highly structured and thus inhibiting participation and restraining members from expressing divergent opinions.

The command meeting can be criticized from two basic aspects: the principles underlying it and in terms of its actual practice. The theoretical criticisms of the command meeting spring ultimately from confusion about the nature of authority and responsibility. The assumption that the manager is 'completely responsible' for decisions made at the command meeting does not seem justified in my experience. Associated with this assumption is the neglect of the concept of corporate accountability. Likewise there has been a failure to recognize that commitment is facilitated by participation. Brown's rejection of the findings of group dynamics, particularly relating to the need for a group to do a certain amount of non-work, has certainly disturbed some Glacier personnel officers.

In practice, the command meeting may be criticized on account of its inefficiency, in terms both of time wasted and of the poor human relations it generates. Finally the operation of the command meeting illustrates the difficulty of applying the task approach to the committee.

THE WORKS COMMITTEE

The legislative system of the Glacier Metal Company which has given rise to the greatest degree of misunderstanding, requires that policy shall be agreed by the General Manager and the elected representatives of the factory. As already described, these meetings at the London factory are called Works Councils, but at Kilmarnock, they are known as Works Committees. The Works Council at the Kilmarnock factory was disbanded after the 1957 strike and when it was revived it was known as the Works Committee presumably to show that the workers regarded the previous system with a degree of suspicion. In fact the Joint Shop Stewards Committee has only recently accepted the Company Policy Document, and previously had only formally acknowledged its existence.

The method of investigation consisted of analysing the minutes of the Works Committees over a number of years, interviewing executives and shop stewards to determine their attitude towards the Works Committee, and analysing one meeting of the Works Committee in detail.

A great deal of the discussion that takes place at the Works Committee is concerned with methods of pay, conditions of work, accidents, safety and canteen matters. Even in the Glacier canteen questions loom large; apparently trivial issues such as getting the right proportion of sugar, milk and tea can on occasions occupy their time. In fact, most matters relating to important issues are settled between the management and the stewards before they reach the Works Committee. A great deal of discussion on matters such as wage rates and conditions of service takes place in the various staff committees and in the Joint Shop Stewards' Committee. It is not uncommon for members of the personnel staff to be 'called in' to help to resolve such problems. There are also frequent meetings between the General Manager and the Convener of the J.S.S.C.

At each meeting of the Works Committee, the General Manager presents a report showing the current state of business, but this elicits little response. In the London Works Council, according to an article describing Glacier, entitled 'Glacier's Experiment in Management', Austen Albu,[2] M.P., reports:

241

Although the annual report and accounts are circulated to all council members, there is rarely any discussion on them. Even the allocation of profits or new investment decisions, until they begin to impinge on conditions in individual departments, do not seem to arouse much interest. Nor does trading policy, unless it has some political connotation when the more militant members of the works committee may raise it. Some members objected to the purchase of German machine tools, but were persuaded that buying tools was a purely executive responsibility. A resolution in general terms was recently passed in favour of east-west trade with the support of the management member.

Austen Albu[2] goes on to say that

judged by the usual but not necessarily conclusive, criteria of managerial efficiency, such as productivity, labour turnover and absenteeism, Glacier does not differ significantly from similar firms in the area, but most of the managers believe that the system does help to get changes accepted and to overcome the problem of the definition of managerial responsibility. To that extent managerial authority has been strengthened. On the other hand, employees feel that they can always get a hearing on any matter. Nevertheless the complicated distinction between executive and representative roles is not always clear.

This difficulty, distinguishing between executive and representative role-behaviour, produced difficulties at the Kilmarnock Works Committee.

THE DETAILED STUDY OF A
WORKS COMMITTEE

A detailed study was made of one meeting of the Works Committee which started at 2.30 p.m. and ended at 3.40 p.m. The method of the study required recording the content of the discussion. Each contribution was timed and recorded under the name of the contributor.

The meeting was in no way remarkable. After the reading of the minutes, the first matter for consideration was a Draft Standing Order, dealing with absence due to sickness. The Convener of the J.S.S.C. objected to the Company personnel.

department interfering in the process and 'stopping' it from going through. The Convener put it like this:

> I think it is a poor show that the P.D.M. (Personnel Divisional Manager) from London can stop it going through. We are back to 'square 1' after three years. I want to record the J.S.S.C.'s disapproval.

Other topics discussed included the revision of the Company Policy Document, and the introduction of three weeks' annual holiday. The J.S.S.C. has no great interest in the revision of the Company Policy Document. Illustrative of this attitude is the fact that during a recent conflict over wages the stewards 'did not have time to discuss the revision'.

FIGURE 9.1. SEATING ARRANGEMENT OF MEMBERS OF THE WORKS COMMITTEE

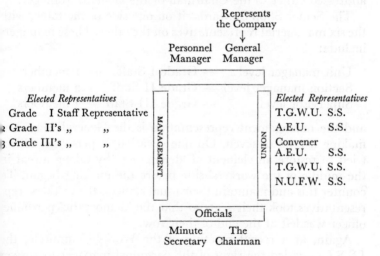

The topic of canteen prices came next, then the Manager's report on the state of trade. Questions were invited, but with no response. A change in wage rates was then formally moved by the General Manager, and seconded by the Convener of the J.S.S.C. On wages most of the negotiation takes place outside the Works Committee and in the particular negotiation discussed, a trial of strength took place between the Company and the workers. During this confrontation all formal contact was broken off and communication between the General Manager and the Convener had to be by neutral third parties. (At this stage of the proceedings research workers may have some value as intermediaries.) Nevertheless, in general terms, wages are settled elsewhere and only formally ratified at the Works Committee.

After dealing with the appointment of the Deputy Chairman the Committee turned to the question of canteen services and prices. The discussion ended by considering a particular accident that had taken place recently.

Table 9.2 shows who the contributors were, for how long they spoke, and to whom they spoke. The General Manager and the Chairman together spoke for nearly three-quarters of the time. The representative of the J.S.S.C., on the other hand, took up a fairly small proportion of the time. Most of the remarks were addressed either to the Chairman or the General Manager.

The Senior Shop Stewards sit on one side of the table, with the six managerial representatives on the other. These managers include:

Unit manager level	— Grade I Staff	— 1 member
Section manager level	— Grade II Staff	— 2 members
Supervisor level	— Grade III Staff	— 3 members

and the management representation is the General Manager making a total of seven. On one occasion, a personnel officer tried to restore an element of 'democracy' by taking a seat in the middle of the workers' side before the meeting began. To counter this and maintain their usual stances, the workers' representatives took their seats so that the 'democratic' personnel officer was left at the end of their row.

Again, at a recent meeting of the Works Committee, the J.S.S.C. queried the right of the personnel manager to answer questions addressed to the General Manager who, in turn replied:

that it was in the Constitution of the Committee that he was entitled to have any of his Staff Officers present to give specialist advice on any situations that might arise, and in a Company of such increasing numbers of personnel the person most readily equipped to answer most queries happened to be the Personnel Manager. It would greatly add to the time taken to conduct the business if the meeting had to be adjourned every time a decision was required on matters pertaining to personnel, rates etc., until the Management Member had had a discussion with the Personnel Manager.

However, it was conceded that, on such occasions, the Management Member (i.e. the General Manager) would formally state that he wished the personnel manager to answer on his behalf, this assuming that it was with his full agreement and approval. Management Member agreed that the point was well taken. The J.S.S.C. also agreed that the existing procedure represented the best method of conducting the business, providing the foregoing was observed.

TABLE 9.2. ANALYSIS OF CONTRIBUTIONS BY LENGTH OF TIME
(Expressed in percentages)

Who	To whom										
	PERCENTAGE	Meeting as a whole	Chairman	General Manager	Personnel Manager	Convener	Assistant Convener	T.G.W.U. Steward	Grade II	Grade III	TOTAL
Chairman	36	53		4	7	4		16	16		100
General Manager	38	60	16			8		12	4		100
Personnel Manager	4	100									100
Convener	6	33	66	1							100
Assistant Convener	3	50	50								100
T.G.W.U. Steward	8	100									100
The Rest	5	100									100
TOTAL	100										

In other words, from the point of view of the stewards there were too many management spokesmen. The balance of power had been disturbed. It is important to make it clear that this disturbance in the balance of power does not relate to questions of voting.

Joint consultation, of which the Works Council is the principal formal instrument, is still a matter of controversy and debate not because, as was once believed, that joint consultation would abrogate management's right to manage but mainly because it frequently began as a 'tea and bun' party and ended in council apparently locked in endless debates on such issues as 'canteens and latrines'. More briefly, councils were more likely to pass away quietly from sheer boredom rather than to expire from over-exertions arising from efforts diverted at formulating Company policy.

Theoretically it may be regarded as a formal arrangement whereby the management and representatives of the employees can exchange information and advice, and in Glacier under particular conditions and on certain topics, discussions can take place and policy decided. Two important advantages of joint consultation to management lie in the fact that it provides top management with the opportunity of meeting representatives of all levels of employees, including those who represent management, and secondly it enables employees to be represented whether they are members of a union or not.

Even a quick glance at the history of joint consultation gives no grounds for assuming that it is an institution with strong survival characteristics. During the First World War joint consultation was foisted on British industry virtually by *fiat*, only to suffer a massive contraction in the inter-war period.

There was great enthusiasm for joint consultation both during and immediately after the Second World War in Great Britain. But in many firms it was found to be an inadequate solution to the complex problems of industry, as W. H. Scott[136] observes in *Industrial Democracy*:

> It frequently failed either to evoke any noticeable response from employees in general or to lead to any concrete results in terms of productive efficiency.

Why do some firms take to joint consultation and others not? In Glacier's case, they went into joint consultation in late 1941 in the great furore of enthusiasm for better co-operation between management and labour generated by the anguish of war, sustained by the belief that democracy was fighting autocracy. 1941 was a significant year for British wartime industrial relations; after June 1941, when Russia was invaded, those workers who previously might have had some reservations about throwing themselves into a capitalist's war, began to play a more active and co-operative role. This was the time of the factory front and victory council. The enthusiasm for consultation survived the war, at least into the immediate post-war period, nourished by a Labour government. The great surge in Glacier consultation took place in the late 'forties. But why do some managing directors get enthusiastic about works councils and others not?

The answer in the case of Wilfred Brown must be related to his earlier belief in an industrial philosophy that favoured democracy. While this was probably true during and immediately after the war, the most important value of the Works Council (disregarding the considerations that the Council has a 'show piece' aspect), lies in the fact that it enables the management to gain sanction from the employees for certain policies. The management may then realistically assume that the employees have assumed certain contractual obligations, which have moral though not legal force.

A useful starting point for understanding the function of the Works Council at Kilmarnock is to be found in the apparently trivial change of name which the shop stewards required before this institution could be reintroduced at Kilmarnock after the 1957 strike. The term Works Committee is used in the formal agreement between the Engineering Employers' Federation and the trade unions.[45] In this document Works Committee refers to a meeting consisting or not more than seven representatives of the management and not more than seven shop stewards. Two comments are appropriate here. The 'seven a side set up' corresponds exactly with Glacier's arrangement; secondly the Kilmarnock stewards in opting for 'Works Committee' instead of 'Works Council' were rejecting Glacier dogma that this institution has a policy making function. This latter point warrants closer examination.

As has previously been mentioned it was assumed by Jaques that when the workers' representatives balked at the prospect of the Works Council in 1948 becoming the policy making organ of the Company, that the root cause of the difficulty lay with their fear of responsibility. Yet the passage of time and events have vindicated their reservation about the Works Council.

In Glacier top-policy making is the prerogative of the Board of Directors and Management. The directors authorize capital expenditure, decide dividends, appoint the Managing Director, decide directors' fees, confirm senior appointments and thus ensure the stable continuity of the Company in relation to technological development, marketing and so on. To say nothing of deciding who will 'take over' the Company and so on. In fact, as well as ensuring that the Company's legal obligations are appropriately discharged, the Board of Directors formulates the general policy of the enterprise. In *Exploration in Management* Brown virtually identifies policy with instructions and thus, rightly, highlights the fact that a major function of a manager is to make policy.

Glacier shop stewards, like their colleagues elsewhere, recognize that 'The employers have the right to manage their establishments and the Trade Unions have the right to their functions'. The workers recognize the right of management to manage, including the right to make policy.

What then is the function of the Works Committee? Excluding both the 'canteens and latrines' element which takes up a certain amount of time even in Glacier, and accepting that the Management Member's report on the Company's trading position arouses little interest, two functions remain: policy making and negotiating. The result of the former activity is enshrined in the Policy Document. Until December 1965, the J.S.S.C. at Kilmarnock did not accept this document, but only recognized its existence. In any case, when the crunch came in 1957 with a strike against the management's handling of a redundancy, the workers did not feel bound by a policy which to their mind loaded the situation against them.

Again, during the recent revision of the Policy Document, the management was much keener to initiate discussions than the stewards were to participate in them. Indeed on one occasion during the wage negotiation already described, when contact between the two sides had been broken, the stewards were 'too busy' to take part in any discussions regarding the Policy Document. On balance, the Policy Document confers more advantages on management than on the shop floor.

These advantages include the fact that it enables management to get sanction for their policies, while providing them with a formal means of communicating with the official representatives of the shop floor, and last but not least it gives a minor function to full-time union officials.

The Works Committee has as a major function the role of negotiation. In fact, judged by the amount of time taken, this would seem to be a minor activity, in the sense that the Works Committee usually merely formally ratifies wage agreements that have been made elsewhere (usually at a meeting between the General Manager and the Executive Seven of the J.S.S.C.).

Glacier is not a member of the Engineering Employers' Federation which in any case forbids its member firms from engaging in plant bargaining. The Engineering Employers' Federation[45] in their evidence to the Royal Commission on Trade Unions and Employers' Association point out that,

> The Industry entered into an agreement during the war years for the establishment on a voluntary basis in federated firms of joint production consultative and advisory committees.
>
> Many of these formal committees still continue but others have lapsed through lack of interest or meetings are held only very occasionally. It is to be noted that these J.P.C. & A.C.s are explicitly prohibited from discussing matters such as wages and like subjects which are covered by agreements with the unions or are normally dealt with by the agreed machinery of negotiation.

This separation of consultation from negotiation is held to be unnatural by many academics. In *Managers and Shop Stewards* (The Institute of Personnel Management, 1963) Arthur Marsh[101] has referred to:

> ... the fate which has befallen many sincere attempts of management to use works councils or joint consultative committees to create direct relationships between themselves and their workers, and to use these to deal with non-negotiable issues such as welfare, safety or production. At some point all these issues are likely to affect earnings or working conditions. At this point workers tend to see them not as matters of common interest for information and discussion, but as subjects about which they must negotiate.
>
> In all probability this explains why the number of joint consultative committees have declined in recent years, why others have become trivial in content or are only kept alive by strenuous efforts of managements, and why some have been frankly turned

into negotiating bodies. Once managements admit the need for collective relations, it appears to workers that it is unnatural to separate consultation from bargaining.

If it can be assumed that the Glacier Works Council does not have a top-legislative function, i.e. it does not produce top-policy, then the joint consultative arrangements in the Company can be said to work well and are useful to both management and labour.

Looking at the operations of the Kilmarnock Works Committee, certain observations may be made: excluding the 1957 strike and its sequel, consultation works in an efficient and fairly civilized way. Nevertheless the 'two sides' of industry have not been removed but formalized. The stewards regard it still as a 'them v. us' situation. As might be expected the General Management and the Chairman dominate the actual discussion.

The Works Committee mainly formalizes decisions that have been made elsewhere. It gives formal recognition to processes that are carried out in all industrial organizations. There is inevitable confusion between executive and representative roles. The General Manager, who is the management member and thus represents the Company, has still executive relationships with the other members of the Council. In particular, he has an immediate executive relationship with the Chairman (a unit manager) and the Grade I and Grade II staff members which, at least unconsciously, must affect their attitudes.

Some General Comments on Committee and Command Meetings

In Brown's eyes, the confusion between these two types of meetings is cultural in origin. According to Brown, in most people's minds the committee procedure is identified with democracy and thus good, while the command meeting's dependence on the manager-subordinate relationship is identified with authoritarianism and thus bad. As Brown[29] notes,

> Industrial Democracy is not another form of Political Democracy but is a completely different thing, whatever it may be. Personally I think that the use of the term 'Industrial Democracy' should be dropped because it can only lead to confusion. It implies that the mechanism of association in both Political and Industrial life are the same, and this is not so.

This rejection of 'Industrial Democracy' represents a virtual volte-face by Brown when it is contrasted with his efforts to set up the Works Council legislative functions. It seems a somewhat bizarre statement for a labour Lord who is a member of a Labour government and who is, or at least was, a member of a trade union (A.S.S.E.T.). This lack of faith in 'Industrial Democracy' by Brown is to be contrasted with Jaques' observation in *Changing Culture of a Factory* (p. 317) in referring to the ultimate basis of joint consultation that 'the beliefs that caused the most argument were those based on ultimate values associated with principles of democratic living'.

Rensis Likert[92] in his *New Patterns of Management* (p. 103) reinforces Jaques' thesis, when he notes that high producing managers use the principle of supportive relationship—i.e.:

The leadership . . . of the organisation must be such as to ensure a maximum probability that in all interactions and all relationships with the organisation each member will in the light of his background, values and, expectations, view the experience as supportive and one which builds and maintains his sense of personal worth and importance.

It is at least questionable whether it is possible to maintain this supportive climate in a command meeting. For a manager, the purpose of command meetings is to work out and set policy to issue orders and such meetings also provide an opportunity for the assessment of subordinates.

But not all meetings are simply concerned with issuing of instructions; information may have to be collected, opinions solicited, and policy argued through. For these purposes, the committee is excellent. Undoubtedly, many workers excel managers in committee work. This is presumably because of their experience in local Labour and trade union branches.

Many executives' first taste of committee work comes at an age when their rate of learning has slowed down. They feel ill at ease with the formal and legalistic aspects of meetings. The rules of debate, the order of voting on amendments, and procedure regarding points of order and frequently outside their experience. While all of this is extremely important in meetings of the Board of Directors, it is much more important to understand the dynamics of discussion leading.

The command meeting has the following characteristics. The purposes include: to collect from and to give information to subordinates, to test out the manager's ideas, to clear up misunderstandings, to state policy, to give instructions, and even on occasions 'to work out and set policy' (p. 136, *Exploration in Management*). The time, place and procedure are decided by the manager. Usually the meeting is between a manager and his subordinates—normally a manager and his immediate subordinates. According to Brown the decisions of the meetings are wholly the responsibility of the manager.

In the committee, on the other hand, responsibility is corporate. The members may elect a chairman. Decisions rest ultimately on a majority vote.

The advantages of the command meeting lie in the fact that its puts the onus of decision-making and responsibility inescapably on the shoulders of the manager calling the meeting. As might be expected in Glacier, having a detailed written statement of how these meetings should be conducted must help subordinates to pursue the purposes of these meetings more effectively. Again it has the effect of concentrating the minds of the members on the tasks to be achieved.

Three major criticisms of the Brown-Jaques concept of the command meeting may be made. These relate to their use of the terms authority and responsibility, their view of subordinates which implies that they are reluctant to accept responsibility and are not adaptable, their reluctance to recognize the relevance of the findings of group dynamics to meetings, their apparent unawareness of the danger that all meetings may be regarded by Glacier executives as command meetings and their use of the term 'requisite responsibility'.

Brown's difficulties over the command meeting have a fundamental source in the semantic quicksands he has created out of the concepts of authority and responsibility. Speaking of the top manager on page 49 of *Exploration in Management* Brown argues that:

His delegation of part of the work in no way affected his total responsibilities. He alone remained responsible to the Company of shareholders. He was, in fact, completely answerable for any failure in the part of his subordinates.

If the top manager is totally responsible, then nobody else in these organizations has any responsibility. In fact, what any manager is held *answerable* for is *managing*, i.e. for ordering and co-ordinating functions which he has delegated to his sub-ordinates. It follows from this definition that his subordinates share this responsibility or accountability. This means that accountability while distributed asymmetrically among the members of the organization according to their rank, is cor-porate. The committee presents an opportunity for this sharing of functions and the making aware, sometimes explicit some-times implicit, of the commitment to this corporate but asym-metrically distributed accountability.

T. T. Paterson[112] defines responsibility as a relation, as he notes in *A Methectic Theory of Social Organisation*:

> The relation of this kind, in which obligation is inherent and specific, is one of responsibility. The word 'responsibility' (or its associative 'responsible') in whatever context it is used, can be shown to imply a relation between two agents, one acting and the other judging action and imposing retribution for failure. It is misleading, though common, to say that A is responsible for another person X. He is responsible only for the ordering and co-ordinating of X's functions.

Brown uses responsibility when it would be better to use the word function. The concept of subordinates which Brown uses implies that they are unwilling to accept any share of the cor-porate accountability with their superior, and that they are unable to distinguish between the permissive relations of a committee and more structured relations of the shop floor. To my mind, both executives and workers are perfectly capable of recognizing this latter distribution and accept that the com-mittee relationship with its reduction of structure and approxi-mation to a peer relationship provides the social atmosphere necessary for the free expression of opinion that is a necessary prerequisite for commitment to take place. Commitment rep-resents the opportunity to formulate new contractual obligations regarding the achievement of further tasks where at least the subordinates' right to be heard has been permitted.

Brown's picture of the subordinate is remarkably reminiscent of the portrait represented by Douglas McGregor[97] in his Theory X. These assumptions include:

The average man is by nature indolent—he works as little as possible.

He lacks ambition, dislikes responsibility, prefers to be led.

He is inherently self-centred, indifferent to organizational needs.

He is by nature resistant to change.

He is gullible, not very bright, the ready dupe of the charlatan and the demagogue.

McGregor has challenged these underlying assumptions of the classical theory with his Theory Y.

Studies in group dynamics have proved particularly useful in improving the conduct of executive meetings. In spite of this, according to one personnel officer interviewed during this research, the Glacier Institute of Management plays down the importance of the subject of group dynamics in their courses. Brown[29] makes his own position clear on page 132 of the *Glacier Project Papers* when he states that:

> The tendency towards escaping the realities of manager-subordinate relationships by means of flights into 'committees' is reflected in much of current social science research on participation and group process in decision-making. It is held to be desirable for groups of subordinates to decide what has to be done, and to do what they decide, with or without informing their manager, who is accountable for the decision, however, and for the results, is never made quite clear.

This rejection of participation by Brown contrasts strangely with Jaques' attitude towards consultation.

Brown in *Exploration in Management* at least implies that most meetings between a manager and his subordinates are, in fact, command meetings. In my experience many Glacier executives are not clear on this point. To argue that a command meeting may be used 'to work out and set policy' makes such gatherings a good deal more important than information collecting (or distributing) or order-giving sessions.

Secondly, saying that 'it is a *requisite responsibility* of subordinates to state his view of the policies' recognizes that this expression of opinion is not only expected but cannot be commanded.

At this point, it may be worth mentioning that Brown makes no reference to any other work in this field. In particular, he assumes that these are only two types of meeting. Since there is no reference to other authorities it would seem reasonable to conclude that his thoughts on meetings are derived from his own personal experience. It is extremely difficult to conclude from the episodes of meetings presented in *Exploration in Management* what roles the anonymous managers hold who are the author's subordinates at these meetings. The point being made is that these subordinates are reported as making statements which imply that there is a considerable difference in rank between them and the author of *Exploration in Management*. This represents a criticism of Brown's method of reaching finality about the principles that should govern the conduct of meetings.

The language, which the Glacier executives use, has a positive ring about it. For example, an instruction frequently used is 'Structure me a meeting with the unit manager'. In this Company the committee has fallen victim to this change of culture.

As Albers[1] observes on page 158 of *Organised Executive Action*:

> Committees have fallen into disrepute. A survey of executive attitudes on the subject of committee organization might well lead to the frustrating conclusion that committees must be the worst and the best means to achieve a goal. One side of the argument is illustrated by such comments as: the best committee is a three-man committee with two men absent; minutes are taken, but hours are wasted.

In spite of such criticism, committees are found in many organizations and, when used properly, are important instruments of managerial action. Why are committees so heavily criticized? Presumably, in the process of sweeping away the permissive management of the 'forties the committee has fallen victim to the axe of positive, direct, task-oriented management. An over-simplification? Perhaps. But what guidance can be given to executives in the light of their critical examination by social psychologists? Perhaps, it would be best to start by stating the disadvantages of committees. Their shortcomings include a tendency to let the number of members in a committee increase without considering the effect on working efficiency. There may be some difficulty in limiting the time of the individual sessions. There tends to be a lack of balance between committee proceedings and other means of internal communication, such as reports and memoranda. From an executive point of view there is the growing difficulty of following up decisions taken at committee sessions, especially when these are attended by an increasing number of people and when the sessions increase both in frequency and duration. As is well within the experience of most practised managers there is a tendency to use committees of already overworked executives as a substitute for staff assistants, for the handling of matters which need the full time attention of a particular executive.

To overcome these disadvantages, three preliminary requirements for the successful operation of committees have been suggested: they must justify their costs; procedural difficulties should be minimized; and they should only be used on the subjects where the committee approach has proved its value.

PART V
CONCLUSIONS

Chapter 10

AN ASSESSMENT OF THE
GLACIER SYSTEM OF
MANAGEMENT

An adequate understanding of the Glacier system of management requires viewing it in broad perspective. Two facts
should especially be kept in mind. First, the Glacier Experiment
has been going since 1948. What is important to understand
here is that the theory and practice of administration which have
been labelled 'Glacier' are in a state of flux and still in the process of development. The validity of this argument may be
examined by contrasting the themes of *Changing Culture of a
Factory* and *Exploration in Management*. Seen in this light, changes
in Glacier philosophy may be viewed as a reflection of the
changes in the dynamics of society as a whole. Put another way,
the Glacier Project may be regarded as a well documented cap-
sule account of the contemporary history of organization theory,
which starts with the classical theory of organization, followed
by the human relations school and then the task approach.
The Glacier Experiment covers the last two phases.

Secondly, it is important to remember that the experiment
developed through the collaboration of Tavistock and Glacier.
A curious symbiotic relationship exists between these two institutions which has produced correlated theoretical changes in
both. Nevertheless, Glacier philosophy differs from Tavistock
thinking in one important respect. This difference has its origins
in Brown's reluctance to accept the relevance of findings of
group dynamics. It is impossible to reconcile his concept of the
task management with the basic assumption of the group
dynamicist that the group has two functions, which have been
designated task and human relations functions. The human function requires that the group does a certain amount of non-work.

From Brown's point of view, this type of group activity would appear to be largely a waste of time. But, in more general terms, no conclusions on causation need be reached on the similarities between the 'task' approach of Brown and the socio-technical systems of Trist and Emery. They are probably both products of the 'garrison state' society.

Again, it might be argued that the concept of socio-technical system and the task approach are only new names for what anthropologists have recognized for a long time, viz. that the form of technology available to a society is a major determinant of the social structure that it develops. Since the end of the Second World War, organization theorists and industrial sociologists have recognized the value of studying enterprises as systems. This return to formal organization as a focus for theorizing and empirical research has been demonstrated by industrial sociologists. Brown, in developing his theory of management, owes much to the social scientists at Tavistock. Nevertheless, it is a fascinating sociological exercise to trace out the forces that helped Glacier to make the switch from the soft human relations approach to the more positive and dynamic task management. With all the advantages of hindsight, it is perfectly possible to see in *Changing Culture of a Factory* the first signs of this mutation. Jaques' research, in the first instance, was mainly concerned with investigating joint consultation and making it more effective. But by the end of the book, he had turned his attention to role theory. Implicit in Jaques' approach to roles is the idea that role behaviour may be defined as the sets of behavioural acts and attitudes which is expected of everybody in a particular position, irrespective of who he is. Therefore, the behaviour and to a lesser extent the attitudes of the role holder are socially ordained and thus defining roles serve to delimit the types of idiosyncratic expressions possible in any given situation.

Formal organizations which may be thought of as giant molecules with roles for atoms have the effect of defining the individual member's function and of circumscribing his activities. Put more briefly, role theory ignores or at least plays down differences in personality. In *Measurement of Responsibility* Jaques[67] changed his relationship with the Company; instead of being an independent social science research worker, he was now employed directly by the Company, notwithstanding the fact that he reported to the Works Council. His interest now shifted to the problem of payment. To solve this problem, Jaques developed his theory of the time span of discretion. What is important in this concept is not that it places the measure of responsibility on a quantitative basis, in terms of time as Jaques claims, but rather that it focuses attention on the location of review mechanisms. The identification and specification of review mechanisms is exactly the semantic stuff out of which effective task oriented management develops. This approach may have been obvious before, in relationship to production roles, but applied to specialist roles it provided a breakthrough.

In Glacier, the coupling of the time span of direction concept and role theory proved a very useful marriage. In the writing of role descriptions, the concepts of prescribed and discretionary work proved very useful as a means of specifying and delimiting the functions and operations of an executive. Here, I think, Glacier has made an important and useful contribution to management practice which many other companies would do well to emulate. Nevertheless, a major criticism of these job descriptions as they work out in practice lies in their failure to acknowledge the weakness of the trait approach to leadership. Two good examples of this criticism are provided by examining the job descriptions of the posts of section manager and supervisor which contain a surfeit of leadership terms for which behavioural correlates are lacking, as demonstrated by empirical examination of these roles.

It is possible to argue that the Company's progress to task management was accelerated by a series of bad returns in terms of profitability in the mid-'fifties. Some of the external causes of these lean years can be seen in the change from a sellers' to a buyers' market, the notorious 'stop-go' economy of Britain, and the fact that Glacier was a supplier of components to the notoriously unstable motor-car industry. But, there were also internal problems. There was the problem of patents. There was a lot of technological development work to do. When the Company's profitability began to falter, they brought in the 'Company doctors', the industrial consultants.

The full implication of this latter development only becomes obvious when the philosophy of administration held by management consultants is considered. Like their first patron saint,

Frederick Winslow Taylor, they accepted at that time the classical theory of organization, i.e. their approach is based on a combination of accounting and engineering model. Mason Haire's[55] comments on classical theory are revealing: 'It breaks the total job down "rationally" and assigns the parts neatly to a group of boxes spread about a family tree. It uses a balanced system of authority and responsibility. In principle, a certain amount of authority is pumped into each one of the boxes, and along with this goes a responsibility to pump out a certain kind of productivity. This kind of double-entry system of input and output seems to be one of the first essentials.'

This was essentially the approach taken by the consultants assisting Glacier. Their contributions were made in three main areas: work study, budgetary control, and programming. Two important consequences emerged from their efforts, one personal and the other theoretical. Taking the former first, a consultant was appointed General Manager of the Kilmarnock factory, which previously had a notorious reputation, both for low profitability and for turnover in General Managers. Aided by fellow consultants, but above all by his own extensive experience of rescuing sick companies, he put the factory on its feet. Indeed, so successful was he in putting the Kilmarnock factory on a sound financial footing that he was soon afterwards appointed Managing Director of the Company. In the factory, he was extensively admired, both by management and the men, especially for his success in saving the factory and also for his fairness. It was widely held that he was a non-believer of the Glacier Cult. Being of an empirical, it somewhat robust, temperament, he felt free when the occasion warranted it to ignore 'the book' if he felt the Company Policy Document was not appropriate. Recently he left the Company to set up his own consultancy business. But even yet the Company is one of his clients.

Glacier theorists have left themselves open to the criticism that they have created an organizational structure where the tasks have been defined and organized with insufficient reference to the people fulfilling them.

Turning to the theoretical consequence of introducing this dose of classical organization theory (in terms of the evolution of management theory – represented a regression), it is my contention that the empirical verification of the pay-offs inherent in this classical injection with its emphasis on the measurement of performance and profitability, must have figured largely in Glacier thinking and must have given Glacier theorists much stimulation as to how to integrate the classical theory with the human relations approach. The result was the task approach to management. All these organizational changes did not take place in a theoretical vacuum. The climate of social science research of the 'sixties has been changing to a position which is generally supportive of task-oriented reality-centred approach to leadership.

Other factors that may have played some part in shaping Glacier's philosophy of task management include the shift from a sellers' to a buyers' market, which must have had the effect of focusing top management's gaze on external markets rather than on the internal problems of production. Secondly, this need to look outwards and adopt a more market oriented approach has been reinforced by the necessity of expansion which has required going to the money market to attract investment. This, in turn, would inevitably reinforce the need to present a more conventional front. Penultimately, management theory and practice have developed considerably of late. Without such a development it is doubtful whether the task approach would be possible.

Finally, the mores of Western society have been moving away from the permissive democratic tradition where the emphasis has been on human relations towards a more positive approach to organizational leadership. This value adaptation is widely regarded as a consequence of living in a 'garrison state' or a society which is under threat. In the process of developing the task approach to management Glacier, in my opinion, has developed a pattern of organization similar to a bureaucracy.

GLACIER AS A BUREAUCRACY

Bureaucracy, the model of formal organization most widely known by organization theorists, was postulated by Max Weber, the German sociologist. While much of his research was historical, his work has made a tremendous impact on the thinking of modern sociologists concerned with organization theory; he is regarded as one of the pioneers in the development of the scientific theory of organization. While his style of writing is often ponderously legalistic, the material which he describes, on the other hand, provides a brilliant description of the institutions of bureaucracy. The term bureaucracy as used by Weber is not intended to have any derogatory connotations. In this context, it is used as a technical term which refers to an 'ideal type' of organization. Because the term bureaucracy is very often assumed to be synonymous with a slavish obsession with standard and uniform procedures which impede progress, with a preoccupation with means rather than with ends, it is often wrongly assumed that bureaucracy represents an undesirable form of organization. Bureaucracy implies a task approach and is classical.

Weber was fascinated with the function and exercise of authority in society. His researches led him to the conclusion that in this context there were three major centres of interest:

(i) the law and traditional taboos of the society
(ii) the charisma, which referred to individual leadership and which he considered to be largely emotional
(iii) the bureaucracy, which referred to the mass of administrators who carried out the laws and policies of the government.

In terms of Weber's classification it is interesting to note that power centres (ii) and (iii) are in opposition, as one symbolizes irrationality and the other rationality. An excellent example of the charismatic leader is Adolf Hitler, who because of his immense personal magnetism, could dominate the decision-making process, irrespective of the situation. In a bureaucracy, authority is not exercised through charismatic leaders.

As Max Weber[50] observes in *Characteristics of a Bureaucracy*, the ideal type of organization, i.e. a bureaucracy, has the following characteristics:

1. an emphasis on form
2. the concept of hierarchy which specifies that each lower office falls under the control of a higher one
3. specialisation of task which requires that role holders are selected

on the basis of merit and ability to perform specified functions of the total task

4. specified areas of competence; this requires that relationships between the various specialisations should be clearly defined and observed in practice

5. established norms of conduct which ensure that the behaviour of organisational role holders would contain minimal elements that were unpredictable.

The indoctrination of the bureaucrats with these policies would ensure that the organization operated effectively and that policies were implemented. In Weber's bureaucracy, all administrative behaviour including discussion and rules would be set down on paper, thereby ensuring that precedents were created which would ensure predictability of performance within the organization.

Weber regarded bureaucracy as a universal phenomenon which could be applied to both the public and private sectors of organization. He argued in favour of a separation of policy and administration in which the idea of a professional executive is emphasized. While there have been numerous criticisms of Weber's bureaucracy in recent years, many social scientists have been reassessing his concepts as a possible basis for developing a theory of organization. Much of the criticism levelled against Weber has stressed that he used the autocratic Prussian form of bureaucracy as a standard by which the world organizations should be judged. Nevertheless, his ideas have had a profound impact on social scientists working on organization theory.

The Characteristics of Glacier Bureaucracy

This contention, that Glacier has developed a bureaucracy, warrants further examination. Consider first the emphasis on form. As Max Weber[50] notes in his *Characteristics of a Bureaucracy*, modern officialdom functions in the following specific manner:

(1) 'The regular activities required for the purposes of the bureaucratically governed structure are distributed in a fixed way as official duties.' In Glacier, great emphasis is placed on the definition of duties which is achieved by giving very careful attention to role descriptions.

(2) 'The authority to give the commands required for the discharge of these duties is distributed in a stable way and is

strictly delimited by rules concerning the coercive means, physical, sacerdotal, or otherwise, which may be placed at the disposal of officials.' The ultimate source of authority in Glacier is the Policy Document, which specifies the part to be played by the Executive System in running the Company.

(3) 'Methodical provision is made for the regular and continuous fulfilment of these duties and for the execution of the corresponding rights; only persons who have the generally regulated qualifications to serve are employed.' Not only in the main administrative office, but in every unit of the Glacier factories, there are to be found organisation charts which spell out and delimit the official 'jurisdictional areas' of the role holder in that particular unit. The authority of incumbents is very carefully defined indeed and while many Glacier executives have reservations on this point, the Company is widely regarded as a meritocracy.

Again Weber[50] argues—'The principles of office hierarchy and of graded authority mean a firmly ordered system of super and subordination in which there is a supervision of the lower offices by the higher ones'. Great emphasis in Glacier, as far as this is possible, is placed on ensuring that each subordinate has only one executive superior whom he knows. Weber goes on to say that such 'a system offers the governed the possibility of appealing the decision of a lower office to its higher authority, in a definitely regulated manner'. This is precisely what Glacier's Appeals System does. When the Appeals System was introduced, it was regarded as a separate system which would ensure that the quality of justice applied to the super-subordinate relations. Now the Appeals System is regarded as part of the Executive System; an appeal is now regarded by personnel officers as a second review. The Appeals System, as an instrument of justice, was conceived in the era of human relations and developed in the period of task approach into a second review as part of the Executive System.

Weber[50] also argues that the management of the modern office is based upon written documents 'which are preserved in their original or draft form'. In Glacier these files refer to the Policy Document, the minutes of the Works Council, standing orders and memoranda.

Weber argues that the bureaucrats should be chosen on the basis of merit and ability. The Glacier Company Policy Document is quite clear in its guidance in this matter. In Glacier, it is also assumed that relationships should be clearly defined and that vagueness and sloppiness in these matters inhibit efficient management. For a start operational management roles have been clearly differentiated from specialist roles. The Glacier senior manager can be under no illusion that he carries final authority for the work of his subordinates. In spite of the logical difficulties of this approach which leaves all the authority in the hands of the top manager, it at least has the utilitarian value of making managers extremely aware of their authority and account-ability for decisions within his specified area of jurisdiction.

The norms of conduct in Glacier are established at Company level, by the Company Policy Document, at the factory level by the Works Council minutes and at a managerial level by the manager's behaviour. On this latter point, Brown in *Exploration in Management* notes that 'a manager's behaviour is an implicit means of setting policies for the subordinates; but this sometimes results in a manager unintentionally setting policies with which he himself is not in agreement'. Again, 'Every act of a manager no matter how trivial contains its content of instructions for his subordinates' (p. 92).

Early in *Exploration in Management* Brown begins his analysis of organization by defining the relation of organization to work in the following manner: 'Effective organisation is a function of the work to be done and the resources and techniques available to do it. Failure to make explicit acknowledgment of this relationship between work and organisation gives rise to non-valid assumptions, e.g. that optimum organisation is a function of the personalities involved, that it is a matter connected with the personal style and arbitrary decision of the chief executive'. In essence what Brown is saying is that optimal organization is a function of the task which in turn is dependent on the resources available to achieve that task, viz. personnel, technological and economic resources. It also tells us that optimal organization is *not* a function of personality. This proposition warrants closer examination and analysis.

Nowhere does Brown prove this assertion. It is widely accepted by anthropologists that the technology (the type of tools or methods of work available to a people) is a major factor deter-mining the structure and beliefs of the society. Joan Woodward[157] in 'Management and Technology' has shown from her work in South Essex that technology and industrial behaviour (at both management and operator level) are closely related. She has demonstrated that the most difficult problems both in organization and industrial relations arise in batch production and assembly line production. Burns and Stalker[31] in *The Management of Innovation* have related the factor of technological innovation to their dichotomy of organization; organic and mechanistic. Thus it may be accepted that there is a relationship between organization and technology. But nowhere is there any proof that optimal organization is not also related to personality. Indeed it might be suspected from commonsense that the personality of the boss would be a major factor affecting the productivity of the work group.

W. W. Daniel[38] in 'How Close Should a Manager Be?' has suggested from 'a study now being carried out at Ashorne Hill that in departments where the managers were the most psychologically distant in Fiedler's sense, being very much task leaders, the assistant managers had to spend a very large proportion of their time and activity running round smoothing people down. Thus the personality and activities of the formally designated head of the hierarchy will be only one, though a very important one, of the factors in the performance of the group.'

Optimal organization is difficult to define. 'Optimal' implies the best—the most for the least. These criteria require to be defined. Best for *whom* requires to be specified. To be meaningful, Brown's use of 'optimal' requires amplification and explanation. If the word 'optimal' is struck out, the first part of his statement is valid, i.e. organization is a function of the task and available resources. The corollary that optimal organization is *not* a function of personality is not supported in any way by Brown.

It is also possible to take the view that the method of research used by Jaques which disregards personal factors, partly to protect the identity of the client but mainly to concentrate on the formal nature of the role, has the inevitable consequence of loading the results and conclusions of his research in the direction of proving that personal factors play only a minimal part in industrial behaviour. Put more shortly, if the research method discounts personality, then it can come as no surprise that the research concluded that personality is not a factor in optimal organization.

Therefore, Brown's central concept stands *not proven*. Thus it must be regarded as an act of faith on his part. Presumably this is the reason Trist (in his foreword to *Exploration in Management*) described this concept as Brown's credo.

Empirical evidence supportive of Brown's thesis that personal factors only play a minimal part in the behaviour of the section managers is provided by the studies of section managers and supervisors. From this behavioural data, it is perfectly clear that managers, who have been assigned approximately the same task, with approximately the same resources, distributed their time in more or less the same fashion irrespective of whether the distribution is by location, function, or according to person. Much of this is reminiscent of Merton's[105] description of bureaucracy, which he defines as 'A formal, rationally organised social structure involving clearly defined patterns of activity in which ideally, every series of actions is functionally related to the purposes of the organisation. In such an organisation there is integrated a series of offices, of hierarchical statuses in which inhere a number of obligations and privileges closely defined by limited and specific rules. Each of these contains an area of imputed competence and responsibility. Authority, the power of control which derives from an acknowledged status, inheres in the office and not in the particular person who performs the official role. . . . The system of prescribed relations between the various offices involves a considerable degree of formality (which) is manifested by a more or less complicated social ritual . . . Ready calculability of others' behaviour and a stable set of mutual expectations is thus built up.' Especially appropriate is Merton's last comment where he refers to the 'ready calculability of others' behaviour and a stable set of mutual expectations is thus built up'.

In Weber's bureaucracy, administration is depersonalized. Weber[50] argues that 'the "objective" discharge of business primarily means a discharge of business according to calculable rules "without regard for persons"'. It is clear from the empirical evidence produced by the activity sampling of the section managers' behaviour that the proportion of time devoted to personnel work is on the small side. In fact, the data shows that he spends only half the time on personnel work that efficient foremen in other studies give to this activity. This lack of concern for the personnel function illustrates how highly task oriented the section manager is. For that matter, when the personnel work of the section manager was analysed further, it was found that a very large proportion of this personnel work was task oriented and a relatively small proportion was concerned with the human relations aspects.

A CRITIQUE OF GLACIER BUREAUCRACY

Social scientists are coming to realize the technical superiority of bureaucratic organizations over any other form of organization. As Weber notes, 'The mature bureaucracy compares with other forms exactly as does the machine with the nonmechanical modes of production. Precision, speed, unambiguity, knowledge of the files, continuity, discretion, unity, strict subordination, reduction of friction and of material and personal costs—these are raised to the optimum point in the strictly bureaucratic administration, and especially in its monocratic form'. Indeed modern sociologists, while aware of the disabilities of bureaucracy, have not been slow to recognize its advantages.

Obviously only a very large complex technological enterprise, which can afford to employ the large numbers of technologists, scientists and social scientists required (that is a monopoly or, perhaps, part of an oligopoly, which in turn finds itself part of a complex technological society) could have the necessary intellectual, social and physical resources to do the necessary theoretical work that the operation of a bureaucracy requires. It is precisely in these areas that Glacier finds itself at a considerable disadvantage. With a relatively small labour force (approximately 5,000), with a record of varying profitability, involved in the stop-go of the British economy and, at that, in its most sensitive spot the motor-car industry, Glacier would seem in a relatively weak position to develop the necessary theoretical constructs of a bureaucracy.

Again the question arises as to what extent is it possible for the mores of the factory to differ from the mores of society? Undoubtedly employees of an enterprise come to it with attitudes already monitored by the beliefs of the society in which the organization operates. In fact, H. A. Simon[138] has argued that 'Organisation theory has been largely culture-bound through failure to attack this problem. The theory of bureaucracy as developed by Max Weber and his followers represents the furthest progress in dealing with it. The historical data appealed to by the Weberians needs supplementation by analysis of contemporary societies, advanced and primitive. A comparison of intracultural uniformity and variation would provide the evidence we need to determine to what extent the co-operative patterns in organizations are independent of the mores of co-operation of the society.'

GLACIER PERSONNEL AND INDUSTRIAL RELATIONS

A bureaucracy, at least as theoretically defined, if not in practice, is inevitably a meritocracy, that is to say appointments will be made on the basis of merit and not on nepotism. On this count Glacier, possibly like many other companies, leaves itself open to the charge of inefficiency. It is only recently that psychological tests have been widely used at Kilmarnock as a means of improving the selection of the operators. Again, much of the internal selection is certainly not free from criticism. This is particularly seen in the selection of section managers. The Company Policy has been to recruit in the main from 'butchers, bakers and candlestick makers' for the machine operative grades. The better ones among these, after a suitable time, float to the surface first as supervisors then as section managers. Some of these may in fact even end up, if only for a short time, as unit managers. This failure to recruit and select suitable people for training as section managers and unit managers has had serious repercussions throughout the Company.

In referring to training, Weber[50] notes that 'Office holding is a "vocation". This is shown, first in the requirement of a firmly prescribed course of training, which demands the entire capacity for work for a long period of time and in the generally prescribed and special examinations which are prerequisites of employment.' On this question of training, the Company has been slow to recognize both the necessity and possibilities inherent in training. While the Glacier Institute of Management may do something to alter this picture in the long run, the failure to train section managers and supervisors in significant numbers in the past has caused many difficulties. Tied to this question of training is the problem of 'tenure for life'.

Weber points out when he is describing the position of the official that normally the position is held for life (as is the case in Japan). This is the case in the public bureaucracy and is increasingly the case in the private sector of the economy, and is frequently regarded as a *sine qua non* for persons employed by modern business enterprises. This is certainly not the case in Glacier. Indeed, this is one of its worst features. Redundancies, perhaps, are an inevitable consequence of car industry economics and the fluctuations of the British economy. When a redundancy is in the offing, a feeling of tension and insecurity passes through the organization. Even a relatively unimportant post, such as a storeman, will attract a fairly large number of applications from those who realize that the chances of a storeman being declared redundant are relatively slight. This fear of redundancy is not confined to the shop floor. On at least one occasion the Company has been known to sack managers and clerical workers. One such managerial and clerical redundancy had such traumatic effects on the organization that it came to be known as 'Black Friday'. This dread of redundancy is aided and abetted by the many promotions that are followed by demotions. All this reduces the chances of establishing a stable bureaucratic organization.

It is useful to re-examine the strikes in the light of Glacier as a bureaucracy. The 1957 strike throws some light on the peculiar nature of Glacier bureaucratic mentality; in fact the analysis of this strike reveals the obsessional belief of top Glacier executives that the form of a situation is more important than its content, which is some ways is the quintessence of bureaucracy. Prior to the strike, a considerable measure of anxiety and indeed tension was brought on by operating a shorter working week. When the strike did break, the Managing Director went around holding up his hands in horror, claiming that the workers had failed to honour the Works Council agreement on redundancies, which was a very complex one. In times of crises very simple statements are to be preferred, as Churchill well knew. When the workers went back, it was on the basis of 'last in, first out'. Here, the failure was to recognize the law of the situation rather than the ponderous legalistic jargon of the redundancy standing order.

If the 1957 strike had only certain bureaucratic overtones, then certainly the 1962 strike arose as a reaction to bureaucracy. In that strike the whole shop floor of the engineering industry, which includes Glacier, was engaged in a series of one day 'political' strikes against the government's pay pause. Because of Glacier's own obsession with its own concepts, the second one day strike was exacerbated into a longer strike. This, as already described, arose in the following manner. The Company argued that a manager is a person who has more work than he can do himself, therefore he is given people to help him; these are his subordinates. When his subordinates are unable or unwilling to work, the manager reverts to his first role and carries on with 'their' work. In spite of warnings from local trade union officials, and in spite of the fact that the mores of our industrial society regards with disfavour managers operating machines, the Company issued an order for the managers to work the machines. The strike followed immediately.

In the Kilmarnock plant even today, many executives find it difficult to discuss in a rational manner this issue of managers operating machines. Certainly, many of the more senior members of management regard it as a loyalty test and conform to the Company's official attitude which seems to spring ultimately from a quasi-legal belief that the managers own the machines. In interviews, it is not uncommon for managers to justify their behaviour by saying, 'After all, I was only operating *my* machines'.

There are many criticisms that can be levelled at Weber's concept of a bureaucracy, especially his belief that the modern bureaucracy is the most rational means of achieving certain ends. Nevertheless, many enterprises have been created in approximate accord with Weberian notions. But these same organizations, or rather the people in them, have on many occasions behaved in an apparently irrational manner and social scientists have a great interest in discovering what the unanticipated consequences of bureaucracy are. In general terms, these studies have shown that Weber's unidimensional view of administration has all the limitations that flow from a failure to view a social institution holistically. In *Administrative Organisation*, Pfiffner and Sherwood[118] have noted that bureaucracy may ensure 'that many of the organisation's prescribed goals have been accomplished, but in the process other events have also occurred. In many instances these unanticipated consequences have appeared to be antipathetic to the prescribed goals of the organisation. Thus the sociologists have suggested a fundamental problem; the attempt to pursue one goal rationally may result in irrational behaviour patterns relevant to the accomplishment of other organisation goals. Furthermore, there is evidence that the natural bureaucratic response, on the part of leaders and participants, is to tighten controls and become even more rigid in adherence to prescribed patterns of behaviour as threats occur.'

The more one studies Glacier in action, the more one realizes the importance of charismatic leadership, the inevitable antibody of bureaucracy. Glacier has had and still has its great men. Wilfred Brown has undoubtedly made a tremendous personal contribution to the organization and operation of the Company. In the United States he is regarded as the English counterpart of Chester Barnard. In the same view, *Exploration in Management* is compared with *The Function of the Executive*.[10] Wilfred Brown is widely regarded as an extremely intelligent and sensitive man of tremendous personal strength, who has made a unique and useful contribution to organization theory. Indeed, all social scientists must be indebted to his courage and good sense which made the Glacier experiment possible. Nevertheless, much of his behaviour, many of his decisions and much of his dogma have a certain charismatic quality that cannot easily be accommodated into any bureaucratic structure.

Secondly, it is doubtful whether the concepts of bureaucracy can be fully applied to a management-labour situation. Indeed, reference to Weber's bureaucracy shows that the 'designation of official by means of an election among the governed modifies the strictness of hierarchical subordination. In principle, an official who is so elected has an autonomous position opposite the subordinate official. The elected official does not derive his position "from above" but "from below" or at least not from a superior authority of the official hierarchy but from powerful party men ("bosses"), who also determine his further career.' Indeed, in some circumstances, it would seem better to regard a factory as composed of two segments of a bureaucracy which are more or less in contact.

A substantial segment of the early literature of organization was devoted to the reaction of the individual to the dynamic forces acting on him in the organizational context. Much of this thinking is a reflection of the human relations school. H. A. Simon,[138] referring to the rational and non-rational aspects of organizational behaviour, has observed that 'Organisations are the least "natural", most rationally contrived units of human association. But paradoxically, the theory of an organisation, whose members are "perfectly rational" human beings (capable of unlimited adaption) is very nearly a perfectly vacuous theory.' Incidentally, it is a curiosity of management theory that it swings like a pendulum from one extreme to another. Since the 'twenties sociologists have been preoccupied with the informal aspects of organization, possibly because of the ease with which they could be investigated. In the last decade, this has led to a neglect of the concept of legitimacy which must be regarded as a philosophical rather than a legal concept. Ironically, this research in Glacier organization has spot-lighted the reaction from an excessive emphasis on human relations to an obsessive preoccupation with formal organization theory.

GLACIER COMMUNICATIONS

This has not been without its effects on informal organizations, considering first the horizontal dimension of communication which provides a neat illustration of the workings of the informal apparatus; it is a truism today that effective communication is vital to the proper functioning of organizations. Communication refers to the systematic use of symbols. Speaking in very broad terms, communications may pass vertically or horizontally. Likewise it is obvious that information is a principal basis for decision. In general, in a bureaucracy, the object is to structure communication flow. Three reasons exist for this structuring: first, it ensures obedience to hierarchical authority; secondly, the aims of the organization have a better chance of being achieved if certain communications are kept secret; thirdly, structured communications produce more effective results than those that are unstructured, provided the main problem of the organization is co-ordination rather than innovation.

In Glacier it is not uncommon to hear executives express a preference for an exclusively vertical form of communication. This impossible ideal is presumably a reflection of their insecurities and a desire to be able to predict the behaviour of their subordinates with complete accuracy. These same executives seem to believe that the existence of the horizontal dimension in communication is a sign of weakness or even a mark of failure. Nevertheless, this present research has produced ample empirical evidence that a substantial proportion of executive communication is horizontal. The need for horizontal communication arises from an inevitable inability of superordinates to make policy sufficiently comprehensive and explicit to cover all contingencies.

Again, supposing it was possible that vertical communication could be made the sole means of transmitting information, which would be inefficient anyway, would it be desirable from the human point of view? It is worth remembering that in terms of human satisfaction that contacts between organizational peers are almost as satisfactory as contacts with superiors. Thus, while communicating with one's superior is likely to be governed from above, in establishing contact with peers one retains a fair measure of initiative. In other words, the horizontal flow of communication meets not only task needs but human needs. In essence horizontal communication, which Glacier executives would seek to minimize, is an inevitable consequence of the failure to make instructions explicit, reinforced by the need of the informal apparatus to have some means of communication.

Another technique of communication, that is finding increasing favour with management, is the 'contraction of executive lines' (a euphemism for by-passing subordinates). This most frequently arises when a negotiation with the workers has run into an insuperable blockage; the manager, usually the General Manager, informs the representatives that he is going to address all the workers. In 'Glacier Speak' the representatives remove their representatives' bowlers and don their workers' bowlers.

Incidentally, the address may be made by Tannoy; sometimes the workers walk out.

In terms of industrial relations, the Company's task approach is revealed in the technique of industrial brinkmanship. This robust approach has produced two important strikes and a number of small strikes in the last ten years. There seems to be an acceptance of the principle 'that casualties are inevitable and must be accepted'.

Glacier Speak

It is only in elementary theoretical textbooks that the determination of the means *follows* the definition of the aim. As in decision theory, the means available affect the selection of the aim. Thus, the methods of operation used by an enterprise are of fundamental importance. The task attitudes of Glacier can be regarded as an inevitable consequence of the Company's official language, policy, organizational structure, communications employed and the type of personnel employed. Each of these warrant closer examination.

The study of the argot of organization which is always very revealing of its sub-culture is of critical significance in the sense that the nature of the language influences the thinking of those who use it. It is obvious that great advantages flow from a standard, uniform, clearly defined nomenclature, especially where the definitions have been carefully thought out. In 'Negotiation between Managers and Representatives', Wilfred Brown notes 'The main contention of this essay is that the vocabulary and the concepts which we use in thinking or talking about industrial organization are often inconsistent with the data available to us, with the consequence that much of our thinking as managers is not as constructive as it could be. This is evidenced by the lack of a language about organisation which has been defined in boundary terms. By boundary terms I mean in a manner which enables any reasonable person to ascertain what falls within or without the ambit of the meaning of the word. Lack of such a vocabulary leaves us unable to define even our problems with clarity, with the result that when we discuss them with others our conversation often turns into a semantic confusion. It is noteworthy, for instance, that neither the British

Institute of Management nor the American Management Association has yet defined the meaning that they attach to the word "manager".'

But if the sources are restricted and the degree of reality testing limited (i.e. verification of the concepts that the words denote), then there is always the danger that the language will become obsolete and that it will eventually regress into the argot of an esoteric cult. Glacier officialese includes: 'conjoint relationship, contraction of executive lines, timespan of discretion, the manager once removed, looped instructions, collateral relationship and adaptive segregation'. Inevitably, these words come to be used as a sort of O.K. prayers.

Many of these terms are commonly used in the factory by Glacier executives. A kind of 'Glacier Speak' has been evolved. Examples of this argot include:

'Structure me a meeting.'

'What are your terms of reference?'

'Who is your immediate superior?'

'I am executively responsible to the Unit Manager and technically responsible to the Personnel Manager' (a Unit Personnel Officer).

'There is an nth option. You can leave the company.'

'Where is your nearest cross over point?'

Wilfred Brown seems to be preoccupied with questions of language. In the 'Glacier Project Papers' dealing with validation, he refers to the 'travel test'. 'If a number of people who are acquainted with a specific concept find that it helps rapid and constructive intercommunication, they will feel that it is useful and continue to use it. In our Company, where we have done a great deal of work in defining organizational entities, I have noticed that these concepts which have later stood the test of usage were usually picked up very quickly by anybody who heard them and spread very rapidly into general use, whereas those that later proved to require amendment did not "travel" in this manner.' Language of this type tends to formalize relationship in a brittle way that some persons find offensive. It would appear, going on impressions, that the word most frequently used in the Company is 'subordinate'.

Indeed, one would suspect that in the Glacier System they set out to achieve the bureaucrats' dream by formalizing the informal structure through the setting up of the Works Councils, which is the basis of the legislative system as a manifestation of bureaucracy. A substantial part of *Changing Culture of a Factory* is devoted to explaining the resistance of the workers to being involved in the Works Council as legislators. The overriding impression left by Jaques' study is that the workers' representatives are reluctant to be involved in the constructive side of making policy. This may not be the case. It could be argued that the workers' reservations about assuming legislative functions flow from their realization that the workers, *per se*, are lacking the necessary sapiential authority, without which it is impossible for the workers' representatives to engage in policy making.

If an examination is made of the minutes of the Works Council, then many instances will be found that illustrate the workers' lack of enthusiasm for the system. Indeed, in the Kilmarnock factory after the 1957 strike, the Works Council disintegrated. When it was resurrected, the stewards insisted on it being called the Works Committee. Another striking illustration of the workers' resentment of the Glacier System was provided by a recent discussion which was concerned with the revision of the Company Policy Document. In this discussion 'The Joint Shop Stewards Committee intimated that they were not prepared to accept the revised document provisionally under any circumstances, and reiterated what had been their argument before–that this was not a project to be entered into hastily, and they also expressed the view that they believed it would be easier to change the document before it had been provisionally accepted than it would be after this had been given. They also again put forward the point that they had never, in fact, accepted the existing Policy Document; the hourly rated members only acknowledge its existence but do not acknowledge acceptance of it. Although it was pointed out to J.S.S.C., that they made use of it for hourly rated members' benefit.'*

In the workers' minds, it is the management's job to manage. If managing involves making policy, which affects the workers, then the workers should be consulted. The workers' advice *ought* to be incorporated in the new policy, but the important point is that while the workers are being consulted and the management advised, the responsibility for policy at the end of the day is

---

* Minutes of 57th meeting of No. 3 factory Works Committee, held 14 May 1964.

management's. This re-establishment of the Works Council as the Works Committee was only possible when the Company had agreed 'that the scope of discussions "shall cover any subject of general concern. Any constituent body has the right to refuse to discuss any subject which they regard as falling within the prerogative of the trade unions".' Put another way this, in effect, meant that a trade union can raise directly with the Company a matter which it considers to be the union's prerogative. 'Previously, the Company had insisted that all matters were governed by its councils and that a trade union, as an outside body, had no part to play.' Thus it might be said that the Company Policy in setting up the Works Councils, as part of its legislative system, ran contrary to the values that govern British industrial relations. In Scotland most local trade union leaders' support for Works Councils has been tepid. Indeed, it is more tolerated than approved.

On the point of manager membership of unions, one of the curious facts that emerged from this research was that 85 per cent of the section managers were members of A.S.S.E.T. Out of a survey conducted in twenty firms in the area only one other firm has a higher proportion of its managers of equivalent status in A.S.S.E.T. This was also a firm renowned for its task efficiency.

In British society, where pluralism is possible, bureaucracies breed other bureaucracies. That is to say, because of the bureaucratic implications of the Glacier System and in particular because of the injunction that managers must set machines when the workers are on strike, managers felt compelled to join a union bureaucracy which in turn demanded that managers should not set machines when operatives were on strike. It is an interesting commentary, on the human condition, that once managers had satisfied this latter condition, they were regarded as being free from the first injunction. Again, it will be recalled that during the 1957 strike the senior managers formed a union and sought registration with the Company as an official union.

The Human Backlash to Task Management

Different personalities have reacted in different ways to the task approach. Some of these variations are of particular interest. A favourite defence mechanism is the technique of enveloping the situation with 'Glacier Speak'. Discussion with such executives produces a surfeit of jargon. This defence is often associated with over-identification with the Company. Another linguistic defence mechanism is the over-formalization of problems. A personnel officer who complained of nepotism in the method of making appointments was told to submit a memorandum on this topic or else forget it.

One strong 'personality's' reaction to stress was depersonalization. The General Manager kept needling him with comments such as:

'What is your scrap figure?'
'You say about 5 per cent. What do you mean "about"?'
'I want a scrap report within a week.'

After the report—

'Your scrap figure must be reduced to 4 per cent.'

After the reduction—

'How long can you keep this up?' etc.

Given this treatment, the victim manager said, 'I try to imagine that it's happening to somebody else.'

The manager, who was being processed, was advised to appeal; he replied, 'No, it would be like playing Russian Roulette. You can lose but you can't win.' Another manager, handed the same treatment, left the Company for a post at half the salary he had with Glacier.

One operator interviewed showed even a stronger reaction. His alleged reaction to bureaucratic strain was to engage in sabotage by spoiling work, by putting the locating nick in the wrong place on the bearing.

Fatigue was frequently reported in these interviews. One unit manager who subsequently left Glacier said, 'I feel so shagged out at the end of a week's work here, that I just lie around the house at the weekend.' A shop steward, when asked about political work outside the plant, replied, 'When I get home at night, my wife sometimes says, "What happened to you?" I just feel all clapped out.' In some cases the strain gets to great, that the manager concerned has a nervous breakdown.

There seems to be a 'Glacier Executive' who can survive in

this task context. The impression one forms is of a personality with the following characteristics:

* He has an extroverted persona; the sort of person who describes sincere personalities as over-earnest, keen types.

* He is usually fairly insensitive. This is required to suppress some of the task signals.

* He is probably bright in terms of intellect, if somewhat unimaginative. His approach is non-theoretical; the type of person who is waiting on Jaques to bring out a *manual* on time-span* to *tell* him how to do *it*.

* He is a good administrator; better at co-ordinating than innovating.

* He is rarely troubled by Super Ego problems. If he advises the management that their actions will cause a strike, and if management does not heed his advice and a strike follows, so what!

* He may be an ex-military officer. Being a Glacier bureaucrat seems the ideal occupation for this type. It gives him an organization to which he can be over-loyal, where he can retain his extroverted, mildly insensitive, practical non-theoretical approach, when his services administrative training will not feel out of place with a standard language, standard role descriptions, command meetings, nuclear commands, with the possibility of contracting executive lines, and conversation about 'role flic' discussed in terms of removing one bowler and donning another.

A Critique of Glacier Organization Theory

In considering the role that Glacier has played in the development of organization theory it is tempting to engage either in blanket acceptance or rejection. Certainly, it was a most interesting and stimulating idea to set up the four systems, viz. the legislative system, the executive system, the representative system and the appeals system. Likewise, the development of more rigorous definitions, in particular the writing of role specifications which was facilitated by the concept of prescribed

* This has now been published—E. Jaques, *Time-span Handbook*, Heinemann, London, 1964.

and discretionary work are particularly useful to practising managers. A particularly good illustration of the Glacier insight into how managers operate is provided by their resolution of line/staff conflict. The drafting of the Company Policy Document is in itself a considerable *tour de force* and commands considerable admiration.

It should be made clear that the empirical evidence for the present research was collected at the Kilmarnock factory of the Glacier Metal Company. This represented an opportunity of assessing a system which was mainly developed at the London factory. The Company's attempt to apply Glacier theory to a relatively similar factory, under the same control, has not been a complete success. If this is so, how then is it possible to give unreserved support for Brown's assertion that his description of organization is valid for industry in general? He argued that because the Company is subjected to 'all the normal cultural pressures of British society and British industy' and 'because we employ 3,600 people with a sample of this size it would be unrealistic to maintain that we are not an average cross-section of the British population'.

Where lies the source of the Glacier theoretical difficulties? Students of organization have turned to the social sciences in search of theories that can be adapted and used in the practice of management. Here Glacier leaves itself open to the charge of being too introverted. There has been a failure to take cognizance of the vast literature on management theory. Some idea of the dimension of this problem may be gained from the following statistics. In 1963, 502 books on management were published in the United Kingdom, and 503 in the United States, and on sociology and economics the numbers were 1,807 in the United Kingdom and 2,487 in the United States. If it is argued that the rate of increase of knowledge is exponential, then Glacier risks the charge of intellectual isolationism, in refusing to acknowledge the developments in organization theory and group dynamics.

Again, criticisms can be directed at their failure to exploit the wealth of methods that the social sciences have provided organizational analysts. The principal method favoured by the Glacier researcher is the technique of 'working through', that is making explicit the psychological forces operative at a factory level, at a group level and at an individual level. As might be expected, from theorists employing a psycho-analytical orientation, all that is required is to make the executives aware of forces at work (of which they may not be aware) and thus render the situation explicit. In this manner, it is possible to spell out the responsibility of each subordinate and thus free them from the internecine strife associated with unclear terms of reference. In contra-distinction to this approach, organization theory is only beginning to escape from the charge of anecdotalism and casual empiricism by the development of theoretically significant empirical research. The development of research techniques in the behavioural sciences has transformed organization theory.

The research reported in this book has been concerned with exploring the empirical possibilities that flow from an observational study of organizational behaviour. Thus more rigorous experimental techniques produce evidence that challenges established beliefs. The rigour of the technique gives us a method of achieving concensus on matters of fact. It also supplies us with a bridge that connects theoretical propositions with the realities of immediate experience.

While speculation in administrative theories is desirable, it is necessary to develop propositions from this speculation, from which we can in turn derive quantitative statistical hypotheses against which data can be collected, which in turn could be analysed and certain conclusions and comparisons reached. It is this capacity to maintain a balance between speculation and empiricism that is so necessary, if the science of organization is to develop. The result of the examination of the Glacier system of organization provides a certain measure of superficial semantic, if not scientific, satisfaction.

GLACIER'S ACHIEVEMENTS

As E. F. L. Brech[21] in *Organisation* points out:

Speaking broadly, however, it would not be untrue to say that these investigations did not produce any startling new findings, either in the field of management practice or in regard to social relationships. They have rendered a very valuable service in analysing what goes on behind the normal facades of management in industry, and in systematically reviewing the significance of many features of everyday practice—features which are taken for granted by most people and thereby cause conflicts and difficulties in relationships: cause them by the very fact that the 'taking for granted' implies inadequate attention and so affords the breeding ground to confusion and misinterpretation. It is, perhaps, important to emphasise that, although the Glacier studies have *not* produced *new* knowledge, they are no whit the less valuable or significant. They have served to confirm what goes into good management practice and to prove to the managers themselves the worthwhileness of systematic adherence to and application of sound principles.

Nevertheless it is useful to list Glacier's achievements in terms of what has been achieved. In terms of organization, the number of levels of management is relatively few. Thus communication from the shop floor to the General Manager is rapid. Conversely the General Manager is fairly 'far forward' and therefore able to exert fairly sensitive control of the production process. The resolution of the conflict between production management and specialists works well. Glacier organization is carefully thought out and considerable effort is expended to ensure that the members of the firm are familiar with its structure. The job descriptions are carefully thought out (subject to the reservation that they require to be checked against behavioural data) and are extensively used and certainly the Company's written policy helps considerably to reduce conflict between managers.

As far as the personnel function at Kilmarnock is concerned the staff, while thin on the ground, is very capable and extensively consulted. The training of apprentices is particularly good. The medical facilities are good; a part-time medical officer, assisted by full-time nursing sisters, is employed in the factory. The policy of filling vacancies 'from within' works well.

Turning to industrial relations, strikes, while they are not non-existent as many people believe, are relatively infrequent. An important reason for this is that rates of pay and conditions of employment are good. On the other hand, labour turnover and absenteeism are at a level to be expected in the engineering industry. But nevertheless there is a large number of applicants for shop floor jobs. Good facilities are provided for the shop stewards. For example, the convener has an office with telephone and is provided with clerical assistance. The Appeals System works well in the case of dismissals, and there is virtually no victimization of shop stewards. One of the most interesting features of the Company, that surprisingly has not been copied generally, is the fact that clocking has been abolished. The canteen facilities are adequate. Glacier has an international reputation for joint consultation and justifiably so. In fact there is a great deal of consultation at every level in the factory. Views and opinions are freely expressed in the Works Committee.

In terms of economics, Glacier has a good record of profitability, especially since 1950. In the vital field of exportings Glacier's record is good. To enable it to remain competitive the Company has engaged in a heavy programme of capitalization. The adaptive nature of Glacier top management is displayed by the rate at which the marketing function is being developed. Again, the fact that Glacier managed to be taken over by a British company rather than by an American firm, confirms Brown's entrepreneurial skill.

In terms of technology Glacier has made a considerable investment in product development, and the production of special machine tools. Glacier has reinforced their technological advantage by the development of new bearing materials; for example, it has pioneered the development of the plastic bearing. Presumably to meet the vagaries of the market, the Company has pursued a policy of product diversification. In terms of organization research Glacier has an outstanding reputation, particularly in the fields of joint consultation, method of payment, and forms of organization.

Some Theoretical Objections to the Glacier System

A major theoretical objection to the Glacier System is the definition of optimal organization in terms that exclude the personality factor. This remains non-proven. The Glacier concept of 'total responsibility of the top manager' leaves the other members devoid of all accountability and reveals a failure to come to terms with modern thinking on the nature of authority and responsibility. Likewise there has been a failure to distinguish between role and role-behaviour; the former refers to the part created by others and the latter refers to how the actor (the role-holder) interprets the part. On the same point there has been a lack of recognition of the importance of personality in defining organization. This unusual attitude to role theory coupled with a reluctance to accept the findings of group dynamics, appears to focus Glacier executive thinking too firmly on the formal aspects of organization at the expense of the informal. Likewise Glacier's concept of 'subordinate' implies that he cannot recognize corporate responsibility or distinguish between committee and executive relationships. Hence the need in Glacier to emphasize the command meeting.

The Glacier philosophy runs the risk of being accused of intellectual isolationalism, of being too introverted and makes too great a departure from the mores of society in formulating policies, e.g. 'contracting executive lines' really means by-passing the shop stewards. The fact that the management minimizes the importance of union officials in Glacier industrial relations reinforces this belief.

Many academics believe that Glacier tries to solve too many problems by definitions, e.g. calling foremen section managers. What seems scarcely credible to these same academics, is that Glacier theorists ignore other management research. Many managers, as well as social scientists, resist the assumption that what is true for Glacier is valid for other industries.

There are inevitable if understandable difficulties of sustaining the idea that 'the factory is the state writ small' which produced the idea of the four systems, legislative, executive, representative and appeals. That the legislative and appeals systems require to be redefined and possibly renamed is at least acknowledged by Glacier theorists. The legislative system requires to be redesigned to take cognizance of the fact that the present arrangements give inadequate recognition of the lack of structural and/or sapiential authority by the workers' representative in the Works Council. Again the charge of paternalism has been levelled against Glacier procedures, by union officials who resent the Company's attitude 'that they know what's best for the workers; that union officials and unions are really a nuisance and that we are all one big happy family'.

In terms of research methods, too much Glacier theoretical work remains at the level of definition and/or hypothesis with insufficient effort devoted to verification. (Excluded from this criticism is Elliott Jaques' work on the time-span instrument.) The dangers of 'travel test' are ignored or minimized. 'Working through', which in any case deliberately excludes the personal factor, requires to be supplemented by other research techniques. Again insufficient use is made of behavioural studies. Finally, argument is too frequently by the loaded dialogue.

The most important charge levelled against Glacier is that Glacier's system of management is unscientific. Linguistic exercises which result in clear definitions are only a prerequisite of a scientific inquiry; they do not represent its sum total. Few of Glacier ideas are subjected to proper validation, either by experiment or controlled observation. The Platonic form of dialogue, with Wilfred Brown as Socrates and the shop steward as Thrasymarchus, can only produce paper victories. Again, the method of research employed by Glacier social scientists is the technique of 'working through' – 'when all is known, all will be well' is just a variation on the Platonic theme that 'knowledge is virtue'. This sanguine hope awaits the realization that 'In industrial life, you can't win: you can only minimize your maximum loss'.

Finally, the conclusion of this research is that the Glacier Project, which began in 1948 with an attempt to understand the human relationships of a whole factory and, in 1965, is largely concerned with maximizing the task effectiveness of the organization, is still worthy of the interest of both social scientists and executives. But the mandates of 1948 are not those of 1965. If the Glacier philosophy (which is ultimately a form of Instrumentalism, i.e. ideas are tools which you use to get somewhere) has changed, then at least social scientists have had the chance to record these changes. On the basis of other, mostly unnamed, organization research, the changes at Glacier cannot be regarded as unique.

A Final Judgment

Is it possible to pass a final judgment on the Glacier system of management? Before this question can be answered it is necessary to define criteria. Possible criteria that suggest themselves include: is it consistent, in the sense in which psychologists use the term reliability? The overall answer must be in the affirmative. The system is applied in a fairly systematic manner. Some managers might regard this consistency test as inappropriate; their argument would be that since all the facts of organizational life are not known, how is it possible to pre-judge the situation by operating an *a priori* determined policy.

The second criterion suggests itself from this last point – Is it a valid theory? To what extent does it correspond with the data of organizational life? In the light of the present researches, the correspondence between theory and fact is limited and incomplete. But it is impossible to reach certainty on this count without further examination of what the facts are. To my mind, Glacier has neither the resources nor the will to carry through such a test of validity.

Validity, to some extent, is measured by comparing a theory with other 'good' theories. While to some extent Glacier theorists leave themselves open to the charge of cultism, nothing but good would come of an attempt to integrate Glacier theory with the considerable body of organization theory that is now emerging from universities and business schools on both sides of the Atlantic.

Does Glacier theory have predictive powers? This is impossible to answer without setting up properly conducted experiments. Nevertheless it would appear that Glacier executives appear to have a useful model which enables them to make dynamic adjustments to organizational events.

This suggests yet another test – what is the utilitarian value of Glacier theory? The answer must be that it has considerable utility. I have been impressed by both Glacier and ex-Glacier executives' ability to structure inchoate and ill-defined situations in their interests as well as their Company's.

Other minor tests suggest themselves such as the travel test and the aesthetic test. On the latter, Glacier theory, especially the Four Systems Concept, is an extremely elegant theme and is well received by most managers. The travel test, presumably a sub-test of utilitarianism, is passed with flying colours by such Glacier terms as time span of discretion and so on.

What is the final verdict? Consistent, yes. Valid, not always. Elegant, yes. Utilitarian value, considerable.

APPENDIX I

Notes

1. GENERAL INFORMATION
   (a) Confidential. This will not be included in report.

   (c) Confidential. In report generalization such as 'Light Engineering Products' would be used.

   (e) For definition of 'supervisor' as meant here, kindly refer to covering letter.

   (f) By 'allied departments' we mean maintenance, millwrights, inspection etc.

2. POSITION & DUTIES OF SUPERVISORS

Questions

Question 1
   (a) Name of Company ....
   (b) Location ....
   (c) Product(s) ....

   (d) Total labour force ....
       (1) Staff ....
       (2) Workers ....
   (e) No. of supervisors in manufacturing departments.................

   (f) No. of supervisors in departments allied to manufacturing..............

Question 2
   (a) Title ....
   (b) No. of subordinates?........
   (c) What is the position held by a supervisor's immediate superior?........

290

Questions (*d*), (*e*) and (*f*) require the yes/no type of answer. Kindly indicate by drawing a circle round the appropriate word, e.g.

YES   NO

(*d*) Do supervisors:
  1. Schedule or re-arrange work of subordinates?
     YES   NO

  2. Carry out fixed programme as set by their immediate superior?
     YES   NO

(*e*) Do supervisors have power to:
  1. Select or reject subordinates?
     YES   NO

  2. Determine standard of subordinate's performance?
     YES   NO

  3. Determine standard of subordinate's behaviour?
     YES   NO

  4. Authorize a subordinate's wage increases?
     YES   NO

  5. Requisition maintenance?
     YES   NO

(*f*) Are supervisors responsible for following:
  1. Safety   YES   NO

  2. Training of apprentices?
     YES   NO

  3. Providing or arranging any further training needs of his subordinates?
     YES   NO

Notes

3. REMUNERATION–
   FINANCIAL

(a) The supervisors referred
to in this question are
those who you have
included in the totals in
answer to questions 1(e)
and 1(f). Therefore the
total No. of supervisors
in this question should
equal the total of 1(e)
and 1(f).

Questions

Question 3

(a) Kindly indicate the
number of supervisors that
lie within each of the
following wage ranges.

Rate p.a.	No. of supervisors
Below £600	...
£600 –£675	...
£675 –£750	...
£750 –£825	...
£825 –£900	...
£900 –£975	...
£975 –£1050	...
£1050–£1125	...
£1125–£1200	...
£1200–£1275	...
£1275–£1350	...
£1350–£1425	...
£1425–and over	...
Total No. of supervisors.........	

(b) Are there clearly defined
limits for supervisors'
salaries?

YES   NO

(c) Indicate in terms of years

(c) If so, how long would it
take the 'average' super-
visor to move from the
bottom to the top of the
scale? ....

Some parts of questions (d),
(e) and (f) require the yes/no
type of answers, others require
specific details.

(d) Are supervisors paid–
    1. weekly?   YES   NO
    2. monthly?   YES   NO

(e) Do supervisors receive–
    1. production bonus?
                        YES   NO
    2. If so, how much?
       ....*per month*

(*g*) (1) and (2) please
indicate thus √
where appropriate.

(*f*) Supervisor's overtime
1. Does he work overtime?
YES   NO
2. If so, average no. of
hours per week? ....
3. Is he paid for it?
YES   NO
4. If so, at what rate?
....

(*g*) Fringe benefits–do supervisors enjoy the following:

1. Sick benefits?
CONTRIBUTORY
NON-CONTRIBUTORY
2. Pension?
CONTRIBUTORY
NON-CONTRIBUTORY
3. Profit sharing?
YES   NO
4. If yes to (3) indicate av.
supervisor share per
year.   £.............
5. Participation in bonus
scheme of non produc-
tive nature?
YES   NO
6. If yes to (5) what is av.
supervisor share per
year?   £.............
7. Long service gratuity?
YES   NO
8. Paid holidays?
YES   NO
9. If yes to (8) how many
days per year?
.............*days*

(*h*) 1. Is it possible for
subordinates to earn
more than supervisors?
YES   NO

2. If yes is this possible
   (a) regularly? YES NO
   (b) only in exceptional
       circumstances?
       YES NO

(i) What are av. no. of hours
    worked by supervisor per
    week? ....

---

4. REMUNERATION– NON-FINANCIAL

All parts of this section
require only a yes/no
answer.

Question 4

(a) Do your supervisors:
   1. Receive free
      protective clothing?
      YES NO
   2. Enjoy rent-free
      company housing?
      YES NO
   3. Enjoy subsidized
      company housing?
      YES NO
   4. Have sports club
      facilities?
      YES NO
   5. Family recreational
      and social facilities?
      YES NO
   6. Have canteen
      facilities?
      YES NO
   7. Have special cloak or
      changing room
      facilities available?
      YES NO
   8. Have separate
      rest-rooms?
      YES NO

APPENDIX II

Production Unit
(Wrapped Bush Unit: Thin Wall Unit)
Short Specification for the Role of
Section Manager (Machining Sections)

The Section Manager (S.M.) is accountable to the Unit Manager (U.M.) who is a subordinate of the General Manager (G.M.). He has as colleagues other S.M.s, the Unit Production Engineer (U.P.E.) and the Unit Production Controller (U.Pr.C.). He has as subordinates approximately 25 hourly-rated members (H.R.M.'s.) and may have one or more Auxiliaries, and one or more staff Supervisors (S.P.'s.).

A. Description of the Work content of the Role
(*1*) *Main Prescriptions Limiting the Role*

1.1 *General:* statutory, Company, factory and his manager's own policies.
1.2 Having agreed the feasibility of a weekly programme and of emergency changes of programme prescribed by the U.Pr.C., produce a specified number of parts (or perform specified operations upon parts) to drawing and to a prescribed standard of quality in the prescribed time. (Parts may be half-bearings ranging from 1½" O.D. to 3½" O.D., wrapped bushes ranging from ⅜" Bore Dia. to 6" Bore Dia., or thrust washers ranging from 1" Dia. to 6" Dia., according to the Section the S.M. manages.)
1.3 Perform the above within limits of material, labour and consumable costs prescribed by the U.M., employing the machines, tooling, equipment, floor area and establishment allocated by the U.M., and following the methods and techniques which may be prescribed by the U.P.E.

1.4 Maintain within standards set by the U.M. or U.P.E. the machines and equipment allocated by the U.M. in a state fit for further production.

1.5 Maintain a labour force adequately trained and motivated to assist him in achieving his current and future programmes within the distribution of skills, the Unit training programme, and the establishment prescribed by the U.M., and within the wage brackets legislated by Works Committee; carry out quarterly wage reviews.

1.6 Maintain the standards of safety, cleanliness and tidiness prescribed by the U.M. and by statute.

(2) Examples of Decisions to be Made

2.1 *General:* how to reconcile apparently conflicting prescriptions; when to refer to the U.M.; how best to use his own time.

2.2 What tasks are feasible, and what changes in resources to recommend to the U.M. to achieve those which are not; what work to do himself and what to delegate; what standards of output and quality to prescribe to his subordinates, and how to inspect their performance; in what order to schedule the work to be done and how to deploy his men, machines, and equipment; when to recommend that work be sub-contracted to other Units and/or externally; how best to use Supervisors and Auxiliaries; when to report difficulties to the U.M., U.P.E. or U.Pr.C., when to request the assistance of technical, programming or personnel specialists; what records to keep.

2.3 What consumables to requisition; when to recommend a change of prescription; what methods and techniques to use within prescriptions or where none are specified; when to request transfers and/or loans of labour from or to his Section; what overtime-working to recommend.

2.4 How to avoid breakdowns; what alternative action to take during a breakdown; when and what maintenance services to requisition.

2.5 Which persons to select as his subordinates; how much time to devote to training, and when to request training services; how to assess his subordinates, and what wage and salary increases to give; when to recommend payment for exceptional performance in excess of the role; when and what corrective action to take when his subordinates do not achieve the standards he prescribes; when to dismiss members from his command and/or from the Company; how to conduct himself towards his subordinates; when to permit absences; when to recommend a loan from the Company, or assistance from the Benevolent Committee; what records to keep.

2.6 What standards to prescribe to his subordinates and how to inspect their performance.

(3) *Some Effects of the Use of Marginally Sub-standard Discretion by the Occupant of the Role*

3.1 Less or more than is required is produced, or required quantities are produced too late.

3.2 Scrap-rate is too high; material, consumables and labour costs are too high.

3.3 Machines break down and capacity is lost.

3.4 Appeals and representations from his command occupy the time of the U.M., Personnel Manager and G.M.

3.5 The U.M., U.Pr.C. and U.P.E. pay excessive attention to him and his command.

3.6 The Company is made liable for personal injuries and is warned by H.M. Factory Inspector.

(4) *Some Mechanisms in Operation for Reviewing the work done by the Occupant of the Role*

4.1 Direct and personal review by the U.M. from day to day in discussions and visits to the Section.

4.2 Appeals and representations to the U.M. from members of the Section.

4.3 Daily and weekly achievement reports; arrears lists; reject and scrap reports; machine utilization reports.

4.4 Personal assessment sheets written by the S.M.; change of wage and salary rate forms; extra wage allowance forms.

4.5 S.M.'s requests for overtime working.

APPENDIX II

Working Conditions

The standard working week is 42 hours, with alternating fortnights of dayshift and nightshift. The G.M.'s policy is that dayshift and week-end overtime shall be limited to the production of urgent orders and shall average no more than 5 per cent. S.M.s are required to work overtime on a rota basis to provide managerial cover according to a prescribed scale. A cubicle type of office is provided for pairs of S.M.s adjacent to their commands.

B. Policy on Filling the Role

Preferred age range: internal applicants   25–40,
external applicants   25–35.

Transit time of occupants to role: 2–25 years. The most usual promotion to U.M. could be undertaken by an exceptional member at the end of two years, although periods as U.Pr.C, U.P.E. and Personnel Officer would make a member a better candidate. For those technically qualified a transfer to a Production Engineer role would be possible. For older applicants the role could provide a lifetime career.

Recruitment to the role may be from the present members of the Company occupying the role of Supervisor who have demonstrated technical ability, from Production Engineer or Work Study Officer roles, or from external applicants who have qualifications at least equivalent to O.N.C. level.

Status and Salary

Grade II status with a salary within the range £986–£1450.

PERCEPTION OF AN EXECUTIVE ROLE

The cognitions of the individual are selectively organized. There are two main kinds of determinants: stimulus factors and personal factors. By stimulus factors are meant those factors which derive from the nature of the external stimulus object. By personal factors are meant those factors which derive from the characteristic of the perceiving individual. It is with the personal factor in perception that this investigation is concerned. The role of such personal factors as mental set in selectively sensitizing the perceptual mechanism has been studied in a number of experiments. D. C. Dearborn and H. A. Simon studied a group of 25 executives on an executive training course who were asked to read a standard case study. Before discussing the case the executives were asked to indicate 'what they considered to be the most important problem facing the company – the problem a new company president should deal with first'. Five of the six sales executives mentioned sales as the most important problem facing the company. Likewise the majority of the production executives stressed organizational problems. The inference is clear, viz. that executives perceiving the same situation select for emphasis those aspects of the problem which relate to the aims and interests of their own departments. The manner whereby the experiment developed is relevant. In an investigation into executive behaviour using a sampling procedure, a difficulty had arisen concerning how certain executive activities should be categorized. In *Exploration in Management* Wilfred Brown defines operational work in conceptual terms:

No instruction given by a manager is complete unless, in fact, or by implication, it specifies who shall carry it out, what technique shall be used and the timing and quantity of activity which are demanded. . . . The contention is, therefore, that operational work is a three dimensional activity and that it can be analysed under three headings

(a)   organizational and personnel work;
(b)   work concerned with the techniques used in production; and
(c)   programming work concerned with balancing, timing and quantification of operations.

The categories Personnel, Technical and Programming were used to describe each of these dimensions respectively. The basic problem is 'Do executives with different backgrounds presented with the same work situation categorize it in the same way?' To test this hypothesis, the following questionnaire was developed.

THE EXPERIMENT

1. Complete the following questionnaire indicating as in the examples given below the content of each situation described.
2. Entries *must* be made in terms of a 10 point total.
3. Thank you for your co-operation.

	Classification		
	Program-ming	Person-nel	Technical
Example 1 Discussing with H.R.O. who has appealed against your decision not to upgrade him at the recent wage review.	—	10	—
Example 2 At end of Friday day shift, checking on the day's production, making arrangements for the Maintenance Engineer to overhaul a machine and discussing with H.R.O. his application for leave of absence on Monday day shift.	2	5	3

APPENDIX III

No.	Item	Classification		
		Program-ming	Person-nel	Technical
1.	Present on shop floor with own supervisor, discussing deployment of machines and operatives in own section.			
2.	Discussing with Unit Engineer a problem of tooling for own section.			
3.	On shop floor with own supervisor, telling him of a change in priorities and instructing him on how to achieve maximum effectiveness of section.			
4.	Completing schedules of production figures, deleting from list jobs which have been completed, and adding new work which has reached section.			
5.	In another section discussing whether other operatives can be borrowed for a short period to deal with a 'rush job'.			
6.	Initial deployment of personnel at start of shift.			
7.	In wages office, collecting wages for own section.			
8.	Alone in office dealing with paper work in connection with a three-monthly wage review.			
9.	In dispatch with supervisor of inspection and own supervisor, checking on completed batches.			
10.	Checking on delivery to own section, a batch which has been lost.			
11.	Discussing with own operative his transfer to another section.			

301

No.	Item	Classification		
		Program-ming	Person-nel	Technical
12.	On shop floor at start of shift discussing with supervisor and N/S section manager a problem of tooling which has been causing a delay in setting up machines for day shift.			
13.	Discussing with shop steward his objection to your supervisor setting a machine on your own instructions.			
14.	Writing notes for N/S section manager and giving details of the day's production, stating requirements in terms of priorities for the N/S in order that the following day shift's programme can be followed through.			
15.	Discussing with Inspector the rejection of a batch and convincing him that it is in fact within the accepted tolerance, so that it is passed by inspection for dispatch.			
16.	Interview an hourly-rated operator for purposes of a wage review.			
17.	In another section, finding out when work will be completed on a batch and delivered to own section.			
18.	In Unit Manager's office, in consultation with Unit Manager, Unit P.E., Unit P.C. and other section managers. The main topic of conversation is the need for overtime.			

No.	Item	Classification		
		Program- ming	Person- nel	Technical

19. In canteen with other section managers, after unit manager's meeting.
20. In production control dept., obtaining information from Unit Production Controller, regarding change of production schedule.

Have you any comments?

H.R.O. = Hourly Rated Operator
N/S = Night Shift
P.E. = Production Engineer
P.C. = Production Controller

The above form was given to a small group of employees of the Glacier Metal Company at the Kilmarnock factory.

RESULTS

TABLE I. MEANS FOR DIFFERENT ROLES

Role	N	Programming	Personnel	Technical
Unit Manager	1	82	89	29
Section Manager	10	92·3	77·1	30·6
Supervisors	4	90	75·75	43·25
Machine operators	5	72	101	27
Unit Engineer	1	88	62	50
Training Officer	1	62	72	66
Personnel Officer	1	90	80	30
TOTAL	23	85·4	81·2	32·8

Tests of significance were based on the t test at 0·5 level because of the small samples.

(a) Perception of the technical aspect. The Unit Engineer's score was almost significant and the Training Officer's score was significant.

(b) Perception of the personnel aspect. Only in the case of the machine operators was there a significant difference in means.

(c) Perception of the programming aspect. The machine operators' score was almost significant. The training officers' score was significantly different.

These results support the view that there is more variation within groups than between groups.

Discussion

It would seem on the basis of the results that on the average the Unit Manager, Section Managers and Supervisors perceived the role of the section manager in the same way. But there are considerable variations within groups. The Unit Engineer and the Training Officer both overestimate the technical aspect of the section manager's job. The training officer has considerable technical qualifications and experience. This would seem to afford support for the view that the role of the perceiver would affect the perception of another executive's role. In the case of the machine operators' perception of the work of the section manager, they would appear to overstress the personnel aspect and understress the programming aspect. This would support the view that the level in the organization occupied by the perceiver affects his perceptions.

Subject to the reservations that arise from the size of the samples being so small, certain observations can be made. The first comment refers to experiments on executive behaviour using the self recording technique. There would appear to be some support for the view that different executives would categorize the same event in different ways. Secondly there appears to be some support for the view that the clash between a functional specialist and the line executive is based on a difference in perception of an executive role. Thirdly it can be argued that the machine operators' perception of the section manager's role represents an expression of the machine operators' need for the section manager to be more personnel conscious.

The questionnaire was given to a group of personnel management students which was made up of eight men and five women.

Six of these students were engaged in a project at that Kilmarnock factory of the Glacier Metal Company.

TABLE II

		AVERAGE			HIGHEST			LOWEST		
Group	No.	Prog	Pers	Tech	Prog	Pers	Tech	Prog	Pers	Tech
Whole Group	13	77	73·4	49·6	98	94	78	55	53	52
Males	8	78·6	70·2	51·1	91	81	78	63	53	33
Females	5	73·7	80·5	45·8	98	94	52	55	70	32
Glacier Group	6	89	71	40	98	78	52	77	68	32
Section Managers	10	92·3	77·1	30·6						

The results are shown in Table II. The scores for section managers are shown for comparison. The score of the Glacier project students are closer to the scores of the section managers. The inference in this case is that knowledge of the role and of the meaning and significance of the terms, programming, personnel and technical, has affected the perceptions of the project students. Comparing the scores of males and females, the scores are in agreement with the studies of sex differences in interests by Terman and Miles, Kuder and Strong which show that men are more interested than women in mechanics and scientific activities while women are more interested than men in people and social work. This is reflected in the females' higher personnel score and the males' higher technical score.

SUMMARY

This study is concerned with an examination of the personal factors that affect the organization of the cognitions of different individuals perceiving the same events of a particular executive role. When the averages of different management and supervisory groups are considered, the differences are not significant but the variation within groups is considerable. Engineers are inclined to overvalue the technical aspect of the job. The machine operators overstress the personnel aspect and understress the programming aspect. Knowledge of the role perceived and the meaning of the terms, programming, personnel and technical, seem to be a factor for outsiders. Lastly, males tend to overstress the technical aspect and females the personnel aspect. In short, the perception of the activities of an executive role is affected by the following factors: the perceiver's position in the organization, his function, his knowledge of the role and its functions, and the sex of the perceiver.

Brown, W., *Exploration in Management*, London, Heinemann, 1960.

Burns, T., 'The Directions of Activity and Communication in a Departmental Executive Group', *Human Relations*, Vol. VII, No. 1, 1955.

Dearborn, Dewitt C., and Simon, H. A., 'Selective Perception: A Note on the Departmental Identification of Executives', *Sociometry 21*, 1958.

Krech, D., Crutchfield, R. S. and Ballachey, E. L., *Individual in Society*, New York, McGraw-Hill, 1962.

Roe, A., *The Psychology of Occupations*, New York, Wiley, 1956.

Strong, E. K., *Vocational Interests of Men and Women*, Stanford, Stanford University Press, 1943.

Terman, L. M. and Miles, C. C., *Sex and Personality*, New York, McGraw-Hill, 1936.

APPENDIX IV

GLACIER SHOP STEWARDS—A SCIENTIFIC SNAP-SHOT*

In general terms, it is possible to predict that behavioural scientists of the 1980s will explain the decline and fall of the shop steward as a consequence of the film 'I'm all right, Jack' and the television series 'The Rag Trade'. Television satire rarely initiates trends, but is most successful when it crystallizes inchoate and unstructured sentiments, directed against pompous, powerful and usually tyrannical father-figures. In public esteem, the shop stewards were at the zenith of their popularity in the period towards the end of the war and immediately afterwards. But the public's enthusiasm began to wane as they suffered as consumers hit by strikes which appeared to them senseless. This reinforced by the onset of affluence with its attendant meritocracy which insisted in a brutal oversimplification that the shop floor was manned by the 11 + failures, put the great mass of the public out of sympathy with the shop steward who was seen most frequently in the behavioural snap-shot of calling a strike over the quality of the tea.

A caricature of the steward exists in the mind of many managers. Such managers frequently complete accounts of particular manager-steward conflicts with—'of course, he was a bloody bolshie'. These same executives have invented a patronizing fable which they use to describe encounters with the shop floor worker who in this class-loaded picture is referred to as Joe Bloggs which is presumable the alias 'Private Snooks' (beloved of officers' anecdotes) used when he was demobilized.

One such executive, who was a personnel manager of a light engineering company, related to me this account of a convener of shop stewards who was sacked for being 'too slow at his work': 'not only was he a commie—he had a direct land line to Moscow.

* This study was completed too late to be included in the main text.

You should have heard him arguing. He used the Marxist dialectic. He was terrific.' Another phrase used to describe shop stewards is that they are a 'crowd of little Hitlers'. Nevertheless, in spite of this loss of status, shop stewards are playing an increasing part in the shop floor industrial relations of our society.

Arthur Marsh in *Managers and Shop Stewards* has explained why this development has taken place:

> One answer is to say that collective agreements in Britain have left a good deal of scope for workplace supplementation and improvement, by a process of 'filling in' at lower levels of negotiation. Some agreements are standard and provide conditions which must be uniformly applied. The wages of busmen are a case in point and also the length of the working week in most industries. But other industry-wide agreements only attempt to lay down minima, or guarantees, or to suggest how certain kinds of provisions might be applied. They were not intended to be rigid in application, but adaptable to local or workplace needs and circumstances. Agreements of this kind clearly leave considerable room for workplace bargaining.

In the paternalistic minds of many managers there has been created a stereotype of the shop steward who is seen as a power-crazy worker who is incompetent at his work, with a chip on his shoulder, who has the gift of the gab but is recalcitrant and intransigent in negotiation, bent on the destruction of the capitalist system. The shop steward is seen as a cross between a barrack-room lawyer and a mob orator. Undoubtedly, for many executives the shop steward seems to act as lightning conductors for their hostilities and anxieties.

WHAT DO SHOP STEWARDS DO?

To try and clarify some of these issues regarding the shop steward, and penetrate behind these stereotypes, it was decided to conduct a behavioural study of a group of Glacier shop stewards. The investigation had three phases: a self-recording exercise which lasted three weeks, followed immediately by an observation study for a further three weeks, and an attitude survey. During the self-recording phase, they were required to note on a precoded diary form their shop steward's activities. To facilitate recording, their activities were broken down into three major categories: Individual Shop Floor Grievances, Meetings, and Union Routines. These were further analysed as follows:

Individual Shop Floor Grievances
- (a) Wages
- (b) Promotion
- (c) Discipline
- (d) Welfare
- (e) Overtime
- (f) Safety
- (g) Appeals
- (h) Others

Meetings
- (a) Shop Committee
- (b) Joint Shop Stewards Committee
- (c) Works Council

Union Routines
- (a) Collecting union dues
- (b) Recruiting new members
- (c) Checking cards of new starters

Responsibilities of Elected Representatives
(according to the Glacier Policy Document)

F.4 A representative is accountable to that constituent group or electoral unit which elects him; and it is his responsibility:

F.4.1 To make himself aware of the main interests of all in his constituency.

F.4.2 To represent the point of view of his constituents in committees and Councils, even where this may mean presenting a point of view contrary to his own personal opinion or his view in his executive role.

F.4.3 To allow Councils or committees to work with the greatest possible realism by judging when to state any views held by minorities within his constituency or committee.

F.4.4 To judge when reference to constituents is necessary, and when to accept responsibility for acting without such reference.

F.4.5 To initiate proposals for change which would be in the best interests of his constituents.

F.4.6 To take appropriate steps when in his judgment executive actions or the actions of his constituents are inconsistent with policy.

F.4.7 To assist his constituents to understand the executive implications of the agreements he has accepted on their behalf.

F.4.8 To familiarize himself with the Constitution and Standing Orders of those bodies of which he is a member and with established rules of procedure.

F.4.9 To know policy, and in particular to understand those aspects of policy which are of most immediate concern to his constituents.

F.4.10 To ensure, before taking up an appeal with and on behalf of a constituent, that the constituent has in the first instance taken up the matter with the manager concerned.

F.4.11 To act as adviser to any of his constituents in cases of appeal when requested to do so.

The self-recording data revealed two basic inconsistencies when contrasted with the observational material. According to the stewards, they were spending only a relatively small proportion of their time on industrial relations. For example, according to the convener, his representative duties occupied him for $7\frac{1}{2}$ hours a week. Whereas the observational studies showed that he spent 31 hours 41 minutes in steward activities. Another steward, according to his diary, spent only $6\frac{1}{2}$ hours a week in his representative role; the observer's record showed his average to be 19 hours 55 minutes a week. The stewards claimed that they had not been aware of any change of tempo over the six-week period. The observers regarded their data as a conservative measure of the time devoted to representative duties. These times are to be compared with the findings of Clegg, Killick and Adams reported in *Trade Union Officers*, where it appears that the steward on the average spends 11 hours a week on union busi-

ness, 6 of them in working time. These figures are in agreement
with our self-recording data, but much less than our observational findings.

The second inconsistency in the diary material relates to the
details of the distribution of their activities. The observers
reported that all the stewards performed a wide variety of functions. The diaries, on the other hand, showed that particular
stewards appeared to specialize in particular functions. For
example, one steward who had established a justifiable first-class
record for his skill in handling grievances recorded his time for
one week as follows:

Grievances	4¼ hours
Welfare meeting	1½ hours
TOTAL	5¾ hours

The observation study, on the other hand, showed that he was
engaged in the following representative activities (based on an
average for three weeks):

Wages	1 hour	50 minutes
Discipline	1 hour	25 minutes
Welfare	1 hour	30 minutes
Overtime		5 minutes
Safety	1 hour	50 minutes
Appeals	1 hour	10 minutes
Meetings	2 hours	45 minutes
TOTAL	10 hours	35 minutes

These inconsistencies illustrate how the reliability of self-
recording studies is affected by the perceptual slant of the
recorders, their liability to 'forget' certain activities, and their
need to attenuate, dramatize, and elaborate their experience.

The Observation Study

The subjects of the investigation were the 'executive seven'
of the J.S.S.C. They were not continuously under observation,
but the observers contacted them frequently during each day to

make a record of their representative activities. In some respects the method of data collecting was nearer to the technique of the critical incident procedure, in the sense that the research was not concerned with the total behaviour of the subjects, but only the representatives' aspect of it. So, in effect, when the stewards understood the nature of the investigation, the observer only needed to say to the steward, 'anything to report?'

TABLE I

	Average No. of hours per day used for shop steward duties	Percentage of working day spent on shop steward duties
Convener	6 hours 21 minutes	77%
Steward 1	3 hours 59 minutes	50%
Steward 2	38 minutes	8%
Steward 3	1 hour 30 minutes	19%
Steward 4	3 hours 00 minutes	38%
Steward 5	2 hours 07 minutes	27%
Steward 6	1 hour 38 minutes	20%
Steward 7	1 hour 55 minutes	24%

Table 1 lists the average number of hours per day spent by each steward on shop floor industrial relations. The convener, who has an office with a telephone, was completely free from production work. The other stewards had operatives' roles but were able to get away to attend to their shop stewards' duties.

The first comment on this table refers to the magnitude of the total time required for representatives' activities. Assuming that the convener was employed full time, that the four chairmen of shop committees devoted one-third of their time, the other stewards one-sixth of their time to representation, it was estimated that the stewards must have been costing the management approximately £200 per week, excluding other administrative costs, such as the expense of the executives with whom the stewards confer. As far as benefits to the firm are concerned it would be necessary to assign a financial value to the avoidance of strikes, the maintenance of the morale of the work force and the efficiency of the communication system. Another way of pricing a service is to ask what would be the cost of its nearest alternative. Perhaps, it would have been cheaper and more efficient to have cut the cost and work of the shop stewards by a half (say) by the appointment of four personnel officers at £25 per week. Pursuing these arbitrary assumptions further, it might have been more efficient to 'have commissioned in the field' some of these shop stewards as personnel officers and to have assigned them as shop personnel officers.

TABLE 2

Percentage of total representative time spent on separate functions.

	Convener	Chairmen of Shop Committees	Other Shop Stewards
	%	%	%
Wages	6	8	10
Promotion	Nil	Nil	4
Discipline	30	18	6
Welfare	4	10	5
Overtime	5	12	10
Safety	2	4	4
Appeals	6	8	8
Unions	20	9	13
Meetings	17	31	40
Miscellaneous	10	Nil	Nil
TOTAL	100	100	100

Table 2 shows the detailed distribution of the stewards' activities.

The Attitude Survey

The attitude survey revealed that most shop stewards in this plant represented about 40 members. With the exception of the convener and one steward, none of the stewards had had any formal training. The convener had taken a correspondence course in public speaking, and one steward had been to an A.E.U. week-end course.

Before this investigation, I had formed the opinion that the men who ran the local Labour Party, sat on the Co-op Boards and as shop stewards organized the shop floor. In fact, our research findings showed that while the stewards, in general, supported Labour, they took no part in political activity and, except in the case of the convener who attended district meetings of the A.E.U., the great majority of the stewards had scarcely had any contact with the union outside working hours. The answers to the question 'Do you feel that you have sufficient say in production and management matters?' revealed two opposing views. The majority of the stewards answered in the negative and a few even indicated that they would like to have a look at the Company's books. None of the executive seven, who sat on the Works Council, shared this view. In the Works Council, the executive seven were kept informed of the Company's trading position, forward plant load and production difficulties. But they appeared to evince little interest in these matters.

To the question, 'What do you consider to be your most important function?' answers were evenly divided between winning good wages and conditions and maintaining good management-labour relations by liaison and representation of grievances etc. The least liked duty was the collecting of union dues. A significant number stated they disliked representing workers on grievances, particularly if they were not soundly based and there was a likelihood of them being rejected.

Other points thrown up by the survey were:

1. Stewards' duties should take preference over operative work if there was a conflict of interests.
2. Two most useful attributes of a steward were:
   (a) Knowledge of Company policies and procedures.
   (b) Fluency of speech.

To supplement this data on attitudes, five of the executive seven, including the convener, were interviewed. Contrary to what many non-Glacier managers hold to be the case, these stewards were technically well qualified and were on the top level of pay in their respective wage brackets. They had the qualifications necessary for promotion but for a variety of reasons had not pursued this matter very actively. It was obvious from discussions with stewards that it is regarded as a mark of distinction to be offered promotion and to refuse it. This reflects to some extent the poor status, both financial and social, of foremen and junior management roles, but it also argued that there is a degree of satisfaction in the steward's role.

Why did they choose to become stewards? The research did not produce much positive information on their motivation. Altruistic considerations, such as political dedication, seem to be of only minor significance. It is possible to view the steward's role as an example of self-created job enlargement within which he can meet certain social and leadership needs. Reflecting on this problem over a number of years, I have been able to identify four different types of stewards.

(a) *The Agitator* fights a hot version of the class war on the shop floor; not always, but frequently, a member of the political *demi-monde*, his attitude and behaviour are monitored from within by ideology. Pragmatic considerations rarely weigh with him. He is the type of unofficial strike leader who is likely to 'up' demands so that management is placed in an impossible position. Union bureaucracy and this type are inevitably in conflict. He abounds in an environment which the unions have not structured. One group of stewards which I encountered in a different context had come together informally 'to fight the comms', as they put it. But their district was 'very well organized' and they had to search hard in 1965 to find a 'comm' seeking office. Fortunately, the anti-comm meeting took place in a pub, on a Saturday morning so that the group's switch from its unique aim to accessory aims created no special difficulties. In a well organized plant, the agitator has a reserve role, in the sense that if the management 'does something mad' such as springing a 20 per cent redundancy on the work force, then there is a good chance that the agitator steward will emerge in response to the crisis which inevitably has the effect of simplifying and dramatizing the issues for the workers.

In brief, the plant culture and the extent of union bureaucracy are the two principal factors determining the style of shop floor leadership likely to emerge. American research findings by Schrag show that in prisons when the inmates are allowed to select representatives, then they choose hostile and aggressive members who have records of violence in the prison including fighting, escaping and assault ('Leadership Among Prison Inmates', *American Sociological Review*, *19*, 1954, pp. 37–42).

(b) *The Constitutionalist* is much more common on the shop

floor of British factories. Usually, he is a first rate craftsman who has considerable seniority, who is regarded by his peers as a 'very canny type' and by his immediate boss as 'sound but deep'. He has an expert knowledge of the union rule book and is particularly knowledgeable about collective agreements, local plant arrangements, company policy precedents and plant grievance procedure. He is expert at reserving his position and is unlikely to take any new initiative until his facts are 'hard', and he has worked through channels. Personnel managers, who have constitutionalists as conveners, are in a good position to tackle their problems of industrial relations in a systematic manner.

(*c*) *The Advocate* or 'prisoner's friend' as he is sometimes called is much sought after by workers who are appealing against particular managerial decisions. They will rarely act unless they are certain of the facts of the case and sure that there are 'grounds for proceeding'. One of the stewards in this research had an established reputation as an expert on appeals; he preferred the level of the appeal which involved the General Manager.

(*d*) *The Nondescript* refers to the many stewards who are drafted for this kind of work and who approach it with varying degrees of skill and enthusiasm. This explains the fact that there is such a wide degree of variation in the total amount of time different stewards devote to representative activities.

A general comment on how Glacier treats its shop stewards may not be inappropriate at this stage. In general terms, the climate within which the stewards operate is excellent. The facilities for the convener are first class and enable him to discharge his function very effectively. Victimization of stewards is virtually unknown. Consultation with managers is free and frequent. Their reservations in regard to appeals against wage reviews and the Glacier practice of 'contracting executive lines', I have already discussed. But, in general, Glacier shop stewards and managers seemed to function very well together.

The overriding impression left by this research is the need for a new definition of the union-steward-employer nexus. In any case, if the unions cannot set their house in order on this count, some other agency will. The Ministry of Labour's written statement to the Royal Commission on 'Trade Unions and Employers' Associations' states 'that 90 per cent to 95 per cent of all strikes are unofficial, and more than half of them are due to matters other than wages—dismissals, unsatisfactory working conditions, and demarcation disputes' and goes on to say that in many cases the union is doing less than it could to prevent unofficial strikes. The Memorandum notes—'The argument would be that it is then desirable in the national interest that pressure should be exerted on trade unions to give more attention to the activities of shop stewards and other subordinate bodies. In the case of unofficial strikes the trade union concerned should be subject to defined penalties, according to the length of time the strike lasted, unless they could show to some independent tribunal that they had taken all the steps open to them to prevent the strike taking place, or to bring it to an end as soon as possible.'

BIBLIOGRAPHY

1. Albers, H. H., *Organised Executive Action*, New York, Wiley, 1961.
2. Albu, A., 'Glacier's Experiment in Management', *I.W.S. Journal*, 1964.
3. Anonymous, *Understanding How Groups Work*, Adult Education Association of the U.S.A., 743 N. Wabash Avenue, Chicago 11, Illinois.
4. Argyris, C., *The Impact of Budgets on People*, New York Controllership Institute, 1952.
5. Argyris, C., *Personality and Organisation*, New York, Harper, 1957.
6. Bales, R. and Slater, P., 'Rôle Differentiation in Small Decision-Making Groups', T. Parsons, R. Bales *et al.*, *Family Socialisation and Interaction Process*, Illinois Free Press, 1955.
7. Bales, R. F., 'In Conference', *Harvard Business Review*, Vol. 32, No. 2, April 1954, pp. 44–50.
8. Bales, R. F., 'Some Uniformities of Behaviour in Small Social Systems', S. E. Swanson, T. M. Newcomb, E. L. Hartley (Eds.), *Readings in Social Psychology*.
9. Banton, M., 'Rôle', *New Society*, 7 May 1964.
10. Barnard, C. I., *The Function of the Executive*, Harvard University Press, Cambridge, 1938.
11. Barnes, R., *Motion and Time Study*, New York, Wiley, 1953.
12. Bavelas, A., 'Communication Patterns in Task-oriented Groups', D. Cartwright and A. Zander (Eds.), *Group Dynamics: Research and Theory* (2nd ed.), Evanston, Illinois, Row Peterson, London, Tavistock, 1960.
13. Berkowitz, N. H. and Bennis, W. G., 'Interaction Patterns in Formal Service-oriented Organisations', *Administrative Science Quarterly*, Vol. VI, 1961–62.

14. Berliner, J., 'A Problem in Soviet Business Management', *Administrative Science Quarterly*, Vol. 1, June 1956.

15. Bertalanffy, L. Von, 'The Theory of Open Systems in Physics and Biology', *Science*, III, 23, 1950.

16. Bird, C., *Social Psychology*, New York, Appleton-Century, 1940.

17. Bion, W. R., *Experiences in Groups*, London, Tavistock Publications, 1961, New York, Basic Books, 1962.

18. Bion, W. R., 'Experiences in Groups', *Human Relations*, Vol. III, 3, 1950.

19. Blau, P., *Dynamics of Bureaucracy*, Chicago, University of Chicago Press, 1955.

20. Blau, P. M. and Scott, W. R., *Formal Organisations*, London, Routledge and Kegan Paul, 1963.

21. Brech, E. F. L., *Organisation*, London, Longmans, 1965.

22. Brown, W. and Raphael, W., *Managers, Men and Morale*, London, MacDonald and Evans, 1948.

23. Brown, W., 'Principles of Organisation', *Monographs on Higher Management, No. 5*, Manchester Municipal College of Technology, December 1946.

24. Brown, W., 'Some Problems of a Factory', *Occasional Papers No. 2*, Institute of Personnel Management, London, 1952.

25. Brown, W., 'Can There be Industrial Democracy?', *Fabian Journal*, March 1956.

26. Brown, W., *Exploration in Management*, London, Heinemann, 1960.

27. Brown, W. 'Selection and Appraisal of Management Personnel', *The Manager*, Vol. XXVIII, No. 6, 1960.

28. Brown, W., *Piecework Abandoned*, London, Heinemann, 1962.

29. Brown, W. and Jaques, E., *The Glacier Project Papers*, London, Heinemann, 1965.

30. Burns, T., 'The Directions of Activity and Communications in a Departmental Executive Group', *Human Relations*, Vol. VII, 73–97, 1954.

31. Burns, T. and Stalker, G. M., *The Management of Innovation*, London, Tavistock, 1961.

32. Carlson, S., *Executive Behaviour*, Stockholm, Stromborgs, 1951.

BIBLIOGRAPHY

33. Cartwright, D. and Zander, A., *Group Dynamics in Research and Theory* (2nd ed.), Evanston, Illinois, Row Peterson, London, 1960.

34. Chambers, S. P., 'Statistics and Intellectual Integrity', Inaugural Address of the President, delivered to the Royal Statistical Society, 25 November 1964.

35. Coch, L. and French, J. R. P., 'Overcoming Resistance to Change', *Human Relations*, Vol. I, 512–32, 1948.

36. Combey, P. G. and Rackham, 'Rewards and Punishment in Industry', *New Society*, 16 September 1965.

37. Crichton, A., 'Personnel Management in Working Groups', *Occasional Papers No. 18*, Institute of Personnel Management.

38. Daniel, W. W., 'How close should a Manager be?', *New Society*, 7 October 1965.

39. Davis, K., *Human Relations in Business*, London, McGraw-Hill, 1957.

40. Drucker, P. F., 'The Employee Society', *American Sociological Review*, *58*, 358–63, 1952.

41. Dubin, R., 'Business Behaviour Behaviourally Viewed', G. B. Strother (Ed.), *Social Science Approaches to Business Behaviour*, London, Tavistock Publications, 1962.

42. Dubin, R., *The World of Work*, Englewood Cliffs, N.J., Prentice-Hall, 1958.

43. Emery, F. E., *Characteristics of Socio-Technical Systems*, London, Tavistock Institute, Doc. No. 527, 1959.

44. Emery, F. E. and Trist, E. L., 'Socio-Technical Systems', Proceedings of 6th Annual International Meeting of the Institute of Management Sciences, London, New York, Paris, Los Angeles, Pergammon Press, 1960. *Management Science Models and Techniques*, Vol. II.

45. Engineering Employers' Federation, *Evidence to the Royal Commission and Employers' Associations*.

46. Fiedler, F. E., 'The Leader's Psychological Distance and Group Effectiveness', D. Cartwright and A. Zander (Eds.), *Group Dynamics, Research and Theory* (2nd ed.), Evanston, Illinois, Row Peterson, London, 1960.

47. Flanders, A., *Fawley Productivity Agreements*, London, Faber and Faber, 1964.

48. Fleishman, E. A. and Harris, E. F., *Leadership and Super-*

vision in Industry, Columbus, Ohio State University Press, 1955.

49. Fleishman, E. A., Harris, E. F. and Burt, H. E., 'Leadership Climate Human Training and Supervisory Behaviour', *Personnel Psychology*, VI, pp. 205–22.

50. Gerth, H. H. and Wright Mills, S. C., *From Max Weber*, A Galaxy Book, Oxford University Press, 1946.

51. Gouldner, A. W., *Patterns of Industrial Bureaucracy*, Glencoe, Illinois, 1954.

52. Guest, R. H., 'Of Time and Foremen', *Personnel*, May 1956.

53. Hacon, R., *Management Training, Aims and Methods*, The English University Press, 1961.

54. Haire, M., *Modern Organisation Theory*, New York, Wiley, 1959.

55. Haire, M., 'The Concept of Power and the Concept of Man', G. B. Strother (Ed.), *Social Science Approaches to Business Behaviour*, Tavistock, London, 1962.

56. Haire, M., *Psychology in Management*, London, McGraw-Hill, 1964.

57. Halpin, A. W., 'The Leadership Behaviour and Combat Performance of Airplane Commanders', *Journal of Abnormal Social Psychology*, *49*, 19–22, 1954.

58. Hanson, B., *Work Sampling for Modern Management*, Englewood Cliffs, N.J., Prentice-Hall, 1962.

59. Hill, J. M. M., 'A Consideration of Labour Turnover as the Resultant of a Quasi-Stationary Process', *Human Relations*, Vol. IV, No. 3, 1951.

60. Hill, J. M. M., 'The Time-Span of Discretion in Job Analysis', London, *Tavistock Pamphlets No. 1*, Tavistock Publications, 1957.

61. Hill, J. M. M. and Trist, E. L., 'A Consideration of Industrial Accidents as a Means of Withdrawal from the Work Situation', *Human Relations*, Vol. VI, 357, 1953.

62. Hill, J. M. M. and Trist, E. L., 'Changes in Accidents and Other Absences with Length of Service', *Human Relations*, Vol. VIII, 121, 1955.

63. Holmes, R., 'Review of *Exploration in Management*', *Occupational Psychology*, Vol. XXXV, 1 and 2.

64. Jaques, E., 'Studies in the Social Development of an

Industrial Community', *Human Relations*, Vol. III, No. 3, 1950.

65. Jaques, E., *The Changing Culture of a Factory*, Tavistock Publications, London, 1951.

66. Jaques, E., 'On the Dynamics of Social Structure', *Human Relations*, Vol. VI, No. 1, 1953.

67. Jaques, E., *Measurement of Responsibility*, London, Tavistock Publications, Harvard University Press, Cambridge, Mass., 1956.

68. Jaques, E., 'Fatigue and Lowered Morale Caused by Inadequate Executive Planning', *Royal Society of Health Journal*, Vol. 78, No. 5, 1958.

69. Jaques, E., 'An Objective Approach to Pay Differentials', *The New Scientist*, Vol. 4, No. 85, 1958.

70. Jaques, E., 'Standard Earning Progression Curves: A Technique for Examining Individual Progress in Work', *Human Relations*, Vol. XI, No. 2, 1958.

71. Jaques, E., *Equitable Payment*, London, Heinemann, 1961.

72. Jaques, E., *Time-Span Handbook*, London, Heinemann, 1964.

73. Jaques, E., Rice, A. K. and Hill, J. M. M., 'The Social and Psychological Impact of a Change in Method of Wage Payment', *Human Relations*, Vol. IV, No. 4, 1951.

74. Kahn, R. L. and Katz, D., 'Leadership Practices in Relation to Productivity and Morale', D. Cartwright and A. Zander (Eds.), *Group Dynamics*, Tavistock, London, 1960.

75. Kay, B. R., 'Prescription and Perception of the Supervisory Rôle', *Occupational Psychology*, Vol. 37, No. 3.

76. Kay, B. R., *Leadership in Supervision*, Cleveland, Howard Allan.

76(b). Klein, L., 'Review of *Time-Span Handbook*', *Journal of Management Studies*, Vol. 2, No. 3, 1965.

77. Kelly, J., 'Group Dynamics: Searching for the Hidden Agenda', *Technical Education*, August 1963.

78. Kelly, J., 'Changing Views of Management Efficiency', *Journal of Industrial Economics*, April 1964.

79. Kelly, J., 'A Study of Leadership in Two Contrasting Groups', *The Sociological Review*, November 1963.

80. Kelly, J., 'The Study of Executive Behaviour by Activity Sampling', *Human Relations*, Vol. XVII, No. 3.

81. Kelly, J., 'Scottish Foremen', *Scotland*, January 1964.
82. Kelly, J., 'Evolution of Management Theory', *Scientific Business*, March 1964.
83. Kelly, J., 'New Approach to Discussion Leadership', *Times Review of Industry*, August 1964.
84. Kelly, J., 'The Manager in No Man's Land', *The Supervisor*, May 1964.
85. Kelly, J., 'The Efficient Manager Puts the Job First', *The Manager*, February 1965.
86. Kelly, J., 'Group Dynamics: a New Approach to Leadership', *Technical Education*, February 1965.
87. Kelly, J., 'Observing Organisations: Methods', *Scientific Business*, March 1966.
88. Landsberger, H. A., *Hawthorne Revisited*, Cornell University, 1958.
89. Landsberger, H. A., 'The Horizontal Dimension in Bureaucracy', *Administrative Science Quarterly*, Vol. VI, 1961–2, pp. 299–322.
90. Lewin, K., 'Defining the Field at a Given Time', *Psychological Review*, 50, 1943.
91. Likert, R., 'Motivational Dimensions of Administration', R. Walker (Ed.), *America's Manpower Crisis*, Chicago Public Administration Service, 1952.
92. Likert, R., *New Patterns of Management*, London, McGraw-Hill, 1961.
93. Linton, R., *The Study of Man*, New York, Appleton-Century-Crofts, 1936.
94. Linton, R., *The Cultural Background of Personality*, New York, Appleton-Century-Crofts, 1945.
95. Lippit, R. and White, R. K., 'An Experimental Study of Leadership and Group Life', E. E. Maccoby, T. M. Newcomb and E. L. Hartley (Eds.), *Readings in Social Psychology* (3rd ed.), New York, Holt, 1958.
96. McCusker, R., 'Ice Cold at Glacier Metal', *Trade Union Affairs*, Autumn/Winter 1961.
97. McGregor, D., *The Human Side of Enterprise*, New York, McGraw-Hill, 1960.
98. Malinowski, B., Introduction to H. I. Hogbin's *Law and Order in Polynesia*, New York, Harcourt, Barce, 1934.
99. Malinowski, B., *A Scientific Theory of Culture and other*

Essays, Chapel Hill, University of North Carolina Press, 1944.

100. March, J. G. and Simon, H. A., *Organisations*, New York, Wiley, 1958.

101. Marsh, A., *Managers and Shop Stewards*, London Institute of Personnel Management, 1963.

102. Mayo, E., *The Human Problems of an Industrial Civilization*, New York, Macmillan, 1933.

103. Mayo, E., *The Social Problems of an Industrial Civilization*, Boston, Harvard University, 1945.

104. Merrett, A. J. and Sykes, A., 'Incomes Policy and Company Profitability', *District Bank Review*, September 1963.

105. Merton, R. K., 'Bureaucratic Structure and Personality', *Social Forces*, 18, 560–8, 1940.

106. Murchison, C., *Handbook of Social Psychology*, Clark U.P., Worcester, Mass., 1935.

107. National Institute of Industrial Psychology, *The Foreman*, London, Staples, 1957.

108. National Institute of Industrial Psychology, *Joint Consultation in British Industry*, London, Staples, 1952.

109. Parsons, T., 'Some Ingredients of a General Theory of Formal Organisation', Chapter 3, A. W. Halpin, *Administrative Theory in Education*, Chicago, 1958.

110. Paterson, T. T., 'Towards a Theory of Retribution in Industry', *The Manager*, March 1963.

111. Paterson, T. T., *Authority*, Department of Administration, University of Strathclyde.

112. Paterson, T. T., *A Methectic Theory of Social Organisation*, Department of Social and Economic Research, University of Glasgow, 1957.

113. Paterson, T. T., *Morale in War and Work*, London, Max Parish, 1955.

114. Paterson, T. T., *Glasgow Limited*, Cambridge, at the University Press, 1960.

115. Paterson, T. T., 'Jaques' System: Impractical?', *New Society*, December 1963.

116. Paterson, T. T., 'First Report of the Commission of Enquiry into the Organisation and Development of the Southern Rhodesia Public Services', presented to the Legislative Assembly, 1962.

BIBLIOGRAPHY

117. Pelz, D. C., 'Influence: A Key to Effective Leadership in the First-line Supervisor', *Personnel*, III, 209–17, 1952.

118. Pfiffner, J. M. and Sherwood, F. P., *Administrative Organisation*, Prentice-Hall Inc., Englewood Cliffs, N.J., 1960.

119. Piersol, D. T., 'Communication Practices of Supervisors in a Mid-Western Corporation', *Advanced Management*, XXIII, 20–1, 1958.

120. Ponder, A. D., 'The Effective Manufacturing Foreman', *Proceedings of the Tenth Annual Meetings, Industrial Relations Research Association*, pp. 41–52, Madison, Wis.

121. Renold, C., *Joint Consultation over Thirty Years*, London, Allen and Unwin, 1950.

122. Rice, A. K., 'The Use of Unrecognised Cultural Mechanisms in an Expanding Machine Shop', *Human Relations*, Vol. III, No. 2, 1951.

123. Rice, A. K., 'An Examination of the Boundaries of Part-Institutions', *Human Relations*, Vol. IV, No. 4, 1951.

124. Rice, A. K., 'The Relative Independence of Sub-Institutions as Illustrated by Departmental Labour Turnover', *Human Relations*, Vol. V, No. 1, 1952.

125. Rice, A. K., *Productivity and Social Organisation*, London, Tavistock Publications, 1958.

126. Rice, A. K., Hill, J. M. M. and Trist, E. L., 'The Representation of Labour Turnover as a Social Process', *Human Relations*, Vol. III, No. 4, 1950.

127. Rice, A. K. and Trist, E. L., 'Institutional and Sub-Institutional Determinants of Change in Labour Turnover', *Human Relations*, Vol. V, No. 4, 1952.

128. Richardson, F. L. W. and Walker, C. R., *Human Relations in an Expanding Company*, Yale Labour and Management Center, New Haven, 1948.

129. Ridgway, W. F., 'Dysfunctional Consequences of Performance Measurement', Rubenstein and Haberstroh (Eds.), *Some Theories of Organisation*, Irwin-Dorsey, 1960.

130. Robson Brown, W. and Howell-Everson, N. A., *Industrial Democracy at Work*, London, Pitman, 1950.

131. Roethlisberger, Fritz J., 'The Foreman: Master and Victim of Double Talk', *Harvard Business Review*, XXIII, pp. 285–94.

BIBLIOGRAPHY

132. Roethlisberger, Fritz J., *Management and Morale*, Harvard University Press, Cambridge, Mass., 1943.
133. Roethlisberger, F. J. and Dickson, W. J., *Management and the Worker*, Harvard University Press, Cambridge, Mass., 1959.
134. Rubenstein, A. H. and Haberstroh, L. J., *Some Theories of Organisation*, Irwin-Dorsey, 1960.
135. Seashore, S. E., 'Administrative Leadership and Organisational Effectiveness', R. Likert and S. P. Hayes, Jr. (Eds.), *Some Applications of Behavioural Research*, Paris, U.N.E.S.C.O., 1957.
136. Scott, W. H., *Industrial Democracy*, Liverpool University Press, 1955.
137. Selznick, P., *T.V.A. and Grass Roots*, Berkeley, 1949.
138. Simon, H. A., 'Comments of the Theory of Organisations', A. H. Rubenstein and C. H. Haberstroh (Eds.), *Some Theories of Organisation*, Homewood, Illinois, Irwin-Dorsey, 1960.
139. Simpson, R. L., 'Vertical and Horizontal Communications in Organisations', *Administrative Science Quarterly*, Vol. IV, pp. 188–96, 1959.
140. Stebbing, L. S., *A Modern Introduction to Logic*, London, Methuen, 1930.
141. Stogdill, R., 'Personal Factors Associated with Leadership: A Survey of the Literature', *Journal of Psychology*, Vol. 25, 1948.
142. Stogdill, R. M. and Shartle, C. L., *Methods in the Study of Administrative Leadership*, Columbus, Bureau of Business Research, Ohio State University, 1955.
143. Strother, G. B., *Social Science Approaches to Business Behaviour*, London, Tavistock, 1962.
144. Taylor, F. W., *Scientific Management*, New York, Harper, 1947.
145. Thouless, R. H., *General and Social Psychology*, London University Tutorial Press, 1951.
146. Torrance, E. P., 'Function of Expressed Disagreement in Small Group Processes', A. H. Rubenstein and C. J. Haberstroh (Eds.), *Some Theories of Organisation*, Homewood, Illinois, Irwin-Dorsey, 1960.
147. Trist, E. L., Forword to W. Brown's *Exploration in Management*, London, Heinemann, 1960.

148. Trist, E. L. and Sofer, C., *Exploration in Group Relations*, Leicester, Leicester University Press, 1959.

149. Weiss, R. S., *Process of Organisation*, Ann Arbor, Survey Research Center, University of Michigan, 1956.

150. Whitehead, T. N., *Leadership in a Free Society*, London, Oxford University Press, 1936.

151. Whyte, W. F., *Street Corner Society, the Social Structure of an Italian Slum*, University of Chicago, 1943.

152. Whyte, W. F., 'Applying Behavioural Science Research to Management Problems', G. B. Strother (Ed.), *Social Science Approaches to Business Behaviour*, Homewood, Illinois, Doresy Press, London, Tavistock Publications, 1962.

153. Whyte, W. H., Jr., *The Organization Man*, New York, Simon and Schuster, 1956.

154. Willmott, P., *The Evolution of a Community*, London, Routledge and Kegan Paul, 1963.

155. Wilson, A. T. M., 'Some Contrasting Socio-Technical Production Systems', *The Manager*, December 1955.

156. Wilson, V. F., 'Some Personality Characteristics of Industrial Executives', *Occupational Psychology*, Vol. XXX, 4.

157. Woodward, J. 'Management and Technology', H.M.S.O., *Problems and Progress in Industry*, 3, 1958.

158. Wray, D. E., 'Marginal Men of Industry: The Foremen', *American Journal of Sociology*, 54, pp. 298–301.

159. Zinck, C., 'The Foreman and Productivity', *Advanced Management*, XXIII, pp. 12–16.

INDEX